Leading

WITH

PASSION

AND

KNOWLEDGE

For Allan Vann,
my sixth-grade teacher, retired
principal extraordinaire, and lifelong friend.

NANCY FICHTMAN DANA

Foreword by Michael Fullan

Leading

WITH

PASSION

AND

KNOWLEDGE

The Principal as Action Researcher

A JOINT PUBLICATION

CORWIN
A SAGE Company

AMERICAN ASSOCIATION OF SCHOOL ADMINISTRATORS

For information:

Corwin
A SAGE Company
2455 Teller Road
Thousand Oaks, California 91320
(800) 233-9936
Fax: (800) 417-2466
www.corwinpress.com

SAGE Ltd.
1 Oliver's Yard
55 City Road
London EC1Y 1SP
United Kingdom

SAGE India Pvt. Ltd.
B 1/I 1 Mohan Cooperative
   Industrial Area
Mathura Road, New Delhi 110 044
India

SAGE Asia-Pacific Pte. Ltd.
33 Pekin Street #02-01
Far East Square
Singapore 048763

Printed in the United States of America

Library of Congress Cataloging-in-Publication Data

Dana, Nancy Fichtman, 1964–
Leading with passion and knowledge: The principal as action researcher/Nancy Fichtman Dana; foreword by Michael Fullan.
      p. cm.
"A Joint Publication with the American Association of School Administrators."
Includes bibliographical references and index.
ISBN 978-1-4129-6704-4 (cloth)
ISBN 978-1-4129-6705-1 (pbk.)
   1. School principals. 2. School management and organization. 3. Action research in education. I. Title.

LB2831.9.D36 2009
371.2'012—dc22   2008049666

This book is printed on acid-free paper.

      10   11   12   13   10   9   8   7   6   5   4   3   2

Acquisitions Editor:	Carol Chambers Collins
Editorial Assistant:	Brett Ory
Production and Copy Editor:	Jane Haenel
Typesetter:	C&M Digitals (P) Ltd.
Proofreader:	Caryne Brown
Indexer:	Nara Wood
Cover and Graphic Designer:	Michael Dubowe

Contents

List of Figures and Tables

FIGURES

TABLES

Foreword

Action research has by now an established reputation in education. Nancy Dana's book does two things beyond anything available in the literature. First, no one has written on what the principal's role is in action research. Second, if you just take action research per se as a strategy in itself, this book does a better job of explaining, unpacking, and providing comprehensive help than anything in the wider literature. But let's stick with the principalship.

Recently, on the twentieth anniversary of the publication of *What's Worth Fighting for in the Principalship* (WWFFP), I produced a second edition. I set out to revise the first edition but very quickly ascertained that I had to start from scratch (Fullan, 2008). So much had happened with respect to the role of principals that one had to step back and recast the whole matter. The good news is that almost everyone (including politicians) agrees that the principal is key to successful student learning and achievement. The bad news is that all the new responsibilities for leading change and for accountability have been added to an already full plate. The principalship in a word is overloaded.

In WWFFP, I recommended six Action Guidelines for principals:

1. Declare deprivatization of teaching as a main goal (opening up the classroom)

2. Model instructional leadership

3. Build capacity first (knowledge, skills, and competencies)

4. Grow other leaders

5. Divert the distracters (things that take the school away from the focus on learning)

6. Be a system leader (contribute to the growth of other schools and the district)

Nancy Dana's *Leading With Passion and Knowledge* puts practical tools in the hands of the principal to do the things I was getting at in WWFFP. First, the flow of the book is clear, compelling, and ever beckoning. The book starts with defining inquiry and then guides the principal on the journey—how to get started, data collection and planning, data analysis, implementing and ending the (initial) journey, and assessing the overall enterprise "to become the best administrator and researcher you can be." *Leading With Passion and Knowledge* has a strong conceptual core.

Second, the level of depth is pitch perfect—deep enough to get at the real substance of change but not overwhelming with unnecessary detail. This is a book that is very accessible and very meaningful.

Third, the book contains plenty of direct, targeted examples of actual principals doing what Dana is talking about. These samples make the book interesting to read and additionally helpful. Because the examples are coupled with clear explanations of the central concepts, the link between theory and practice is constantly being forged chapter after chapter.

Fourth, at the end of each chapter, there are sets of exercises, tools, and reflective and action suggestions that insist on engagement. I very much value the emphasis on *doing* something while supplying the necessary ideas and strategies.

These four features—a strong conceptual core, good depth, case vignettes, and tools for action—make *Leading With Passion and Knowledge* a powerful resource for handling the new principalship that I wrote about in WWFFP. Dana has produced a book steeped in passion and strategy that makes action research not an ad hoc project but, rather, a way of life. This project is not a linear one. It is about becoming and continually cultivating what it means to become the best possible leader you can. Without question, Dana has made a significant new contribution to the principal's role as instructional leader.

Michael Fullan
Ontario Institute for Studies in Education
University of Toronto

REFERENCE

Fullan, M. (2008) *What's worth fighting for in the principalship.* New York: Teachers College Press.

Preface

The concept of action research has been around for ages, its roots in the work of John Dewey (1933), popularized by Kurt Lewin in the 1940s (Adelman, 1993), and shortly thereafter applied to the field of education by Stephen Corey (1953). Since its inception, many educational innovations have come and gone, but the systematic study of educators' own practice is a concept that has proved its staying power! Whether we refer to this process as action research, practitioner research, practitioner inquiry, or some other name, three main reasons exist for the longevity of this concept: (1) it has proven to be a powerful tool for teacher professional development (Zeichner, 2003), (2) the process has become an important vehicle for raising teachers' voices in educational reform (Meyers & Rust, 2003), and (3) it is a mechanism for expanding the knowledge base for teaching in important ways (Cochran-Smith & Lytle, 1993).

While the concept of practitioner research was originally developed primarily with the teacher in mind, action research has recently gained favor among administrators, other school leaders, and school-based management teams as a way to improve schools (Glanz, 1998). Although there exists a plethora of books written to take teachers though the action research process, endless collections of teachers' reports of their classroom research, and numerous research studies published on the teacher as practitioner-researcher in educational journals, comparatively few materials exist that focus on the administrator:

- How do we apply what we know about the success of the teacher research movement to the field of administration?
- What actually *is* administrator action research, and what does it look like?
- Why is it important for administrators to engage in action research?

- What is the relationship between administrators' engagement in action research and their professional growth?
- In what ways can administrator action research inform school improvement efforts and enhance student achievement?

If you are a current assistant principal, principal, superintendent, or other school administrator or are studying to earn your principal certification and/or an advanced degree in educational leadership with the intention of joining the administrator ranks, the answers to these questions can help you grow, develop, and succeed in ways you may never have imagined. This book was thus created to take administrative professionals step by step through the process of inquiry, from developing an initial understanding of the process to completing and sharing your first piece of action research.

ABOUT THIS BOOK

Using a journey metaphor, this text will take you through the process of inquiry step by step. You begin your journey with a brief introduction to administrator inquiry in Chapter 1 and then move in Chapter 2 to define your first research question. This chapter, appropriately titled "The Passions That Drive Your Journey: Finding a Wondering," gets you started by exploring nine areas in a principal's work life that are ripe for inquiry—staff development, curriculum development, interactions and relationships with individual teachers, interactions and relationships with individual students, community/culture building, leadership skills, management, school performance, and social justice. These nine areas, referred to as "passions," are explored using examples from real administrator-inquirers I have worked with to illustrate how their wonderings emerged from the intersection of their real-world school experiences and one of the particular passions defined in Chapter 2. Exercises at the end of the chapter help you articulate and fine-tune your research question.

With a wondering developed, nine different strategies for collecting data to help you gain insights into your wondering are explored in Chapter 3, beginning with the quantitative measures of student achievement so prevalent and readily available in today's schools and moving beyond this common form of data to explore field notes, interviews, documents/artifacts/student work, digital pictures, video, reflective journals or Weblogs, surveys, and literature. Throughout the discussion of these data collection strategies, I point to the ways each of them connects to what you already do in your life and work as an administrator. For example, the concept of Classroom Walk-Through notes as a form of field notes is discussed. This discussion is important for you to be able to see how administrator inquiry is *a part of,* not *apart from,* the work you do as a principal. It is also important, in your incredibly busy life as an administrator, to see that the process is realistic and doable.

Chapter 4 tackles one of the most mysterious steps for administrator-researchers—data analysis. The use of metaphor serves to demystify and, once again, makes the process of administrator inquiry seem doable. If you enjoy jigsaw puzzles or scrapbooking, you will particularly enjoy your journey through this chapter as these metaphors are fully developed to describe the data analysis process step by step. In addition, one principal-inquirer's work is used to illustrate what data analysis might actually look like in practice.

Chapter 5 takes a close look at the who, what, when, where, and why of sharing your research with others. This chapter includes tips on developing and delivering PowerPoint presentations and multiple ways to present your research in written form, including the traditional dissertation or thesis (for those engaging in action research as a requirement for advanced study), journal articles, Weblogs, one-page bulleted summaries, templates, brochures, and executive research summaries.

Finally, Chapter 6 discusses how engagement in inquiry is connected to every individual administrator becoming the best he/she can be! One part of becoming the best you can be is reflecting on the quality of the practitioner research you produce. Chapter 6 offers five quality indicators and questions you can ask yourself as you reflect on your own and your colleagues' research.

As in Chapter 2, Chapters 3–6 end with exercises designed to guide you through each step of the process. These exercises will be extremely useful for incorporating into administrative team meetings, leadership team meetings, learning community work, or coursework at the university.

WHO IS THIS BOOK FOR?

Across the nation, administrators vary greatly in their experience with practitioner inquiry. Perhaps you are brand-new to the concept. Perhaps you have been engaged in inquiry for years as a teacher and wish to apply the process to your new role as an administrator. Perhaps you wish to further the development of action research in your school and realize that that process must begin with you. This book is for all administrators, wherever they are in their inquiry journey.

In addition, this book is for students in higher education (as well as their faculty advisors) who are pursuing graduate study to obtain an advanced degree in educational leadership. Inspired by the Carnegie

Initiative on the Doctorate, many institutions of higher education are currently rethinking their advanced degree programs, with a particular emphasis on the differences in doctoral degree programs and requirements for those preparing to be researchers at institutions of higher education and for those preparing to remain practitioners and take on significant leadership responsibilities in the world of schools. The completion of a rigorous, extensive piece of action research to fulfill the requirements for a dissertation or master's thesis is a sound alternative to engaging in traditional forms of research for those students planning to remain in schools, as well as a meaningful way for the student to fulfill the research requirement for an advanced degree. This book, coupled with other texts on educational research, can provide a solid start to the master's paper, thesis, or dissertation endeavor.

Finally, this book is for superintendents and other district leaders who are serious about providing meaningful professional development for their principals. Roland Barth (2001) described professional development for principals as a "wasteland." He called for those in charge of principal professional development to depart from traditional questions such as, "What should principals know and be able to do, and how can we get them to know and do it?" to "Under what conditions will school principals become committed, sustained, lifelong learners in their important work?" Engagement in principal inquiry is one way principals can achieve the latter. With this book as a guide, you can institute a meaningful program of professional learning and growth for the principals under your charge.

Whoever you are and wherever you may be in relationship to practitioner inquiry, I hope this text provides the impetus to develop as an inquirer and an innovative leader in our schools. Happy inquiring!

Acknowledgments

I have had the honor and privilege to work with many tremendous administrators throughout my career, and it is through these administrators' work that I have witnessed the process of inquiry come alive and the power of inquiry as a tool for principal professional development and school improvement speak for itself. Two of these special administrators became the closest of friends and wonderful mentors as I theorized the concept of administrator inquiry and put this concept into practice with many principals over the years—Allan Vann and Fran Vandiver. I met Allan when I was an eleven-year-old sixth grader at Circle Hill Elementary School in Commack, New York. He was the type of teacher you are fortunate to get once in a lifetime if you are lucky. I was incredibly lucky for half of my sixth-grade year, at which time Allan left the classroom to finish up his dissertation studies at Teachers College with Gary Griffin and Ann Lieberman; he subsequently became and served as an extraordinary administrator for nineteen years before retirement. Little did I know as a sixth grader that this teacher would later become a mentor and colleague as I began my own teaching career, pursued advanced study, and began working at the university to understand meaningful professional development for teachers and principals. I thank Allan, to whom this book is dedicated, for the countless discussions, conversations, advice, letters, e-mail messages, and most of all friendship over the years and his many contributions to the framing of this book.

I met Fran Vandiver much later in my life, as I was making the move from my position at the Pennsylvania State University to the University of Florida. As director of one of the few (and finest) remaining lab schools in the nation, the P. K. Yonge Developmental Research School, Fran warmly welcomed me into her school, as well as her work leading thirteen principals in a reading initiative for the state. Familiar with my work with teachers on practitioner inquiry, Fran queried soon after I arrived in Florida, "Why don't you come with me to our next principal meeting? I'll introduce you to some wonderful administrators, and maybe you can share a little bit about inquiry and we can get something going with these principals." That meeting was a wonderful start to five years of developing and fine-tuning how the concept of teacher as researcher can be applied to administration. Without this connection, this work would never have evolved to where it is today. I thank Fran for her warm welcome to the sunshine state, the many thought-provoking conversations we have had about teaching, administration, and schools, and her many insights, wisdom, and encouragement as this work with principals took root and grew.

Throughout my career, I have always been passionate about raising the voices of practitioners in educational reform, which I attempted to do within this text by providing many rich examples of administrator inquiry as I describe the process step by step. Hence, this book would not have been possible without the inquiries that only administrators can provide. I am grateful to all the administrators I have worked with over the years, especially from the North East Florida Educational Consortium's Tier III Principal Leadership Academy (Mark Bracewell, Teri Buckles, Mike Delucas, Ann Hayes, Denee Hurst, Lynette Langford, Marion McCray, Phyllis Pearson, Chris Pryor, Ted Rousch, and Patrick Wnek), the P. K. Yonge Developmental Research School (Amy Hollinger, Brian Marchman, and Randy Scott), the School Board of Alachua County–University of Florida Professional Development Community Collaborative (Jim Brandenburg, Kathy Dixon, and Lacy Redd), the Pinellas County Schools (Carol Thomas and Robert Poth), and the State College Area School District–Pennsylvania State University Elementary Professional Development School Program (Deirdre Bauer and Donnan Stoicovy). I thank these principals for embarking with me on the inquiry journey and the tremendous learning I acquired as I watched them tackle each step in the process. I continue to admire their devotion and am grateful for their dedication to the education profession and their support in writing this book.

In addition, the North East Florida Educational Consortium (NEFEC) has provided invaluable support for teacher and administrator inquiry work to grow and thrive in sixteen districts in north-central Florida. I am grateful to NEFEC's Bob Smith, Marsha Hill, Jason Arnold, and Mark Bracewell for their vision in building their Principal Leadership Academy around the notion of practitioner inquiry and inviting me to partner with them in this endeavor. Their support and passion for providing powerful professional development for principals was instrumental to the writing of this book.

A number of my colleagues provided thoughtful feedback during the conceptualization and writing of this text; thanks to Diane Yendol-Hoppey, Jennifer Jacobs, David Quinn, Chris Sessums, and Katie Tricarico.

In addition, for their tremendous support in all the technical aspects of getting this manuscript written and prepared for publication, I thank Susan Stabel, senior secretary at the Center for School Improvement at the University of Florida, Carol Chambers Collins, senior acquisitions editor at Corwin, and her editorial assistant, Brett Ory.

Finally, no book could ever be written without the love and support from one's family. I thank the best husband, children, and parents ever— Tom Dana, associate dean for academic affairs at the University of Florida, for his support, encouragement, ideas, and computer help; Greg and Kirsten Dana, for unselfishly sharing their mom with a computer as this book was being written; and Ken and Anita Fichtman, who graciously hosted their grandchildren for a week's vacation at Grandma and Poppy's house so Mom could finish this book. I love you all!

PUBLISHER'S ACKNOWLEDGMENTS

Corwin gratefully acknowledges the contributions of the following reviewers:

Roland S. Barth
Author of *Lessons Learned*
Alna, ME

Sister Camille Anne Campbell
Principal, Mount Carmel Academy
New Orleans, LA

Nic Cooper
Faculty, Baker College
Coauthor of *How to Keep Being a Parent When Your Child Stops Being a Child*
Jackson, MI

Margarete Couture
Principal, South Seneca Central School District
Interlaken, NY

Gary Highsmith
Principal, Hamden High School
Hamden, CT

William A. Sommers
Past President, National Staff Development Council
Austin, TX

About the Author

 **Nancy Fichtman Dana** is currently a professor of education and director of the Center for School Improvement at the University of Florida (http://education.ufl.edu/csi). Under her direction, the center promotes and supports practitioner inquiry (action research) as a core mechanism for school improvement in schools throughout the state. She began her career in education as an elementary school teacher in Hannibal Central Schools, New York, and has worked closely with teachers and administrators on action research, building professional learning communities, and school-university collaborations in Florida and Pennsylvania since 1990. She has authored numerous articles in professional journals focused on practitioner inquiry, as well as two additional books (with Diane Yendol-Hoppey) on the action research process from Corwin—*The Reflective Educator's Guide to Classroom Research: Learning to Teach and Teaching to Learn Through Practitioner Inquiry*, and *The Reflective Educator's Guide to Professional Development: Coaching Inquiry-Oriented Learning Communities*. Nancy Dana may be reached via e-mail at ndana@coe.ufl.edu.

Sustaining the development of school leaders is crucial to the quality of life and to the best interests of all who inhabit the schoolhouse—and to their development as a community of learners. Principals, no less than teachers, need replenishment and invigoration and an expanded repertoire of ideas and practices with which to respond to staggering demands. . . . The principal need no longer be the "headmaster" or "instructional leader," pretending to know all. The more crucial role of the principal is as head learner, engaging in the most important enterprise of the schoolhouse—experiencing, displaying, modeling, and celebrating what it is hoped and expected that teachers and pupils will do.

—Roland Barth

1 Administrator Inquiry Defined

Whether you are a twenty-year veteran principal, a brand-new administrator, or studying to complete your degree in educational leadership with an aspiration to become principal of your own school one day, you cannot help but be struck by the staggering demands that a principal faces each day, referred to by Roland Barth in the opening quote. These demands for a principal's time and attention come from an astonishing number of constituencies he or she must serve simultaneously—teachers, students, parents, the superintendent and district office, the board of education, and the community at large. For example, within a given day, a principal might interview and hire a new teacher, provide feedback to a veteran teacher whose lesson was recently observed, discipline a student, lunch with the kindergarten students of the week, complete a newsletter for staff and parents, calm a parent who is upset she wasn't selected as a chaperone for the upcoming field trip to Washington, DC, work on a state-mandated report for the superintendent, meet with the district business manager to discuss the budget, and explain to the disgruntled head of the local Boy Scouts organization that it can no longer hold its weekly Tuesday night meetings in the cafeteria because of a conflict with another school activity. Layer on top of this same day any of a number of "emergencies" that can surface at any time without warning—a break-in to your school's computer lab the night before resulting in twelve stolen computers, the discovery of vandalism in the boy's bathroom, a power failure, a leaking roof, renovations to your building, a teacher who tripped in the parking lot on her way into the building and broke her arm, or an impending snowstorm that threatens early dismissal with no way to notify parents.

With all of the never-ending demands on a principal from a large and diverse number of constituencies, coupled with the numerous emergencies that surface on an almost daily basis, it is easy for principals to lose sight of why they aspired to be principals in the first place—leading and inspiring the teaching and learning that occur within their schoolhouse, a task that has become increasingly more complex in recent years. According to Ken Leithwood and Carolyn Riehl (2003), leading researchers in the field of educational administration:

> Curriculum standards, achievement benchmarks, programmatic requirements and other policy directives from many sources generate complicated and unpredictable requirements for schools. Principals must respond to increasing diversity in student characteristics, including cultural background and immigration status, income disparities, physical and mental disabilities and variation in learning capacities. They must manage new collaborations with other social agencies that serve children. Rapid developments in technologies for teaching and communications require adjustments in the internal workings of schools. These are just a few of the conditions that make schooling more challenging and leadership more essential. (p. 2)

Historically, principals have not had access to tools that can help them untangle the complexity of their work as administrators and bring the focus of their work back to their leadership in teaching and learning. Rather, principals often find themselves focusing on the routine management jobs that must get done and, to survive, responding haphazardly and unsystematically to the constant demand after demand for their time and attention. Administrator inquiry is one tool that can be used by principals to untangle the intricate web of demands in which they become entangled each day, take charge of their own professional development, and become the "head learner" of their school. Transforming the profession is really the capstone of the principal inquiry story. Let's begin our journey into the what, why, and how of administrator inquiry with a simple definition of this very complex, rewarding, transformative, provocative, and productive process!

WHAT IS ADMINISTRATOR INQUIRY?

Simply stated, administrator inquiry refers to the process of a principal engaging in systematic, intentional study of his/her own administrative practice and taking action for change based on what he/she learns as a result of the inquiry. Inquiring professionals seek out change and reflect on their practice by posing questions or "wonderings," collecting data to gain insights into their wonderings, analyzing the data along with reading relevant literature, making changes in practice based on new understandings developed during inquiry, and sharing findings with others. Hence, whether you are studying to be a school administrator or are a veteran administrator with years of experience but faced with new educational challenges every day, administrator inquiry becomes a powerful vehicle for learning and school improvement.

The notion of principal inquiry is adapted from the work on teacher action research (see, for example, Dana & Yendol-Hoppey, 2008, 2009; Zeichner, 2003; Cochran-Smith & Lytle, 1993, 1999, 2001). In fact, you may already be familiar with teacher research as a mechanism for staff development for your teachers if you are currently a practicing administrator or have engaged in the process yourself as a classroom teacher. We know a good deal about the value of teachers' engagement in studying their own practice from the literature and work of many prominent scholars in this area. For example, engagement in teacher research, also referred to as teacher inquiry, action research, and practitioner inquiry, has been touted as a powerful tool for teacher professional development (Zeichner, 2003), an important vehicle for raising teacher voices in policy making (Meyers & Rust, 2003), and a mechanism for generating knowledge about teaching and learning and furthering educational reform efforts (Lieberman & Miller, 1990; Cochran-Smith & Lytle, 1993; 1999; Carr & Kemmis, 1986; Kincheloe, 1991; Miller, 1990). The promise that engagement in administrator action research holds for the principalship lies in the documented strength of this approach for teachers. Teacher researchers gain a better understanding of why they behave as they do and consequently make better choices in their classroom practice (Oberg, 1990). In a fashion similar to the ways teachers utilize this process to gain better understandings of themselves and their teaching practice, administrators can use it to gain deeper insights into their practice as administrators and their leadership role in school improvement efforts.

Another reason administrator action research holds promise as a powerful professional development tool for principals is that this movement is consonant with guidelines and suggestions for effective principal professional development. For example, Sparks (2002) cites the Educational Research Service's 1999 publication *Professional Development for School Principals*, which advocates that "effective staff development for administrators is long-term, planned, and job-embedded; focuses on student achievement, supports reflective practice; and provides opportunities to work, discuss, and solve problems with peers" (p. 8.3). Furthermore, Sparks and Hirsh (2002) state that school systems committed to improved student learning will provide principals professional development in which they participate as members of ongoing study groups analyzing instructional issues for their schools. As you will see in the remainder of this text, engagement in administrator action research is aligned with each of these recommendations. In fact, many exemplary leadership development programs utilize action research as a component of the overall professional development of school principals (Darling-Hammond, LaPointe, Meyerson, Orr, & Cohen, 2007). If you are using this text, you are joining hundreds of other prospective and practicing administrators across the nation who are committing to becoming the "head learner" in their school through the process of action research.

HOW IS ADMINISTRATOR INQUIRY OR ACTION RESEARCH DIFFERENT FROM TRADITIONAL EDUCATIONAL RESEARCH?

Two paradigms have dominated educational research on schooling, teaching, and learning over the past several decades. In the first paradigm, the concept of "process-product research" (Shulman, 1986) portrays teaching as a primarily linear activity and depicts teachers and principals as technicians. The practitioners' role is to implement the research findings of "outside" experts, almost exclusively university researchers, who are considered alien to the everyday happenings in schools. In this transmissive mode, principals are not expected to be problem posers or problem solvers; rather, administrators negotiate dilemmas framed by outside experts and are asked to implement with fidelity a curriculum designed by those outside their school. Based on this paradigm, many principals and teachers have learned that it is sometimes best not to problematize their lived school experiences or first-hand observations because to do so may mean an admission of failure. In fact, the transmissive culture of many schools has demonstrated that principals can suffer punitive repercussions from highlighting areas they find problematic. The consequences of pointing out problems have often resulted in traditional top-down "retraining" or remediation from the district office or being placed in the superintendent's "doghouse." Our educational community does not encourage solution-seeking behavior on the part of administrators in the transmissive framework.

In the second paradigm, educational research drawn from qualitative or interpretative studies, teaching, and schooling are portrayed as highly complex, context-specific, interactive activities. In addition, this qualitative or interpretive paradigm captures critically important differences across classrooms, schools, and communities. Chris Clark (1995) identifies the complexity inherent in the educator's job and the importance of understanding and acknowledging contextual differences as follows: "Description becomes prescription, often with less and less regard for the contextual matters that make the description meaningful in the first place" (p. 20).

Although qualitative or interpretive work attends to issues of context, most of the studies emerging from this research paradigm are conducted by university researchers and are intended for academic audiences. Such university research provides valuable insights into the connections between theory and practice, but like the process-product research, the qualitative or interpretive approach limits practitioners' roles in the research process. In fact, the knowledge about teaching and learning generated through university study of theory and practice is still defined and generated by "outsiders" to the school and classroom. While both the process-product and qualitative research paradigms have generated valuable insights into the teaching and learning process, they have not included the voices of the people who work in the trenches of the school building on a daily basis and are therefore best positioned to understand and better the educational experiences for all members of the schoolhouse—administrators and teachers.

Hence, a third research tradition has emerged that highlights the role practitioners play as knowledge generators. This tradition is often referred to as "practitioner inquiry," "classroom research," or "action research." In general, the practitioner inquiry movement focuses on the concerns of practitioners (not outside researchers) and engages practitioners in the design, data collection, and interpretation of data around their question. Termed "action research" by Carr and Kemmis (1986), this approach to educational research has many benefits: (1) theories and knowledge are generated from research grounded in the realities of educational practice, (2) practitioners become collaborators in educational research by investigating their own problems, and (3) practitioners play a part in the research process, which makes them more likely to facilitate change based on the knowledge they generate.

Elliot (1988) describes action research as a continual set of spirals consisting of reflection and action. Each spiral involves (1) clarifying and diagnosing a practical situation that needs to be improved or a practical problem that needs to be resolved, (2) formulating action strategies for improving the situation or resolving the problem, (3) implementing the action strategies and evaluating their effectiveness, and (4) clarifying the situation, resulting in new definitions of problems or areas for improvement, and so on, to the next spiral of reflection and action.

Note that in my description of this third research tradition, I have used a number of terms synonymously—practitioner research, classroom research, and practitioner inquiry. Although these phrases have been used interchangeably, they do have somewhat different emphases and histories. Action research, for instance, usually refers to research intended to bring about change of some kind, usually with a social justice focus, whereas practitioner research quite often has the goal only of examining a practitioner's practice to improve it or better understand what works. For the purposes of this text and to streamline our discussion of research traditions, I have grouped all these related processes together to represent administrators' and teachers' systematic study of their own practice. I use the term *inquiry* most often, however, because in my own coaching of administrators' and teachers' systematic study of their own practice I became discouraged by the baggage that the term *research* in the phrase *action research* carries when the concept is first introduced to educators. The images that the word *research* conjures up come mostly from the process-product paradigm and include a "controlled setting," "an experiment with control and treatment groups," "an objective scientist removed from the subjects of study so as not to contaminate findings," "long hours in the library," and "crunching numbers." Practitioners, in general, weren't overly enthusiastic about these images, and it took a good deal of time to deconstruct those notions and help practitioners see that they are antithetical to what action research is all about. So, over time, I began replacing the terms action research and practitioner research with one simple word that carried much less baggage with it—inquiry—and I will continue to use the word *inquiry* most often both in this section on research traditions as well as throughout the remainder of this text.

Now that we have explored three educational research traditions (Table 1.1), acknowledged the limitations of the first two traditions, and introduced practitioner inquiry, our brief history lesson might suggest that practitioner inquiry is just another educational fad. However, although the terms practitioner research, administrator inquiry, and action research are comparatively new, the idea of teaching as inquiry and the role of practitioners as inquirers are not. Early in the twentieth century, John Dewey (1933) called for teachers to engage in "reflective action" that would transform them into inquiry-oriented classroom practitioners. Similarly, distinguished scholar Donald Schon (1983, 1987) depicts professional practice as a cognitive process of posing and exploring problems or dilemmas identified by practitioners themselves. Influenced by Donald Schon's work, the role of reflection in improving the learning and performance of schools received considerable attention throughout the 1980s and 1990s (Senge, 1990). During this time, many school administrator professional preparation programs adopted reflection as an instructional methodology for preparing principals to understand and

Table 1.1   Comparison of Research Paradigms

	Process-Product	**Qualitative or Interpretive**	**Practitioner Inquiry**
Practitioner	Practitioner as technician	Practitioner as story character	Practitioner as storyteller
Researcher	Outsider	Outsider	Insider
Process	Linear	Discursive	Cyclical
Source of question	Researcher	Researcher	Principal
Type of research question	Focused on control, prediction, or impact	Focused on explaining a process or phenomenon	Focused on providing insight into an administrator's own practice in an effort to make change and improve the school
Example of research question	Which teacher professional development strategy is most effective?	How do principals' knowledge of teacher leadership and their interaction with teacher leaders contribute to principals' support for teacher leadership? (Mangin, 2007)	In what ways can I as a principal help facilitate the professional growth of the teachers within my building through engagement in action research?

meet the changing social and political demands placed on schools (see, for example, Hart, 1993; Osterman, 1991; Short & Rinehart, 1993). Clearly, the concept of reflection as an essential skill for administrators to possess and use for understanding and improving schools has stood the test of time.

Administrators' engagement in inquiry is one vehicle for making reflection purposeful and visible. Given the complex environments of today's schools, where much of the decision making and discussion regarding what happens in the schoolhouse occur outside the walls of the school (Darling-Hammond, 1994; Cochran-Smith & Lytle, 2006), the time seems ripe to equip administrators with the tools of inquiry and thus enable them to cultivate the expertise residing within the schoolhouse itself and to utilize these critical, untapped resources to improve their schools from the inside out rather than the outside in. In the words of Mark Bracewell, one middle school principal-inquirer I have worked with, administrator inquiry is powerful:

> It's interactive, it's practical, and it's designed by student need and teacher need and principal need. Inquiry is different from traditional professional development I've experienced as a principal because it's introspective; it's not me sitting down in a chair and somebody else, who doesn't know me, my school, my teachers, my community, or my kids, telling me what I should be doing—the traditional "sit and get" or "spray and pray" professional development where you go, you listen, you get what you get, and maybe you use it or maybe you don't. Rather than someone else telling me what I should be doing *to* my teachers and *to* my students, through engagement in inquiry I'm learning *with* my teachers and *with* the students in my building by closely taking a really hard look at what I'm already doing and what I need to do to change it. (Personal communication, August 2008)

If this is the goal, we now need to understand how administrator inquiry can serve as a tool for achieving professional growth and educational reform. I believe that the best-stated definitions of administrator inquiry come from principal-researchers themselves. This section ends with a few descriptions from principals I have collaborated with on inquiry:

> Principal inquiry is a process that allows me to do three things I need and like to do but rarely make time for—be a reflective practitioner, work with a true professional learning community, and model instructional leadership.
>
> —Mike Delucas, Principal, Williston High School

> Principal inquiry is when a principal stops and takes a breath, takes a look at the changes or decisions they have made, and gathers information needed to decide if success on the goals that were set has been achieved. That information may be test scores, teacher input, student input, parent input, evidence seen in classrooms, lesson plans, etc. . . . Compare the results to the goals, talk with all the stakeholders, then actively use this information to plan the next steps, maybe a new direction or keep on keeping on!
>
> —Lacy Redd, Principal, Newberry Elementary School

Engagement in principal inquiry enables me to see things I wouldn't ordinarily see in my school or building when I don't make the time to step back, pose questions, really look at all kinds of data, read, talk with other administrators as well as my teachers and the students in my building, and commit to continuous school improvement. This is hard to do in the midst of the craziness of each school day, but once you engage in the process, you see how incredibly valuable and important it is. Inquiring into practice has become a part of who I am and what I do as a principal, and I can't imagine doing my job without the insights engagement in inquiry can bring.

—Patrick Wnek, Principal, Hilltop Alternative
School and Summit Academy

Inquiry is at the core of everything that I do, whether it is working with students, teachers, colleagues, or our whole school. It is the nagging question (or questions) that stirs me to take action based on data, investigations, instincts, and more questions. It is a never-ending process. It is the process of creating and re-creating my school, my life, and my practice a question at a time.

—Donnan Stoicovy, Principal, Park Forest Elementary School

WHAT IS THE RELATIONSHIP BETWEEN ADMINISTRATOR INQUIRY AND PRINCIPAL PROFESSIONAL GROWTH?

Simply stated, practitioner inquiry is defined as systematic, intentional study of one's own professional practice. Inquiring professionals seek out change by reflecting on their practice. They do this by posing questions or "wonderings," collecting data to gain insights into their wonderings, analyzing the data along with reading relevant literature, making changes in practice based on new understandings developed during inquiry, and sharing findings with others (Dana & Yendol-Hoppey, 2009). Hence, whether you are a prospective principal at the dawn of your career in administration or a veteran principal with years of experience facing new educational challenges every day, administrator inquiry becomes a powerful vehicle for learning and reform.

As a principal-inquirer in charge of your own learning, you become a part of a larger struggle in education—the struggle to better understand, inform, shape, reshape, and reform standard school practice (Cochran-Smith & Lytle, 1993). Administrator inquiry differs from traditional professional development for principals, which has typically focused on the knowledge of an outside "expert"—what principal Mark Bracewell and others have referred to as "sit and get" or "spray and pray." This traditional model of professional growth, usually delivered in the form of workshops, may appear an efficient method of disseminating information but often does not result in real and meaningful change in the schools. Kelline Stevens (2001) captures this sentiment in an article titled "Collaborative Action Research: An Effective Strategy for Principal Inservice":

> Inservice education for school principals is often viewed by principals as something "done to" them by others. Consequently, it is not surprising that inservice is seen in a negative light by many practitioners. A somewhat different approach to meeting the professional development needs of the principals can be found in the concept of collaborative action research. (p. 203)

Like Stevens, those dissatisfied with the traditional model of professional development suggest a need for new approaches, like action research, that enhance professional growth and lead to real change. For example, in the *Journal of Staff Development,* educators from across the country put forth their vision for the "Road Ahead" for professional learning. These ideas included the importance of creating activities, tools, and contexts that blend theory and practice (Darling-Hammond, 2007) and support collaborative learning structures that deepen innovation implementation efforts (DuFour & DuFour, 2007).

Consonant with the movement to change traditional professional development practices is the practitioner inquiry movement. This movement toward a new model of professional growth based on inquiry into one's own practice can be powerfully developed by school districts and building administrators as a form of professional development for all. By participating in practitioner inquiry, the principal develops a sense of ownership in the knowledge constructed, and this sense of ownership heavily contributes to the possibilities for real change in schools.

The ultimate goal is to create an inquiry *stance* toward administrator practice. This stance becomes a professional positioning, owned by the principal, where questioning one's own practice becomes part of the principal's work and eventually a part of the culture within the principal's school. Michael Copland (2003), in his article titled "Leadership of Inquiry: Building and Sustaining Capacity for School Improvement," describes this notion of stance:

Leadership for improving teaching and learning is rooted in *continual inquiry* into the work at the school, inquiry focused on student learning, high standards, equity, and best practice. This process of inquiry does not cease; rather, the work is best thought of as an ongoing effort to build greater *capacity* with regard to instructional practices that improve learning among those who work in the school community. People in the school renorm their basic work around identifying, striving to solve, and continually revisiting critical problems. (p. 376)

By cultivating this inquiry stance toward practice, principals and teachers play a critical role in enhancing their own professional growth and ultimately the experience of schooling for children. Thus, an inquiry stance is synonymous with professional growth and provides a nontraditional approach to administrator development that can lead to meaningful change for schools and all the people who inhabit them—principals, teachers, and students.

WHAT ARE THE BENEFITS OF ENGAGING IN INQUIRY?

In addition to providing principals with a meaningful way to grow professionally, engaging in the process of inquiry reaps other numerous benefits for principals and their schools. First, there have been numerous discussions in the literature about teacher isolation, depicting a lonely profession in which teachers close their classroom doors and have little interaction with other teachers in their buildings (see, for example, Flinder, 1988; Lieberman & Miller, 1992; Lortie, 1975; Smith & Scott, 1990). While teaching has been characterized by norms of isolation, so, too, is the principalship. Professional isolation, defined as the "unpleasant experiences that occur when a person's network of social relations at work is deficient in some important way, either quantitatively or qualitatively" (Dussault, 1997, p. 4), is pervasive in administration for many reasons. First and foremost, there exists a quantitative deficit of colleagues for the principal within his or her own building. Even for those who employ an assistant principal due to the size of their school or administrative structure in their districts, or for principals who have a strong leadership team they collaborate with for decision making, the principal is the *only* person within a school building that holds this unique position, a position that carries with it the ultimate responsibility for all members of the schoolhouse. To find other principals to converse with, administrators must venture outside the four walls of the school sites, and principals feel uncomfortable being away from their buildings for any extended period of time. In addition, in some districts, principals compete with one another for scarce resources, and it can be perceived as risky to share anything but the very best that is happening at your school in an effort to protect your fair share of resources. In still other districts, the times set aside for principals to come together on a regular basis are jammed packed with new information coming from the central office. Principals sit and listen at these gatherings, leaving little time to converse with colleagues in any meaningful ways beyond congenial niceties such as, "Good to see you again," and "How is your family?" Hence, perhaps even to a greater extent than for teachers, norms of isolation surround the principalship. Roland Barth (1990) writes:

> Principals, like teachers, need and treasure collegiality and peer support. Yet, perhaps even more than teachers, principals live in a world of isolation. . . . There is often a huge distance between adjoining classrooms; the distance across town to the next school is even greater. When principals associate with peers, it is often at an administrators' meeting. But just as it is forbidden for principals to "not know" within their individual school, principals often have trouble "not knowing" with peers. Seldom is time or setting conducible to collegial support or the exchange of ideas and concerns. (p. 83)

These very norms of isolation keep principals from learning, growing, and becoming the best administrators they can be and can even lead to professional atrophy (Smith & Scott, 1990; Rosenholtz, 1989). Engagement in administrator inquiry challenges these norms. By engaging in the process of administrator inquiry with other principals, or even in collaborative inquiry with a group of teachers within your own building, you are forced out of isolation and surround yourself with other professionals conversing about practice in systematic and meaningful ways. I'll talk more about powerful structures that support inquiry and connect principals with others in the last section of this chapter.

A second benefit of principal inquiry is that, by engaging in this process, principals become role models for the teachers and students in their buildings. A critical belief about learning is ownership. Learning must be something teachers and students *do*, not something that others do *to* or *for* them. According to Roland Barth (1990), "School principals have an extraordinary opportunity to improve public schools. A precondition for realizing this potential is for principals to become head learners" (p. 84). He also states:

point and time to sit down and say, "Ok, what does this information say?" and "What decision do I need to lead the way in light of this information?" That was hard for me to do because I was fighting fires all the time. . . . I'm not going to lie about that. But as far as the inquiry process itself, I think an effective principal participates in inquiry and finds a way to fit it into his or her schedule because you've got to do it. If your kids are going to excel, . . . you've got to look at what they're doing. Where are they, where do they need to be, how do we get them there? That's essentially what inquiry is. (Personal communication, August 2007)

HOW DO I FIND TIME TO ENGAGE IN INQUIRY AS A PRINCIPAL?

In the harried, everyday firefighting experience of the principal, a definite and very real impediment to engaging in inquiry is time! It is very normal and natural for principals to like the sound of inquiry and believe in it theoretically but to find it difficult to make time for inquiry in practice. There are many things a principal can do to create, find, take, and make time to squeeze the process of inquiry onto an already too full plate.

Perhaps most important is acknowledging that time is a factor that must be dealt with rather than pretending that issues of time management don't exist or totally dismissing inquiry because you just don't have the time. In many ways, inquiry is like exercise. When my own work and life became ultra busy, I gave up exercising, lamenting that "I just don't have the time." Yet, I was haunted each year at my annual physical when my doctor asked me what I was doing for exercise and throughout the year by continuing reports on the news and in magazines that exercising is an important ingredient for overall fitness and health. Although it was difficult for me to take the time to exercise, at the start of this school year, I made a commitment to join a gym and work out three days a week. I found that I felt better, I slept better, and even though exercise was dipping into my work time for three or four hours a week, when I returned to my work after exercising, I was more productive. Exercise rejuvenated me, and my hour break three days a week helped me respond to work tasks more productively and efficiently.

Engagement in principal inquiry is just like that. Research tells us that engagement in inquiry is an important ingredient for the overall professional health of an educator (Copland, 2003). Yet, many principals do not engage in the process because they just can't find the time. Even though it is difficult to take the time to inquire, if you make a commitment and safeguard a little time each week to engage in the process, you'll feel better, make important administrative decisions in a more informed, thoughtful way, and return to the never-ending demands of the principalship with more energy to face the challenges of each school day. Roland Barth (2001) informs us that one reason it is so difficult for school leaders to become learners is lack of time, but he reminds us, "For principals, as for all of us, protesting a lack of time is another way of saying other things are more important and perhaps more comfortable" (p. 157). The first step toward finding time to engage in inquiry as an administrator is to acknowledge that lack of time will *always* be an issue that confronts principals and then make a simultaneous commitment to engage in this important and necessary work anyway.

One way to help ease the tension of time is to make inquiry a part of your daily practice rather than a separate part of it. This can occur by reshaping already existing structures in your work. For example, each year Alachua Elementary School principal Jim Brandenburg had a regular meeting with his superintendent to evaluate his work as a principal and set goals for the following school year. In previous years, these meetings were shaped by a lengthy district form that had to be completed by Jim prior to the meeting. Committed to finding time to inquire, Jim asked his superintendent if they might abandon that form and replace it with a report about an inquiry Jim wished to engage in during the following school year. Ironically, Jim's inquiry would be driven by the question, "In what ways can I as a principal help facilitate the professional growth of the teachers within my building through engagement in action research?" The superintendent agreed, and Jim reports that the meeting where they discussed his plans for inquiry was the most productive and meaningful year-end evaluation he ever had! Jim immediately began collecting data to gain insights into his question even before that school year ended by having his teachers complete a survey, which Jim termed "Druthers" (see Figure 1.1). "Druthers" contained a series of questions that Jim asked his teachers based on the idea that, "If you had your 'druthers' (what you'd rather do), what would you choose?"

Another way to create time for inquiry by making it a part of your normal administrative practice is to formulate a study based on something you must do anyway. For example, principal Terry Buckles needed a plan to deal with her school's inability to make her state's Adequate Yearly Progress (AYP) requirement the previous school year and, thus, being placed on corrective action. She writes:

This is my sixth year of being a principal at Mellon Elementary in Palatka, Florida. The test scores have shown a slow increase each year during this time, however Mellon Elementary has not been

Figure 1.1   Druthers Survey

Please return to Jim by Monday, May 19.

DRUTHERS

Teacher _____

Please take a few minutes and share your thoughts, concerns, plans, or ideas with me.

1. Grade level or teaching assignment preference for next year:
   a. 1st _____
   b. 2nd _____

2. Possible teammates, partners, neighbors that I'd like to work with:
   _____

3. Possible leadership opportunities: _____

4. Openness to change:
   ☐ definitely want to do something different, like _____
   ☐ maybe ready to change, depending on _____
   ☐ please leave me alone because _____
   ☐ none of the above: _____

5. What were some of your successes this year?

6. What was your biggest frustration?

7. The biggest problem that our school needs to address is: _____

8. Share any random thoughts on:
   • technology
   • coteaching
   • master schedule
   • discipline issues
   • ESE class content/scheduling/inclusion
   • professional learning community stuff
   • summer inservice training
   • security
   • clerical support
   • administrative support
   • inquiry
   • subject area needs
   • FCAT/testing issues
   • maintenance
   • front office
   • special class content/schedules
   • etc.

9. The one thing that Jim could do that would make my life easier is: _____
   _____

10. Anything else on your mind: _____

Source: Jim Brandenburg, Principal, Alachua Elementary School, Alachua, Florida.

able to make Adequate Yearly Progress (AYP) or earn an "A" based on the A+ criteria. The teachers and I have worked very hard to try to improve and this is very frustrating for everyone. During the 2005–2006 school year the teachers mapped out the curriculum and identified our bottom quartile students and we were able to make improvements. Even though we improved, we missed making AYP, due to lacking one more student earning a 3.0 on the Florida Writes State Test, which we needed to make the 1% required increase. We met all of the other AYP criteria. In addition, we missed earning a "B" by 4 points. Mellon Elementary is in corrective action this year, because we have not been able to make AYP. This is a serious problem that has to be corrected. If we do not make AYP during the 2006–2007 school year, Mellon will be facing restructuring in 2007–2008. This could mean that the teachers would have to reapply for their positions and that the administration would be replaced.

Another school in our district was required to implement the Florida Continuous Improvement Model (FCIM) during the 2005–2006 school year, because they earned an "F" the previous year. The school earned points to receive a "D," but because fifty percent of their bottom quartile students did not make a year's growth in reading they were dropped to an "F." After implementing the Florida Continuous Improvement Model (FCIM), they moved from an "F" to an "A" in one year. I presented this model to our teachers at the end of the 2005–2006 school year, after this school's test scores and "A" status was published in the newspaper. They were all very receptive to fully implementing the Continuous Improvement Model (CIM) during the 2006–2007 school year. Therefore, the purpose of my inquiry is to address the question, "In what ways will implementing the continuous improvement model help increase student achievement at Mellon Elementary School?" (Buckles, 2008, pp. 229–230)

In this most extreme, but very real, example, Terry had to address that her school was being placed on corrective action. Terry turned to the process of inquiry to find insights into what she needed to do anyway, enabling her to more naturally engage in practitioner research as part of her administrative work.

One final helpful hint in finding time to engage in inquiry is to schedule at least some time that you will commit to doing *something* for your inquiry each week—whether it is spent reading an article related to the topic of your study, writing in your journal about a piece of data that puzzles you, or collecting a new piece of data that will glean insights into your question. For example, just as many people block out Monday, Wednesday, and Friday afternoons to go to the gym to exercise, commit to every Thursday afternoon from 4:00 to 5:00 (or any other consistent time each week) to be your "reflection and inquiry time." Write it into your calendar, and be sure your secretary knows that this time each week is valuable to you and that you don't wish to be disturbed unless it is absolutely necessary. Principal Mary Ann Chapko (2006) writes:

> The never-ending excitement of [the principalship] lies in the unexpected events, life-altering decisions, and controlled chaos that occur at regular intervals throughout the day. As principal, my best defense is to control what I can control, for example: selling 12 kinds of ice cream at lunch, consistently greeting my afternoon kindergartners at 12:40, or scheduling a monthly "Make Your Own Sundae Birthday Party with the Principal." Scheduling events from which I rarely deviate allows me to better deal with the multitude of unscheduled events that occur daily. At the very least, it leaves me with the feeling that I have some control over my day. (p. 30)

By scheduling a planned, consistent time for reflection and inquiry in the same way that you schedule menu items for the lunchroom, your greeting of afternoon kindergarteners, and the monthly special events with students in your building, you'll be surprised at how much you can accomplish and how you will feel a greater sense of control over all of the other line items on the principal's ever-growing "To Do" list.

WHAT ARE SOME CONTEXTS THAT ARE RIPE FOR PRINCIPAL INQUIRY?

With an understanding of what administrator inquiry is, how it differs from traditional educational research, how it contributes to principal professional development and other benefits for the principal, and how to find time in the busy administrator's life to engage in research, let us now consider the kinds of contexts that support administrator inquiry. As previously discussed, administration is full of enormous complexities, and, hence, administration itself invites inquiry. Never a day goes by without at least one problem, issue, tension, or dilemma arising for a principal that beckons for the deep exploration and insights that the process of inquiry can bring! However, even as inquiry beckons each and every administrator, becoming a "lone inquirer" is difficult. For this reason, it is important to explore four particularly ripe contexts for facilitating the development of inquiry stances for practicing and prospective school administrators—university coursework, superintendent/district meetings, leadership teams, and professional learning communities. You may currently be a part of one of these four contexts, or you may wish to seek them out as you begin and continue your career in administration.

University Coursework

Many principals and aspiring principals enroll in coursework at a local college or university or online as they pursue an advanced degree (master's, specialist, or doctorate) or an initial principal certification in their state. Many of these exemplary leadership development programs utilize action research as a component of the overall professional development of school principals (Darling-Hammond et al., 2007). Sometimes engagement in practitioner research serves as the culmination of the program, with master's, specialist, or doctoral students engaging in action research as a portfolio project, paper, thesis, or even dissertation. Although sometimes learning practitioner research skills are a part of coursework, some institutions devote an entire course to practitioner inquiry, with aspiring and/or practicing administrators either completing a proposal for action research or actually completing an entire inquiry project within a sixteen-week semester timeframe. Students who enroll in these courses or have these experiences bond with one another as they share with each other and help their classmates and colleagues through each aspect of the inquiry process.

Superintendent/District Meetings

In an effort to find meaningful professional development activities for their principals, some districts, such as Florida's Pinellas County, are re-creating the bonding that often occurs among classmates at the university within the districts themselves. They are accomplishing this task by reconceptualizing their traditional monthly administrative team meetings to being entirely devoted to, or at least a portion of the meeting devoted to, principals' engagement in action research. Rather than sit passively at meetings and listen to a long list of announcements, many announcements are now taken care of through e-mail, and principals are organized into small groups to complete a series of interactive tasks to help each principal identify an area to study about his or her own practice. At the end of the school year, Pinellas County holds an "Inquiry Celebration" where principals and teachers who have engaged in the process of inquiry during the school year share their work with others. Principals (and teachers) in this county often speak of inquiry as the most rewarding and powerful professional development they have ever experienced as educators!

Leadership Teams

While the first two contexts for inquiry occur outside the principal's school building, a third context ripe for inquiry exists right within the principal's own backyard—the leadership team. A focus in schools in recent years on building a culture of collaboration coupled with educational reform, accountability, and improved standards that require visionary and strategic planning, not only from the principal but also from the whole school community, have led to a leadership team phenomemon (Zappulla, 2002). Leadership teams are instituted by principals and usually include any assistant administrators and at least three teachers who also have classroom responsibilities. The leadership team shares problems, responsibilities, and decision making with the administrator. In fact, according to Pauline Zappulla (2002) and other leading scholars in educational administration, leadership teams may be used for consultative purposes, participative decision making, strategic planning, policy development, monitoring and coordinating programs, and maintaining a commitment to collaboration and shared leadership. In whatever ways principals utilize their leadership teams, however, one vital component for the success of the team is its ability to engender learning: "Team learning is vital because teams, not individuals, are the fundamental learning unit in modern organizations. This is where the 'rubber meets the road': unless teams can learn, the organization cannot learn" (Senge, 1990). Engagement in inquiry with the leadership team is a natural way the principal can be assured that his or her leadership team is learning and is another way to make inquiry a part of, rather than apart from, the regular practice of an administrator. Some principals have even gone as far as organizing their leadership teams as a professional learning community.

Professional Learning Communities

Professional learning communities (PLCs) serve to connect and network groups of professionals to do just what their name suggests—*learn* from practice. In recent years, there has been a proliferation of discussions in both the education and business literature as well as in schools across the nation about PLCs and their ability to help institutions improve. For example, in *Professional Learning Communities That Work*, Dufour and Eaker (1998) argue, "The most promising strategy for sustained, substantive school improvement is developing the ability of school personnel to function as professional learning communities" (p. xi). PLCs took hold across the nation as many top scholars and leaders in education, including Linda Darling-Hammond and Milbrey McLaughlin (1995), Michael Fullan (2001), Peter Senge (1990), and Andy Hargreaves (1994), claimed that schools must become "learning organizations." However, according to Whitford and Wood (in press), there is a stunning lack of clarity about what actually is being proposed. "A wide variety of distinct professional development approaches, school social groupings, and change and improvement strategies appear in the literature labeled as 'professional learning communities.'" For this reason, it is important to clarify the meaning of PLC as it is used in this book.

In this book, I define PLCs generically as small groups of faculty who meet regularly to study more effective learning and teaching practices, with their time together often structured by the use of protocols to ensure focused, deliberate conversation and dialogue by teachers about student work and student learning. Protocols for educators provide a script or series of timed steps for how a conversation among teachers on a chosen topic will develop.

A variety of different protocols have been developed for use in PLCs by a number of noteworthy organizations such as the National Staff Development Council (see, for example, Lois Brown Easton's *Powerful Designs for Professional Learning* [2004]), the Southern Maine Partnership (see, for example, www.usm.maine.edu/smp/teaching.htm), and the National School Reform Faculty (www.nsrfharmony.org), who developed one version of a PLC called Critical Friends Groups (CFGs). In its work conceptualizing CFGs, the National School Reform Faculty laid much of the groundwork for shifting the nature of the dialogue that occurs between and among teachers and their principals about their practice in schools, and it is responsible for training thousands of teachers and an increasing number of principals in developing collegial relationships, encouraging reflective practice, and rethinking leadership in restructuring schools. The CFGs provide deliberate time and structures dedicated to promoting adult professional growth directly linked to student learning.

By their own nature, then, PLCs enhance the possibilities for conducting an inquiry and cultivating a community of inquirers. In fact, in a companion book to this text titled *The Reflective Educator's Guide to Professional Development* (Dana & Yendol-Hoppey, 2008), my colleague and I name a model for school-based professional development that combines some of the best of what we know about action research and PLCs and, in the process, rectifies a weakness that has been identified in traditional professional development practices. We name this new entity the "inquiry-oriented professional learning community." We define this community as a group of six to twelve professionals who meet on a regular basis to learn from practice through structured dialogue and who engage in continuous cycles through the process of action research (articulating a wondering, collecting data to gain insights into the wondering, analyzing data, making improvements in practice based on what was learned, and sharing learning with others).

Many principals are instituting this model in their schools as a powerful form of professional development for their teachers, as well as for themselves. In addition, some principals gather with other principals to form their own inquiry-oriented learning communities where they support each other in the study of one another's school and administrative practice (Dana, Tricarico, Quinn, & Wnek, 2008; Byrne-Jimenez & Orr, 2007). Whether principals are instituting this model in their own buildings or replicating this model with groups of other principals to serve as role models for their teachers back in their own buildings, the success of inquiry-oriented learning community work within a school is directly tied to how aware and connected principals are to the PLC work unfolding in their buildings. What better way for you as a principal to be connected and aware than to join one of your building PLCs yourself or, if appropriate to the goals of your leadership team, to run your leadership team as a PLC?

Whatever context you find yourself in as a principal-inquirer, your first step in your inquiry journey is to develop a question or "wondering" you wish to study, a step we'll discuss in detail in Chapter 2. To illustrate the power of a PLC or lead team functioning as a context for principal inquiry, however, I end this chapter with the story of Marion, an exemplary elementary school principal I worked with, and the ways her wondering developed with the help of her lead team.

PRINCIPAL INQUIRY IN A PLC: CASE STUDY

Elementary school principal Marion and five of her faculty members met regularly to reflect on the teaching and learning that was occurring in their school building for all members of the community—students, teachers, and administrators. Through the use of protocols to examine student and educator work, they uncovered and addressed problems and took action to address them. The group was facilitated by Adam, a veteran fourth-grade teacher who had been through the National School Reform Faculty's intensive, weeklong training on PLCs three years earlier.

About to embark on a new school year, teachers reported to work one full week before the students after summer vacation to prepare for their students' arrival. During this planning week, Marion called her PLC together to look at their students' results on standardized test scores from the previous school year. Along with Marion, all members of the PLC concluded that they really needed

(Continued)

(Continued)

to focus on the bottom quartile of students in their school and that they could utilize the process of action research to make a difference for this population.

Marion shared with Adam and the group, "I've been thinking about this a lot over the summer, and I'm also thinking of a lot of ongoing initiatives in our building. I played around with a question that might guide us this year." She handed out a paper with the following words typed across the top:

Will focusing on the lowest student quartile through teacher culture awareness, mentoring, progress monitoring, intervention by the reading teacher, and the afterschool program be sufficient to raise our percentage making AYP (Adequate Yearly Progress) in reading from 47 to 65 percent?

There was a pause as members of the group silently read and considered the wondering statement, and then Marion queried, "Is this too wordy, or is it even where we should be headed?"

Adam began the dialogue.

Marion, thank you so much for getting us started! This actually comes at a great time—I just finished reading an article about teacher and principal research in the Madison, Wisconsin, Metropolitan School District. The article shares ideas for what they believe makes a good action research question. I think we can learn a lot from this article. Among other things, the authors believe that good action research questions are clear and concise, are "doable," and require a more complex answer than yes or no [Caro-Bruce & McCreadie, 1994]. I think we should play with this research question with these three things in mind. To start, how might we rephrase this question so it is not stated as a dichotomous question?

PLC member Rita gave it a try, saying, "How about something like: What role do teacher culture awareness, mentoring, progress monitoring, reading teacher intervention, and afterschool program participation play in raising the AYP of our lowest student quartile?"

Adam wrote the question on the whiteboard as Rita spoke. He stepped back and looked at what he had written and responded, "I think that's good. Now it reads as an open-ended question. By carefully wording questions so they are open-ended, we open ourselves up to frame the design of our research to uncover lots of possibilities. When a question is posed in a dichotomous fashion, we force the design of our research to fit into narrow categories."

Marion replied, "OK, I see that. But I still think the question is really wordy—not clear and concise like that article shares."

Adam responded, "Well, what if we broke that question down further into an overarching wondering with subquestions? Would that make it more clear and concise?"

All members of the PLC agreed that this was a good plan and contributed to the discussion for ideas about how to "pare down" the wondering on the whiteboard. After lots of crossing out and erasing, their discussion led to the following revision of Rita's question, which Adam inscribed on the whiteboard for all members of the group to view:

Overarching Wondering: What actions can our faculty take to improve reading achievement for our lowest-quartile students?

Subwonderings:

- What is the relationship between teacher culture awareness and raising the AYP of our lowest quartile?
- What is the relationship between progress monitoring and raising the AYP of our lowest quartile?
- What is the relationship between mentoring and raising the AYP of our lowest quartile?
- What is the relationship between reading teacher intervention and raising the AYP of our lowest quartile?
- What is the relationship between afterschool program participation and raising the AYP of our lowest student quartile?
- How do our lowest-quartile students experience and benefit from engagement with each of these strategies (teacher culture awareness, progress monitoring, mentoring, intervention, afterschool)?

The group all agreed that they were making progress, but Rita expressed that it still didn't feel quite right to her.

The process of breaking down this wondering has helped me realize how many initiatives we are participating in. No wonder our faculty was feeling so overwhelmed and stressed at the end of the last school year. Morale was low. I think we should consider the feasibility of this research—are we trying to do too much all at once? And if we attempt to do too much at once, can we really do anything well? And if we end up not really doing anything well, how can we get good data to understand how various initiatives are working? If we do too much at once, we'll only drag ourselves down. We ought to consider this before we proceed.

All members of the group nodded in agreement. As it was nearing 4:00 p.m., Adam drew attention to the clock and reminded everyone that one of their ground rules was that they always started and ended on time and that they were scheduled to end in five minutes. Through discussion, the group members decided that they shared a commitment to focus on the bottom quartile of students this school year but needed to work further on framing their question and research plan. Adam agreed to look through his book of protocols and find one that might help accomplish this goal at their next meeting.

In this story, Marion was well on her way to beginning the process of inquiry with five teachers at her side. Just as Marion began her inquiry journey by exploring possibilities for her research questions, you will begin question exploration in Chapter 2—"The Passions That Drive Your Journey: Finding a Wondering."

CHAPTER 1 EXERCISES

1. Taking some time to reflect on who you are or plan to be as a principal is a critical first step in becoming an inquirer. To begin this process, complete the following open-ended sentences and share your responses with a principal colleague, your lead team, a few trusted teachers, or even a member of your own family. If you are not yet a principal, project into the future and answer these questions as if you were the principal in the school in which you are currently working as a teacher or assistant administrator. After completing these sentences, consider what you have discovered about yourself as a principal and how these discoveries might lead to your first inquiry.

Open-Ended Sentence Completion Activity

My greatest accomplishment as a principal is _____
_____.

One thing I wish I could change about my school is _____
_____.

One thing I'd like to learn to do better as a principal is _____
_____.

One thing my faculty can do to make me happy is _____
_____.

If I were forced to leave the principalship tomorrow, three things I would most want my faculty to say about me:

1. _____.

2. _____.

3. _____.

What the phrase "principal as inquirer" means to me: _____
_____.

2. As you embark on your inquiry journey, you will be doing a lot of thinking about what you want to study and how to best study it! A wonderful way to think about your inquiry is to write. Noted educational ethnographer Harry Wolcott (1990) goes as far as to state that writing

and thinking are synonymous: "The conventional wisdom is that writing reflects thinking. I am drawn to a different position: Writing *is* thinking" (p. 21). Begin a journal to help you keep track of your inquiry journey. This journal may also become one source of data collection you will use to gain insights into your inquiry as the process unfolds for you within your school.

Here are four prompts to help you start your journal:

Prompt 1. Write about something that happened during the last week that you could turn into an inquiry. Discuss what this particular inquiry might lead you to discover and improve about yourself, your faculty, your students, your district, and/or your school.

Prompt 2. Write about something that intrigues or puzzles you about the inquiry process (i.e., defining a wondering, collaborating with others, data collection, data analysis, taking action for change). What components of the inquiry process will be the easiest for you? What components of the inquiry process will be the most challenging for you?

Prompt 3. Write about the key people in your school with whom you might collaborate on your inquiry. What opportunities will you have or can you create for this collaboration to occur?

Prompt 4. One word that describes how I feel about conducting my own personal inquiry into my administrative practice this school year is _____. I chose this word because_____

_____

_____

_____

_____.

2

The Passions That Drive Your Journey

Finding a Wondering

Ⅰn Chapter 1, you were welcomed to the world of administrator inquiry as we explored the definition of practitioner inquiry and how it differs from traditional research conducted at the university, how it is related to principal professional growth and other benefits for the administrator, and how to find time to engage in practitioner research as well as explore the contexts in which your engagement in administrator inquiry can unfold. This welcome to inquiry places you, as current and future administrator, in charge of your own growth and development. Leading your own learning is likely quite different from the majority of your past experiences in "sit and get" or "spray and pray" principal professional development. By taking charge of your own learning, therefore, you are entering uncharted territory!

Charting new territory can be exciting but also quite frightening when beginning a journey in which you are unfamiliar with both the terrain and your final destination. It becomes less daunting after you do some initial preparation and take your first steps, however.

Just as hikers gather information and prepare themselves mentally for a hike or climb—What territory do I want to explore? What do I hope to find?—as a principal-inquirer, you, too, will need some mental preparation before you embark on your first inquiry journey. The groundwork for this journey is what Kettering refers to as the welcoming attitude toward and active seeking of change: "Essentially research is nothing but a state of mind, . . . a friendly, welcoming attitude toward change, . . . going out to look for change instead of waiting for it to come" (Kettering, in Boyd, 1961).

This attitude lays the foundation for your journey. The compass that provides the direction for your inquiry comes from critical reflection in and on your own administrative practice. When administrators seek out change and reflect on practice, the first steps of their journey begin with brainstorming questions or wonderings they wish to explore. To start this process, principals consider the phrases "I wonder . . . ," "I think . . . ," and "What if . . . ?"

WHERE DO I FIND MY WONDERINGS AND QUESTIONS?

A principal's completion of the phrases "I wonder . . . ," "I think . . . ," and "What if . . . ?" do not materialize out of thin air. According to Hubbard and Power (1993), wonderings and questions come from "real world observations and dilemmas" (p. 2). Similarly, researchers Sherman and Webb (1997) state that qualitative research questions come from "felt difficulties." These felt difficulties are direct concerns that emerge from one's own experiences.

Wonderings materialize at the nexuses of the real-world observations, dilemmas, felt difficulties, and passions that you develop in your work as an administrator. In this section, I point to nine different but related areas of passion where you may find your first wondering:

1. Staff development

2. Curriculum development

3. Individual teacher(s)

4. Individual student(s)

5. School culture/community

6. Leadership

7. Management

8. School performance

9. Social justice

In some ways, each of the nine passions overlap each other, but they are presented as distinct entities to help you view an array of different possibilities for finding and defining your first wondering. Each passion is illustrated with the work of one or more principal-inquirers and ends with exercises designed to help you explore that particular area. Because discovering the passions that will drive your inquiry journey will take some time, I suggest you pause at the end of each passion's description, take a break from reading the text, and consider and/or complete one or more of the exercises as you progress through the chapter. A brief pause at the end of each passion is a way to "refuel" during this leg of your journey toward discovering the particular passions that will drive your inquiry work as an administrator and subsequently creating, or perhaps recognizing, the wonderings that reside within you.

In addition to the exercises at the end of each passion, this chapter ends with some general cautions to consider, as well as two over-arching exercises designed to help you look across all the nine areas explored. By the end of this chapter, I hope you will have articulated at least one burning question you have about your administrative practice that you may be interested in exploring and can celebrate the completion of what is often the most difficult component of practitioner inquiry—getting started!

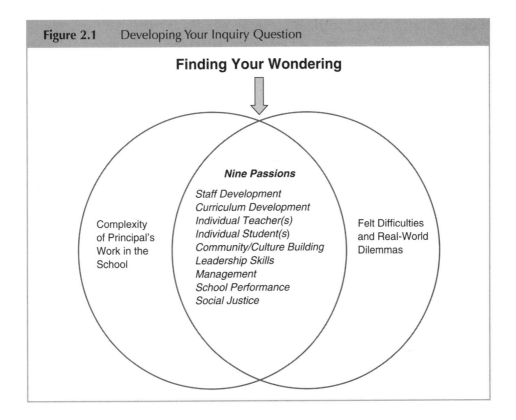

Figure 2.1   Developing Your Inquiry Question

Finding Your Wondering

Nine Passions

Staff Development
Curriculum Development
Individual Teacher(s)
Individual Student(s)
Community/Culture Building
Leadership Skills
Management
School Performance
Social Justice

Complexity of Principal's Work in the School

Felt Difficulties and Real-World Dilemmas

Passion 1: Staff Development

According to Roland Barth (1981):

Nothing within a school has more impact upon students in terms of skills development, self-confidence, or classroom behavior than the personal and professional growth of their teachers. When teachers examine, question, reflect on their ideas and develop new practices that lead towards their ideals, students are alive. When teachers stop growing, so do their students. (p. 145)

As the principal, you have been charged with the awesome responsibility of facilitating the learning and professional growth of the teachers in your school. The job of keeping teachers alive and growing throughout their careers is more important than ever! Given the pressures of high-stakes testing and national, state, and district mandates, coupled with the charge to meet the endless list of student needs, teachers are leaving the profession in record numbers (Luekens, Lyter, Fox, & Chandler, 2004). Those that remain are hungry for support as they strive to meet the endless challenges of teaching in today's schools. In your administrative role, you are uniquely positioned to fulfill the professional development appetites of teachers in your building, keeping them in the profession and, most important, keeping them vibrant in their work. Principals who keep teachers invigorated keep learning vibrant and alive for students each school day. In fact, according to Richard Dufour (1991):

Again and again, the commitment and support of the principal is described as essential to successful staff development programs. . . . In light of these findings, it is distressing that principals have often limited their involvement in staff development programs to arranging for speakers at disjointed inservice programs. Too often, principals have looked upon staff development as a secondary consideration, an aspect of the operation of the school which warranted little, if any, of their time and attention. In fact, the principal as staff developer is an integral part of the concept of the principal as instructional leader. One of the very best indicators of instructional leadership is the presence of an ongoing, school-based staff development program and a school climate in which that program can flourish. . . . Principals who wish to fulfill the role of instructional leaders must recognize their responsibilities in the development of the staffs they are attempting to lead.

They must assume an active part in staff development if meaningful school improvement is to take place. (pp. 9–10)

Given the critical nature of staff development and the important
role principals play in its facilitation, it is not surprising that many
principals find their first wondering for exploration by thinking deeply
about their faculty members and ways they can help fulfill their
professional needs. For example, during her second year as building
principal at Radio Park Elementary School in State College, Pennsylvania,
Deirdre Bauer was reminiscing about her experiences in peer coaching as
a teacher and as an administrator in her previous positions. She had found
peer coaching to be a very satisfying professional growth activity and had
witnessed its potential power as a trainer for teachers and as an alternative
to the traditional teacher evaluation process. In her new position at Radio
Park, she quickly noticed two exemplary first-grade veteran teachers.
Their outstanding practices led Deirdre to wonder about the nature of
professional development for accomplished veteran teachers and what
role the principal could play in facilitating continued professional
development for such consummate professionals. Deirdre decided to ask
Marcia and Judi if they might be interested in trying peer coaching as a
professional development activity. Having already established a strong
professional and trusting relationship, Marcia and Judi agreed, and
Deirdre formulated her first inquiry wonderings: *How does the process of
peer coaching help veteran teachers continue to learn and grow?* and *What role
can the principal play in facilitating this process?* (Bauer, 2001).

Like Deirdre, Jim Brandenburg had been introduced to the power of
prospective and practicing teachers engaging in action research as a
form of teacher professional development in his building. His school was in
the process of becoming a Professional Development School site in
collaboration with the University of Florida, and he wished to unleash the
tremendous potential he saw in instituting engagement in inquiry with his
entire faculty. Over time, Jim thus developed and explored the following
wonderings as he modeled the process of inquiry for his entire staff: *In what
ways can I as a principal help facilitate the professional growth of the teachers within
my building through engagement in action research?* and *How can the process of
teacher research become a part of my teachers' professional development plans?*

Like Deirdre and Jim—principals at the elementary level—high school
principal Jeanette Johnson became passionate about facilitating staff
development in her building while bringing her school's career and
technical education (CTE) offerings into alignment with the academic
course offerings. Jeanette writes:

One curricular area of focus in efforts at high school reform has been in the realm of career and technical education (CTE), which brings learning into context for students and, in doing so, is seen as a promising way to link curriculum, instruction, and student engagement (Hughes, Bailey, & Karp, 2002, p. 275). Unlike traditional academic courses, it is argued, career education classes are more inherently interesting to students, and provide instruction using methodologies to which a broader range of students are more responsive—thus, apparently, increasing both student engagement and success in school. However, CTE courses are often criticized for a lack of intellectual rigor, and are identified as a resulting disservice to students in terms of their intellectual growth and skill development (Perin, 2001, p. 304). This issue is identified as particularly problematic for students who may elect direct entry into the workforce, or a two-year degree or technical certification, as these students are entering careers which are requiring ever-increasing levels of complexity, knowledge, and ability (Krei & Rosenbaum, 2001, p. 825).

From this difficulty comes the suggestion that an integration of academic and CTE concepts may provide the best of both worlds, increasing both engagement and achievement. At the high school level, schools struggle to maintain student interest and focus in their coursework, particularly toward academic subject matter (Leithwood & Jantzi, 1999, p. 685). The separation of fields of study into isolated, discrete courses is critiqued for its failure to mirror the integrated, messy world outside the school walls, so that even students who manage to remain engaged in school are perhaps poorly served by secondary schools' false dichotomy between academic and applied concepts, and so an integration of these curricular components is seen as a possible and promising solution (Stone & Alfeld, 2004, p. 29).

Such is the case in my school as my faculty and I approach combining and aligning our CTE and academic course offerings. I, as well as the teachers in my building, recognize that this is a very large and noble undertaking. With the attainment of this goal looming ahead, the teachers in my building have expressed a need to better understand concepts associated with CTE as well as become knowledgeable about ways our faculty could work together to attain our goal. My inquiry question was born: *In what ways can I, as principal, best facilitate teacher professional development to aid in their integration of CTE and academic concepts throughout our high school curriculum?* (Johnson, 2007)

PASSION 1 (STAFF DEVELOPMENT) EXERCISES

1. Think back over your entire career as an educator. What was the best staff development experience you had? What were the characteristics of this experience that made it meaningful? How can you use your personal knowledge about meaningful staff development in the design of an inquiry to target staff development needs at your school?

2. Review the Web site of one of the leading organizations in staff development—the National Staff Development Council (NSDC)—by pointing your browser to http://www.nsdc.org/. In particular, review the standards for powerful professional development put forth by this organization. In what ways are your school's staff development practices in alignment with these standards? How do your school's staff development practices depart from these standards? How might engagement in inquiry help bring you and your school closer to the recommendations put forth by this organization?

Passion 2: Curriculum Development

In his book *The Principal as Curriculum Leader*, Allan Glatthorn (2000) notes that even though several problems confront school administrators interested in being a curriculum leader—including clarity on what this role means, increases in state standards that create an administrative attitude of "curriculum is not my job," lack of time, and an overabundance of literature focused on instructional leadership at the expense of curriculum leadership—principals should pursue curriculum leadership in their buildings for two important reasons:

> First, a quality curriculum is essential in achieving educational excellence. Though this assumption has the appeal of common sense, it is also supported by sound research. By reviewing more than 3,000 studies of student achievement, Fraser, Walberg, Welch, and Hattie (1987) identified the quality of the curriculum as one of ten factors influencing student achievement. The best teaching methods used in delivering poor content result only in a great deal of mislearning.
> Second, though both the state and the district have key roles to play in the development and implementation of curricula, there is widespread agreement among the experts that meaningful change takes place primarily at the school level (see, for example, Glickman, 1993; Murphy, 1991; Newmann & Wehlage, 1995). . . . The best curriculum work integrates curriculum functions at several levels— state, district, school, and classroom. (p. 25)

Principal Donnan Stoicovy understood the importance of serving as curriculum leader and found her first inquiry wondering at the nexus of her passion for environmental education, the unique setting of her school (twenty-two acres of a mostly wooded schoolyard), and meeting the Pennsylvania Academic Standards for Science and Environment and Ecology. At the time of her inquiry, the Pennsylvania Academic Science Standards included the following:

3.1.4   Illustrate patterns that regularly occur and recur in nature.

3.3.4   Know the similarities and differences of living things.

3.5.4   Know basic weather elements.

In addition, the Pennsylvania Academic Environment and Ecology Standards included the following:

4.3.4C   Understand that the elements of natural systems are interdependent.

4.6.4A   Understand that living things are dependent on nonliving things in the environment for survival.

4.6.4C   Identify how ecosystems change over time.

4.7.4A   Identify differences in living things.

4.7.4B   Know that adaptations are important for survival.

Donnan knew that her school's setting offered a unique resource for meeting these curriculum standards and that students and teachers could become involved in much more engaging instruction by utilizing their setting rather than using the traditional textbook. She therefore worked with a group of teachers in her building to design and implement a yearlong Schoolyard Project at Park Forest Elementary. To begin, Donnan and her teachers enrolled in a course on field natural history that addressed the Pennsylvania standards. In the course, they obtained numerous materials and knowledge about place-based education, biodiversity, and phenology (the study of regularly recurring biological phenomena such as animal migration or plant budding, especially as influenced by climate or other environmental factors that can influence the conditions). Next, working from the standards, the team designed a curriculum that focused on four different sites on the Park Forest Elementary School property that each classroom would visit eight different times at regular intervals over the course of the school year. The students would collect observational data at the sites, recording their observations on age-appropriate student observational sheets as well as in a journal. As principal, Donnan kicked off the entire unit for the students in her building by using a PowerPoint presentation and sharing the story *Windows* by Jane Baker, which shows change over time to a piece of property outside a window (see Figure 2.2). Classroom teachers then helped students collect and make sense of their observational data over the course of the school year, thus meeting the state standards. Donnan writes:

> As teachers and students began to embark on this year-long journey to record phenology, observations and data about our Park Forest Elementary schoolyard, I began to wonder just what the impact of this project would be. I wondered how student observational skills would improve. I wondered if there were areas other than science and environmental education skills that would be addressed from the Pennsylvania Academic Standards. I wondered how the project might impact us as a school community since there were common activities going on from Kindergarten through fifth grade. I wondered how student journal skills would be improved. I also wondered whether students might be able to draw conclusions about the sites based on the data that was collected and organized. (Stoicovy, 2006, p. 5)

Figure 2.2   Principal Donnan Stoicovy Introduces Schoolwide Curriculum Project

Source: Donnan Stoicovy, Principal, Park Forest Elementary, State College, Pennsylvania.

These wonderings led Donnan to engage in administrator inquiry framed by the questions: *In what ways has the Park Forest Elementary School Environmental Schoolyard Project affected student learning (development of observational, journaling, and drawing conclusion skills)?* and *In what ways has engagement in a cross-school curriculum project affected our school community?*

A second example of finding a wondering that relates to curriculum leadership comes from Newberry Elementary School principal Lacy Redd. Observing that the teaching of writing was not an area that her faculty had explored in depth for some time, Lacy hoped to provide opportunities for her faculty to learn more about the teaching of writing, to collaborate across grade levels, and to build a writing curriculum that was coherent and aligned with best practices advocated by leaders in the field. She felt that, if she could cultivate knowledge among her faculty about the best writing practices advocated by leading experts and if her faculty had ownership in designing a curriculum for each grade level that aligned with those best practices and allowed children to experience a cohesive approach to writing as they moved from one grade level to the next, the fourth-grade state writing assessment would "take care of itself." Yet, as a former middle school science teacher, Lacy felt the first place to begin was to develop her own understanding of the teaching of writing. Lacy embarked on an inquiry to accomplish this goal. Her wonderings became: *How can I build my own knowledge of exemplary writing practice?* and *How do I use learning communities as a tool for teachers and me to utilize in the transformation of the writing curriculum at Newberry Elementary?*

A third example of a principal finding her wondering in relationship to the curriculum comes from a middle school principal I worked with in Florida whose passion for developing a new and meaningful curriculum for the students in her building was stimulated by the addition of Section 1003.4156 to the Florida K–20 Education Code. This law required middle-level students to complete a career-based class to graduate from middle school and enter high school. The Florida Department of Education hoped that this career pathways curriculum would give direction and motivation to students and enhance their futures with exciting career opportunities. But this principal was haunted by a tension developing between creating a developmentally appropriate career-based curriculum course that would meet the unique needs of young adolescents and fitting this newly developed course within the already overwhelming curriculum demands at her school. Her wondering became: *In what ways can a career pathways curriculum be developed at my school to simultaneously satisfy our state's new requirement for career education, meet the developmental needs of our middle school students, and integrate seamlessly into our already established middle school curriculum?*

PASSION 2 (CURRICULUM DEVELOPMENT) EXERCISES

1. Browse through your textbooks, district's curriculum documents, and any curriculum guidelines or documents produced by your state. As you browse, generate a list of the topics covered at your school each year that you feel need to be enriched in some way. Next to each entry on your list, jot down a few words that describe your dissatisfaction with how this curriculum area is delivered in your building and/or the ways this curriculum area might be embellished. Select one item from your list to focus a potential inquiry on, and begin the process of brainstorming questions related to the teaching of this curriculum.

2. Visit the Web sites of the leading national organizations for the teaching of specific subject matter, such as the National Council for Teachers of Mathematics (www.nctm.org), National Science Teachers Association (www.nsta.org), National Council for the Social Studies (www.ncss.org), and National Council for Teachers of English (www.ncte.org). View each organization's standards for best practice in that field. How does the delivery of your curriculum mesh with best teaching practice as advocated by these associations?

Passion 3: Individual Teacher(s)

In *What Great Principals Do Differently: Fifteen Things That Matter Most*, author Todd Whitaker (2003) reminds administrators of *the* most important factor in the determination of school quality:

> Each of us can think of many innovations that were touted as *the* answer in education. Too often, we expect them to solve all our woes. When they do not, we see them as the problem. However, we must keep in mind that *programs are never the solution and they are never the problem*. If we cling to the belief that programs are the solution or the problem, we will continually lose sight of what really makes a difference. Back to basics—whole language—direct instruction—assertive discipline—open classrooms—The Baldridge model—state standards—mission statements—goal setting—site-based management. There is nothing inherently right or wrong with any of these ideas. We may have a fondness for one that has met with success, or deep-seated resentment because another has been forced down people's throats. If we take a closer look at some examples, however, we might see that effective principals never forget: It is people, not programs, that determine the quality of a school. (p. 8)

Given that people, not programs, determine the quality of schools, many principals find their first wonderings by looking closely at individual teachers within their buildings and ways they can serve as mentors for both new and veteran teachers.

In light of teacher shortages, coupled with grim statistics on teacher retention that reveal that "after just three years, it is estimated that almost a third of new entrants to teaching have left the field, and after five years almost half are gone" (National Commission on Teaching and America's Future, 2003, p. 19), a principal's support of new teachers in his/her building becomes more important than ever. According to Matthews and Crow (2003):

> The support and development of a new teacher are highly moral acts of leadership every administrator should take seriously. The principal's role in a person's life and career is a substantial responsibility. Although hiring and placement of new teachers are extremely important, the leadership role in supporting and developing new teachers is even more important. . . . Newly prepared teachers need administrative support and help with the types of assignments, the nature of the school's norms and values, and their development in making the transition from novice to experienced professional. Such support and development fall heavily on principals, who must be both mentors themselves and facilitators of mentoring by veteran teachers. (p. 80)

When considering individual teachers they recently hired, two high school principals I worked with in an administrator learning community explored the following questions through inquiry: *What types of support help my new teachers succeed?* and *How can I best help an out-of-field teacher succeed?*

While a typical assumption by many administrators is that only new teachers need mentoring, "effective principals recognize the importance of continued mentoring of teachers in mid-career" (Matthews & Crow, 2003, pp. 94–95). Mid-career professionals have their own unique set of special needs, including the challenges of remaining fresh and energetic as teaching becomes more and more routine with years of experience and of confronting a sense of urgency as they realize their careers are half over. For veteran teachers, "mentoring as an 'awakening' to a new way of seeing things can be a powerful learning resource for improving their teaching" (Gehrke as cited in Matthews & Crow, 2003, p. 94). For example, when approached by a twenty-six-year veteran first-grade teacher lamenting that she felt she was in a rut and didn't know what to do to regain her passion for teaching, her principal suggested they explore options together. After many discussions, this principal and veteran teacher decided to team up and use the process of collaborative action research to explore the question: *What is the relationship between changing a veteran teacher's grade-level assignment and getting her out of a rut?*

PASSION 3 (INDIVIDUAL TEACHERS) EXERCISES

1. Gather all the teachers in your building who have been teaching five years or less. Lead these teachers in a discussion of their hopes and dreams for their careers in teaching. Ask: What will help you attain success in your teaching careers? What barriers/hurdles do you anticipate along the way? What types of support are important for you to receive from the principal?

2. Gather all the teachers in your building who have been teaching twenty years or more. Lead these teachers in a discussion of the changes and improvements they have seen in the school, in students, and in curriculum since beginning their careers. Ask: How have you changed over the course of your careers as our school, our students, and our curriculum have evolved? What changes/school improvement efforts do you hope for in the future? What types of support are important for you to receive from the principal as you continue to tackle change and improvement and take on leadership roles in the building?

Passion 4: Individual Student(s)

You are likely familiar with a very common saying that many educators display on mugs, have framed in beautiful calligraphy, or even print on note cards:

> A hundred years from now, it will not matter what my bank account was, the sort of house I lived in, or the kind of car I drove. But the world may be different because I was important in the life of a child.

In fact, you probably entered teaching and the field of administration on the basis of your passion for children, your talent for connecting with them, and your willingness to commit yourself to touching children's lives.

Each year, administrators encounter particular groups of learners who stand out from the rest for a variety of reasons—perhaps they are struggling learners, perhaps they are learners who exceed the typical expectations for grade-level performance, or perhaps they are learners who are not behaving in ways conducive to your school environment.

These students are puzzles that administrators struggle with throughout the year as they try to figure out how all the complex pieces of these children's lives fit together, and they strive to help make a difference for these learners within and outside the school building. Students who puzzle or intrigue you can be a wonderful source for defining your first wondering. A few examples from elementary, middle, and high school principals follow.

As a first-year principal at Anderson Elementary School, Denee Hurst (2007) believed strongly that to succeed in the principalship, one of the first things she needed to do was to familiarize herself with the available data on every kindergarten through fifth-grade student in her school. She had a particular interest in the primary-grade students since her state mandated retention in grade three for any learners who did not obtain a certain score on the annual achievement test, and she was passionate about reducing the amount of mandatory retentions to a bare minimum. While looking at the student data, Denee noticed both successes and pitfalls related to the subject of reading, and she began to wonder about her school's policy regarding placement in a reading remediation program. A particular group of learners intrigued Denee—the kindergarten students placed in reading remediation based on the progress monitoring tool her school utilized, DIBELS (Dynamic Indicators of Basic Early Literacy Skills). She began to wonder, "How effective is our kindergarten reading remediation program?" "In what ways do our school's kindergarten reading remediation practices help these young learners develop as readers?" "What is the relationship between kindergarteners who receive reading remediation and their performance on the third-grade Florida Comprehensive Achievement Test?" and "Whatever happens to these students after they leave kindergarten anyway?" These wonderings led Denee to turn to the process of inquiry to explore the question: *What happens to struggling readers in our school after they leave intervention programs?*

While Denee and many other principals are often drawn to inquiry in an effort to gain insights into struggling learners, middle school principal Mark Bracewell had a passion for making sure his average and brightest students were also flourishing. He found engagement in administrator inquiry a powerful mechanism for gaining insights into the learning experiences of his average and high achievers, especially in the midst of the inclusion movement. Mark writes:

> This wondering began as a discussion among inclusion teachers, administrators, staffing specialists, and guidance counselors at my school. We were new to inclusion, and were in the "trial and error

phase," still trying to figure out how to make inclusion work for our students. The things we discussed the most revolved around questions like "Are we watering down the curriculum, or are these students getting the same in terms of rigor?" We were also concerned (as were parents and others in our school community) about the effect that this model would have on the achievement of the regular education students. Would our highest achievers (the Florida Comprehensive Achievement Test Level 4 and 5 students) still get the type and level of enrichment that they needed? This was of particular interest, since we had seen a trend of decreasing growth in our upper level students. Would their "infusion into inclusion" further exacerbate this problem? We also felt that there was a plethora of data that supported the value of inclusion to the exceptional education student, but there wasn't much that told us what that value was for the standard education student. So, that led us to this question: *"What effect does the inclusion environment have on the reading achievement of eighth grade Language Arts students at Lake Butler Middle School?"* (Bracewell, 2008, p. 239)

An additional example of a wondering that emerged with an individual student focus comes from high school principal Mike Delucas (2008). Mike was passionate about helping students who had fallen behind retrieve credits to increase their likelihood of graduation. Relying on his ingenuity, research, and inventive resource management, he created a school-within-a-school (SWAS) for these learners to accomplish this mission. Mike turned to inquiry to evaluate the SWAS program and focused on the question: *What is the relationship between students' participation in Williston High's SWAS Credit Retrieval Program and their success in high school?*

Of course, an area that begs for many administrators' attention at all levels is behavior management. It is therefore natural that principals' attention will be drawn to students who are not behaving in ways conducive to a positive learning environment in their schools. For example, principal Lynette Langford (2008) noticed from the school's discipline reports that a large percentage of exceptional student education (ESE) students were receiving out-of-school or in-school suspension as a consequence of discipline referrals. It seemed to Lynette that there must be a better way to discipline students in her seventh- through twelfth-grade school than to take the very students who needed to be in class the most out of class. Working closely with her lead team as well as her entire faculty, Lynette led her school in a schoolwide inquiry that focused on the question: *In what ways are out-of-school or in-school suspensions as a consequence for discipline referrals affecting student performance?* Over the course of their inquiry, Lynette and her faculty's wondering evolved into: *What are some alternative behavior management plans we could implement in our school, and in what ways are they effective for decreasing student tardiness, increasing student attendance in class, and, subsequently, increasing the chances of our students succeeding as learners at our school?* Lynette writes about her faculty's implementation of "Friday and Saturday School":

> For excessive tardies we set up Friday school which ran from 3:15 to 5:30 and students would have trash detail, cleaning floors, pulling weeds, etc. Students would be assigned Friday School for every 3 times they were late to class. The first Friday Day School we had 43 students present. At the time of this writing, our last Friday School only had 7 students.
>
> For unexcused absences, students were allowed to make up the work they missed, but their grades remained "0" unless they attended Saturday School. Saturday School is from 8:00 to 12:00 (we did this one Saturday each month). During this time students could make up their missed work, get help with any school work, or they could bring reading materials. After the Christmas break we decided to tweak this a little and offer the option that if the parent attended and participated with the child they only had to stay for 2 hours instead of the four. We thought this would be twofold in trying to get parents more involved with their student academic success. In the beginning we had few students attend, but when parents realized their grades were suffering, the numbers increased and the numbers nearly doubled when the parents started attending.
>
> The part that I am most proud of is the fact that every single teacher (except one) bought into this plan and the Friday and Saturday Schools were run by the teachers. There were always two teachers and one administrator present. But the teachers took ownership and took two Fridays and one Saturday each semester.
>
> For alterative discipline consequences (how this wondering actually started then evolved), our school district started a Neighborhood Accountability Board (NAB) where a group of 8 community leaders sit and hear cases from students and their parents. The students must admit guilt if they appear before the board and the board places sanctions which may include, but not be limited to, community service, anger management or other counseling, and/or letters of apology. We had approximately 25 students that went through NAB this year.
>
> We also implemented a teen court this year where students received sanctions from their peers. This could be chosen in lieu of

suspension. Another option was for parents to attend class with their student instead of the student being suspended.

Our wondering started out in one direction and actually took on another direction as well. That's what is so wonderful about the inquiry process, it keeps us constantly looking for better ways to serve our students and help them become successful. (Langford, 2008, p. 181)

PASSION 4 (INDIVIDUAL STUDENTS) EXERCISES

1. Gather your lead team and brainstorm different groups of students in your school that are receiving special attention for various reasons (i.e., ESE students, second language learners, gifted learners, struggling readers). Discuss: In what ways is your school succeeding in meeting the special needs of these learners?

2. Now turn your attention to students in your building who are not receiving special attention for any particular reason (the average learner). Discuss: What can you do as a school to be sure that average learners who receive no special attention thrive?

Passion 5: School Community/Culture

In their book *The Principal's Role in Shaping School Culture*, leading researchers and scholars in educational administration Terrence Deal and Kent Peterson discuss what the concept of culture means for the school administrator:

Principals know from experience that piecemeal reforms, reforms which ignore the inner realities of schools, will have limited effect. They understand by instinct that to build a successful school one must work simultaneously on staff needs and skills, the organization's goals and roles, and the dynamics of political power and conflict.

Beyond that, there is something else about a school—something beyond staff skills, goals, roles, power, and conflict—that is vital to performance and improvement. It is hard to define this something, to put your finger on it, but it is extremely powerful, often neglected, and usually absent from our discussions or assumptions of how to improve schools.

Each school has its own character or "feel." You can sense it as you approach the building. You can almost smell and taste it as you walk through the doors. You can see it in the pictures on the walls and the students in the halls. You can hear it in exchanges between students and teachers in the classroom and in students' talk with one another on the playground.

For many years the terms "climate" or "ethos" have been used to try to capture this powerful yet elusive force. . . . We call it *school culture*.

The concept of culture is meant to describe the character of a school as it reflects deep patterns of values, beliefs, and traditions that have been formed over the course of its history. Beneath the conscious awareness of everyday life in any organization there is a stream of thought, sentiment, and activity. This invisible, taken-for-granted flow of beliefs and assumptions give meaning to what people say and do. (Deal & Peterson, 1990, p. 7)

Given that school culture undergirds everything teachers and students in a school building say and do, understanding school culture and reflecting on the role one plays as principal in shaping it is critical to the success of the daily functioning of a school:

When principals have reflected to the point they feel they understand a school's culture, they can evaluate the need to *shape* or reinforce it. Valuable aspects of the school's existing culture can be reinforced; problematic ones require revitalizing. Shaping the culture is *not* an exact science. Shaping a culture is indirect, intuitive, and largely unconscious. (Deal & Peterson, 1990, p. 20)

Because shaping culture is not an exact science, many principals find that exploring school culture through the process of inquiry is a tremendously valuable and insightful experience, and they subsequently find that vital wonderings are emerging from their consideration of the existing culture in their workplace and the actions they are taking to shape it.

For example, after discovering through inquiry the previous school year that engagement in a cross-school curriculum project helped students in her building meet the state standards in science, environment, and ecology and, as a by-product, affected her school community in a positive way, principal Donnan Stoicovy set out to capitalize on the positive cultural outcomes the following school year. Turning her attention explicitly to the culture of her school, Donnan reflected on her many observations during classroom walk-throughs of positive classroom cultures after teachers had received training in the Responsive Classroom approach and instituted Morning Meetings at the beginning of each school

day, one of ten practices at the heart of that approach (http://www
.responsiveclassroom.org/about/aboutrc.html). Morning Meetings consists
of gathering as a whole class each morning to greet one another, share
news, and warm up for the day ahead (Kriete, 2002). Seeing the powerful
ways Morning Meetings worked in individual classrooms, Donnan charted
a course for a new inquiry that focused on applying the Morning Meeting
concept to the entire school by instituting a weekly whole-school gathering.
Donnan and a team of teachers from her building who helped design,
institute, and evaluate the schoolwide meetings utilized the process of
inquiry to provide both formative and summative data to understand the
impact the meeting was having on teachers and students. This inquiry was
framed by Donnan's overarching question: *What role does a weekly schoolwide
meeting play in creating a caring school culture?* Donnan writes about the
process and how she and her teachers worked together to institutionalize
both the schoolwide meeting as well as their wonderings about the process:

> As we explored building a school community, we based our ideas
> on the following question, "How can the school itself, as a collec-
> tion of families, be more like a neighborhood?" (Sergiovanni, 1994).
> Some basic tenets we based our thinking upon were developing a
> feeling of being small, having a sense of community among staff,
> providing multiple opportunities for cross grade level experiences,
> opening frequent communication among all community members
> and sharing celebrations with all. These activities helped us to
> frame ideas for All-School Gatherings. . . .
>
> Our All-School Gatherings began immediately at the start
> of the 2006–07 school year. Our first meeting was centered on an
> introduction to the Lifelong Guidelines for our Tools for
> Citizenship (Pearson, 2000) program of trustworthiness, truthful-
> ness, active listening, no put-downs and personal best. These
> became the themes for future meetings with 18 additional Life
> Skills such as caring, common sense, cooperation, courage, curios-
> ity, effort, flexibility, friendship, initiative, integrity, organization,
> patience, perseverance, pride, problem solving, resourcefulness,
> responsibility and sense of humor. The use of these materials is
> supplemental to what a teacher uses to encourage positive interac-
> tions within his/her classroom.
>
> Over time, some routines began to develop and the framework
> for our gatherings had the following core elements of pledge of
> allegiance, opening songs, presentation of awards for previous
> week's citizenship awards and community service awards, an intro-
> duction of the new citizenship quality, current event information or

presentation, awarding of penguin awards for best community behavior by division for the All School Gathering (Kindergarten, Primary, Intermediate and Upper Intermediate), and a closing song. These became refined and more effective with the involvement of students and teachers.

Our inquiry question was: How does having a weekly All School Gathering help to build our school community? Sub-questions included:

- How does it improve student behavior?
- How does recognizing student accomplishments encourage more student accomplishments?
- What is the relationship between specific seating arrange-ments and the facilitation of a closer, community feeling?
- How can students begin to take ownership of the gatherings? (Stoicovy, 2008, p. 7)

A second example of finding a wondering in relationship to community/culture building comes from aspiring administrator Gabi Nino. As a classroom teacher earning her master's degree in educational leadership at Texas State University, and in the midst of completing her administrative internship in the same school in which she was teaching, Gabi was disturbed when she met one of her former students from the previous year in the hallway and he shared that he was on his way to "Student Assistance in Learning," known by the children as SAIL. SAIL was a pullout literacy intervention program for struggling students.

Immediately, Gabi feel a knot in her throat. She wondered why Ryan was seen as a struggling student who needed additional support. As his first-grade teacher, she had had no concerns about Ryan entering second grade because he was well prepared for it, and he was performing at grade level. After seeing Ryan in the hallway, her concern began to overwhelm her, and Gabi went to find Ryan's second-grade teacher to find out more. The information she learned was bothersome because, before exiting first grade, Ryan was reading at the appropriate grade level. On the first day of second grade, when he was still reading at that same level, he was now considered below grade level and qualifying for reading interventions.

Gabi reflected back to the previous year when Ryan entered her first-grade classroom performing well below grade level. As his teacher, she immediately wanted to gather more information that would help her learn more about his situation. The only data easily accessible on Ryan, however, were his name, date of birth, student ID number, and his end-of-year reading level. The data also included the name of his previous teacher, who had left the school to pursue a career in business. This information was what was on his student placement card, used by teachers to sort and place students in new classrooms. Other than this student placement card, she could find no personal information or any data that documented his progress in kindergarten. Since his kindergarten teacher had left, there was no one available to discuss his previous progress with; therefore, Gabi had started from square one with Ryan.

Ryan and Gabi worked extremely hard all year, and he not only ended the year on grade level, but he also felt successful. As he advanced to second grade, Gabi knew how hard he had worked, and she hoped Ryan would continue with the success he had experienced in first grade. Unfortunately, however, his second-grade teacher started the year with the same inadequate information Gabi had had the previous year. Gabi and Ryan's second-grade teacher had never communicated with each other about his needs. Ryan's second-grade teacher only saw the data that reflected Ryan's name, date of birth, student ID number, and his barely-on-grade-level reading scores. She did not know about the great accomplishments he had made the previous year. Gabi knew just how bright Ryan was, and not only had she been extremely proud of his progress but so had Ryan's parents. Ryan had ended his first-grade year with confidence in his ability to be successful in second grade. More than anything else, Gabi had wanted the celebration of the progress he had made to continue as he began second grade. Instead of this celebration, within the first two weeks of school, Ryan was immediately confronted with feelings of inadequacy and worrying about being academically successful.

After visiting his second-grade teacher, Gabi learned that, although Ryan had met the first-grade reading level expectation, the reading level for the beginning of second grade was even higher. Every student in Gabi's school district was administered the Developmental Reading Assessment (DRA). This assessment is designed around a series of leveled texts that, when used accurately, can guide teachers to the level a child is reading on so that instruction can begin at that level. When first graders meet the DRA level of 16, they have met the end-of-year grade-level expectation. In second grade, the beginning-of-year reading expectation is level 18. In other words, students are expected to make gains over the summer when they are out of a structured educational environment. Furthermore, if they are not at this DRA reading level of 18 when they start second grade, they immediately receive reading interventions.

Gabi worried about the message a student receives when he or she meets the expectations of the first-grade teacher in every way but, on the first day of second grade, he or she is considered academically unsuccessful. Gabi was noticing that not only were there discrepancies in the expectations for students' success, but there was also a lack of communication about student progress data among colleagues. Ryan's new teacher did not realize that he had left first grade on grade level and was doing very well due to several instructional strategies that had been implemented. She did not understand the gains he had made the previous school year. Gabi thought to herself, "As teachers, if we had discussed the information I had collected documenting Ryan's academic and social gains, we would have made better judgments about the type of instruction and strategies that would better meet Ryan's needs in second grade."

As a part of her administrative internship, Gabi turned to the process of action research. She began by gathering some preliminary data to get a feeling for the situation beyond her individual experience with Ryan, and she quickly learned that Ryan was not alone in this situation. Initially, Gabi collected data during an administrative team meeting in January. She took anecdotal notes as she engaged in conversation with the administrative team of principal, assistant principal, and three other aspiring administrators. She supplemented this data with information from informal conversations with several teachers. The data indicated that teachers across campus had two concerns. The first concern was how to effectively communicate student needs from year to year. The second concern was about sharing with other teachers the expectations of the new grade level as students transition. The third-grade teachers in particular felt that students were not prepared for the expectations of that grade level. They expressed concerns about a lack of urgency in teachers from primary grade levels in preparing students for the TAKS (Texas Assessment of Knowledge and Skills). This concern that children were not prepared for new grade-level expectations was prevalent across grade levels 1–3. There was a recognized need to resolve or relieve these concerns so that students did not bear the burden of lack of communication among teachers.

Gabi reflected that one cause for these communication concerns could be related to the changing context of their school. Longhorn Ranch Elementary was an elementary school serving over 1,150 students. The campus had seen tremendous growth in enrollment in a fairly short amount of time. The campus had opened in 2001 with just over 100 students, and because of the low enrollment, the teaching staff was also small. The largest grade level had three teachers working as a team. In just six years, Longhorn Ranch Elementary had grown to sixty-eight teachers, with several grade levels having teams of ten teachers. Longhorn Ranch Elementary is a campus that prides itself on academic success. The TAKS scores in 2005, 2006, and 2007 exceeded the state and district averages, resulting in an "Exemplary" rating by the Texas Education Agency. The strong desire to maintain that rating and the rapid growth had produced many challenges. Gabi writes:

As a direct result of the tremendous growth on campus, developing a collaborative culture has been one of the challenges faced. With teams growing in large numbers every year, the focus has been on developing teams that work collaboratively together within particular grade levels. While this type of collaboration is important, there is also a strong need to work cohesively as a campus between grade levels. To date, vertical collaboration has not been a focus on our campus.

Based on my observations and discussions with teachers and reviewing the students' progress data, it appears that our teaching staff might not have a clear understanding of the expectations of students in consecutive grade levels. Cultivating a culture on campus where teachers can collaborate collectively about student progress and achievement became the focus of my action research. My research questions for my administrative internship became: *In what ways can our school develop a collaborative culture characterized by teachers from different grade levels communicating, understanding, and sharing expectations for all of our students?* and *In what ways can the administrative team facilitate that process?* (Nino, 2008)

Passion 5 (School Community/Culture) Exercises

1. According to Deal and Peterson (1990), it is important for the principal to get an initial cultural read on the school by asking a series of questions about the founding, traditions, building, current realities, and future dreams of the school. Complete a cultural read of your school by addressing these questions:

- How long has the school existed?
- Why was it built, and who were the first inhabitants?
- Who had a major influence on the school's direction?
- What critical incidents occurred in the past, and how were they resolved, if at all?
- What were the preceding principals, teachers, and students like?
- What does the school's architecture convey? How is space arranged and used?
- What subcultures exist inside and outside the school?
- Who are the recognized (and unrecognized) heroes and villains of the school?
- What do people say (and think) when asked what the school stands for? What would they miss if they left?
- What events are assigned special importance?
- How is conflict typically defined? How is it handled?
- What are the key ceremonies and stories of the school?
- What do people wish for? Are there patterns to their individual dreams? (Deal & Peterson, 1990, pp. 18–19)

(Continued)

(Continued)

How might what you've learned from addressing these questions lead to an inquiry?

2. Barth (1990) defines the difference between a congenial school culture and collegial school culture. *Congeniality* refers to the friendly, cordial relationships some teachers have with each other in the workplace (celebrating birthdays, discussing the latest sports event, etc.). *Collegiality* refers to the types of relationships that promote professional dialogue and conversation (i.e., talk about curriculum, teaching strategies, etc.). In what ways are the teachers in your school congenial? In what ways are they collegial? Which types of relationships (congenial or collegial) are in most need of your support right now? Why do you feel this way? What can you do to support the development of both a congenial and collegial culture in your school?

Passion 6: Leadership

Based on a continuing research agenda begun in 1983 with the purpose of understanding leadership through case analyses and survey questionnaires, James Kouzes and Barry Posner in their classic text *The Leadership Challenge* uncovered five practices common to leaders when at their "personal best":

When getting extraordinary things done in organizations, leaders engage in these Five Practices of Exemplary Leadership:

- Model the Way.
- Inspire a Shared Vision.
- Challenge the Process.
- Enable Others to Act.
- Encourage the Heart.

These practices . . . aren't the private property of the people we studied or of a few select shining stars. They're available to anyone, in any organization or situation, who accepts the leadership challenge. (Kouzes & Posner, 2002, p. 13)

Principals are, first and foremost, the leaders of their school building, and they have thus accepted the leadership challenge described by Kouzes and Posner. Many principals find the process of inquiry a prudent way to continue to explore and develop their own leadership skills over the course of their administrator lifetimes. For example, led by administrator Fran Vandiver and colleagues (2005), a group of thirteen elementary, middle school, and high school principals from the North East Florida

Educational Consortium (an organization that connects rural districts in north-central Florida) began meeting on a monthly basis in support of each other while implementing an important reading initiative that would become a model for the entire state of Florida. Although this reading program met with success and began expanding, these principals continued to meet as they had found their work together extremely valuable. Over time, they turned to the process of administrator inquiry to find a new focus for their collective work. Using Kouzes and Posner's Self Inventory as well as their Leadership Practices Observer Inventory, they conducted a group inquiry as they all explored the same question individually: *What do I learn from comparing and contrasting my own perceptions, my teachers' perceptions, my leadership team's perceptions, and my supervisor's perceptions about my own instructional leadership as a principal?* Sharing the personal data they received with one another, each principal was able to reflect on and articulate what he or she had learned—both what was expected and what was surprising. With the support and affirmation of the other principals in the group, each individual set new goals for his or her own leadership development.

Kouzes and Posner (2002, pp. xxiv–xxv) identify ten questions that the leaders they worked with and learned from asked themselves to enhance their leadership capabilities. These ten questions can serve as great wonderings any principal would benefit from exploring through the process of inquiry:

- What values should guide my actions as a leader?
- How do I best set an example for others?
- How do I articulate a vision of the future when things are so unpredictable?
- How do I improve my ability to inspire others toward a common purpose?
- How do I create an environment that promotes innovation and risk?
- How do I build a cohesive and spirited team?
- How do I share power and information and still maintain accountability?
- How do I put more joy and celebration into our efforts?
- What is the source of self-confidence required to lead others?
- How do I go about improving my leadership abilities?

In addition to studying their own leadership skills, some principals find their wonderings as they ponder how they can cultivate the leadership abilities of others in their buildings. For example, assistant principal for the Elementary Division at P. K. Yonge Developmental Research School, Amy Hollinger, reflects on her quest through inquiry to enable the concept of *teacher leadership* to flourish:

When I left the classroom to become an administrator, I always had a very clear vision of being an instructional leader. It is this passion that led me to want to be an administrator at PK Yonge. PK Yonge Developmental Research School is a K–12 school that focuses on the whole child in the learning process. Several years ago, the elementary division started to focus on defining our curriculum so that our students would get what we refer to as a "guaranteed curriculum." This means that as our students leave one grade and enter another, there are certain things that they are "guaranteed" to have learned no matter which teacher they had. As I started to learn more about how to develop this curriculum, it became evident that a large part of the process was in being able to develop teacher leaders within the school. I needed some teachers that were willing to become "experts" in a curriculum area to help lead the faculty as the school continued to evolve and develop a "guaranteed curriculum." At the end of my first year as an administrator, I wondered, "How do I develop these curriculum leaders?"

I began to look at what the definition of teacher leadership was based on the research, and I decided to start with a literature review. The literature was nebulous at best, as according to one article I read by Moller (2003), "Defining teacher leadership is like a good school. It's hard to put into words but you know it when you see it." I saw some very general patterns in the research of what a school with strong teacher leadership looks like. Some of the characteristics that came up repeatedly were: collaborating with administrator, shared decision making, curriculum ownership, student ownership, professional growth, high level of professionalism, focus on student achievement, and teacher roles including choosing curriculum and textbook materials, shaping the curriculum, setting the standards for student behavior, making decisions about whether or not students are tracked into special classes, designing and implementing staff development, setting promotion and retention policies, and deciding school budgets (Furrell and Kelly, April 2001).

At this time I also did reading about the administrator's role in developing and sustaining teacher leaders. Moeller and Pankake (2003) felt that the focus of the position should always be providing leadership that builds an ongoing commitment to continuous improvement in teaching that results in improved learning for students. One thing that particularly struck me about the research on the administrator's role in teacher leadership is that over and over again the indicator of success came down to the administrator's relationship with his/her faculty. This made sense to me because as a classroom teacher and cross-country coach, I always knew that to get the best results out of your students and athletes that you have to have a great relationship with them. Now the relationship piece for me became about having a positive relationship with the faculty. My wondering ended up being: *How can I, as an administrator, promote teacher leadership in the elementary division at PK Yonge?*

Other wonderings that came up along the way were: What things could I deliberately put in place to encourage teacher leadership? and What things needed to be in place to sustain teacher leadership? (Hollinger, 2007, pp. 1–3)

PASSION 6 (LEADERSHIP) EXERCISES:

1. Design a timeline of your growth and development as a principal and a leader, beginning with your first teaching position and noting years and dates of critical incidents that affected your decision to become an administrator and the development of your leadership skills along the way.

2. Follow the guide below to design a Principal's Coat of Arms. In space number 1, draw a real or mythical animal that best describes the leader you want to be. In space 2, choose a real symbol, or create your own design, for an insignia that best describes the leader you want to be. In space 3, choose one color in any shade—or a rainbow effect—that best describes the leader you want to be. In space 4, draw one character, real or fictional, that best describes the leader you want to be. In space 6, choose one word that best describes the leader you want to be. How you write that word should also help describe the leader you want to be.

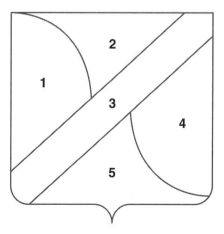

Passion 7: Management

While much of the literature on administration in the past few decades has lamented the administrator's focus on management at the expense of an emphasis on leadership, the truth remains that management is a part of the principal's job. Sergiovanni (1987) states:

> Distinctions between management and leadership are useful for theorists and help to clarify and sort various activities and behaviors of principals. For practical purposes, however, both emphases should be considered as necessary and important aspects of a principal's administrative role. The choice is not whether a principal is leader or manager but whether the two emphases are in balance, and indeed, whether they complement each other. (p. 16)

Hence, another ripe area in which a principal can find his or her wondering for inquiry is in relation to managerial duties and their placement and balance in relation to one's leadership role. The principal's managerial role is defined as "the daily planning, organizing, operating, executing, budgeting, maintaining, and scheduling of numerous processes, activities, and tasks that permit a school to accomplish its goals as a learning community" (Matthews & Crow, 2003, p. 192).

One example of a wondering borne out of the managerial duty of "scheduling" for an administrator comes from Amy Hollinger's colleague at P. K. Yonge Developmental Research School. As the assistant principal for the Middle School Division, Brian Marchman had been intrigued for the past five years with how block scheduling was playing out in the Middle and High School divisions:

> The teachers and administration of P. K. Yonge Developmental Research School made the decision to restructure the schedule in which instruction was delivered beginning in the 2000–2001 school year. Although a groundswell of support existed prior to the formulation of a restructuring committee and a subsequent survey of the high school faculty, the combination of the committee's work and survey results proved to be the necessary impetus to enact the schedule change. (Thirty-five of thirty-eight faculty associated with the high school responded to the restructuring survey.) Beginning in the 2000–2001 school year, P. K. Yonge's high school moved to a later starting time for the school day, in accordance with research in optimal learning times for adolescents. The high school also reduced the number of classes for each student from seven to six. The third major change was to moving from a traditional school day

50-minute periods to a block schedule (three 100-minute classes, four days a week; one day remained a traditional school day schedule). P. K. Yonge's middle school division, for which I now serve as Assistant Principal, followed suit with these restructuring initiatives.

Five years have passed since these major scheduling changes were made, and as issues of scheduling in the middle school are always surfacing and constantly need administrator attention, coupled with the fact that many of the lively discussions I witnessed during the time these scheduling changes were being considered and were initially instituted had quieted quite substantially over the five-year time we've implemented block scheduling, I set out to explore the ways the middle school teachers with whom I worked were currently thinking about block scheduling. I hoped to use what I learned to continue to help teachers explore the best ways to utilize the 100-minute class time period with middle school students. My inquiry wondering became: *What are teachers' levels of satisfaction with the current block schedule in place at P. K. Yonge?* (Marchman, 2006, p. 1)

A second example of an inquiry focused on management comes once again from elementary school veteran principal-inquirer Donnan Stoicovy. Like many principals across the nation, Donnan was frustrated with the ways the lunchroom procedures were going in her elementary school. Donnan articulated a vision beginning with what was already good about lunchtime routines (lunch was a break in the day, time to talk, time to relax, and time to catch up with friends; good lunches were offered; and there were lots of lunch choices). Next, Donnan stated what she believed the school needed to work on collaboratively to smooth out the lunch experience for all (seating that works for everyone, students buy what they want to eat, all students are helpers, respect permeates at lunchtime, students have activities to do when they are done with lunch, paraprofessionals are helpers not enforcers, and the Park Forest Elementary lunchroom is a pleasant place to be for everyone). Once again, Donnan turned to the process of inquiry to engage her whole school in exploring the wondering: *How can we all work together (students, teachers, lunch paraprofessionals, kitchen workers, custodians, and principal) to make lunchtime a cooperative and pleasant time for everyone?* Most noteworthy about this inquiry was the whole school's involvement in exploring this question. Using the already instituted and studied "All School-Gatherings," Donnan used these weekly meetings to assign students at all grade levels, teachers, and herself "tasks" to complete and to collect data on how the school was coming closer to its collective goal of making the lunchtime experience a cooperative and pleasant time in the school day for all.

PASSION 7 (MANAGEMENT) EXERCISES

1. Brainstorm a list of the daily management routines you like the most. What characteristics do these daily management routines share?

2. Brainstorm a list of the daily management routines you like least or have some doubts about. What characteristics do these daily management routines share? What could you do to make them better?

3. Inventory how you spend your time as a principal. What percentage of your workweek is devoted to management routines and tasks? What percentage of your workweek is devoted to leadership activities? What do you believe would be a good balance between management and leadership tasks? What can you do to bring yourself into balance?

Passion 8: School Performance

Marc Tucker and Judy Codding open their book *The Principal Challenge* with the following words:

Why would anyone want the job of principal? Many school principals we know have the look these days of the proverbial deer caught in the headlights. Almost overnight, it seems, they have been caught in the high beams of the burgeoning accountability movement. Now as never before, the public and all the organs of government are insisting that student academic performance improve—and fast. The federal government is putting ever-increasing pressure on the states to that end. The states, in their turn, are busy creating incentives for local boards and superintendents to raise school performance. And the local boards and superintendents are wasting no time in putting as much pressure as they can on the principals. And there it rests.

The principal experiences this set of pressures as a vise that is closing fast. The expectation that the principal will lead the school to levels of student achievement that are unprecedented for that school, for students from that social background, for children for whom English is not their native language, with budgets that are meager—all this seems to be the stuff of fantasy for the principals in the vise. If the principal and faculty had known how to produce unprecedented improvements in student performance before, they would have done it. What, they want to know, makes anyone think they can do it now, with little or no more money than they had before? (Tucker & Codding, 2002, p. 1)

The enormous pressures being placed on teachers and principals to raise students' test scores have resulted in a number of principals embarking on the inquiry journey to determine their relationship to school performance and raising student achievement. For example, recall Terry Buckle's inquiry from Chapter 1. Working in a state that assigns each school a yearly grade based on students' performance on the annual standardized test, principal Terry Buckles needed a plan for dealing with her school's inability to make Adequate Yearly Progress the previous school year and being placed on corrective action. Terry turned to the process of administrator inquiry to gain insights into the following question: *In what ways will implementing the continuous improvement model help increase student achievement at Mellon Elementary School?* In a similar fashion, Terry's colleague from a neighboring county who participated in the same principal inquiry learning community, Marion McCray, found her first wondering by examining her commitment to improving the test scores of her bottom quartile learners:

> At Lafayette Elementary School, the progress of the lowest quartile students in Reading has been declining for the past three years. One of the reasons is that a large percent of those students are ESE students, who cannot read grade level material. In the past, we have been proud of the fact that our lowest students made the most gains. At that time we were more concerned about our above average readers and their progress. Even though this is still a concern, our obligation is to focus on these below average readers to ensure their success in school. Lafayette Elementary School "made the points" for an "A" school grade, but received a "B" for this past year because only 47% (a minimum of 50% is required) of the lowest quartile in Reading made a year's growth. 86% of those students were economically disadvantaged. Because of my concern, as principal, I will work closely with my lead team and our school to focus on the lowest quartile through several different methods. My inquiry question is: *What actions can our faculty take to improve reading achievement of our lowest quartile students?* (McCray, 2007, p. 25)

While Terry and Marion's examples take place in the elementary school context, principals at all levels feel the pressure to increase student achievement. For example, high school principal Jimmy Camp from Collier County Public Schools in Naples, Florida, found his first inquiry wondering at the nexus of the great high school homework debate and his desire to understand the relationship between assigning homework and student measures of achievement at his school. Jimmy writes:

> Homework. The mere mention of the word evokes an array of intense emotion and opinion. Students wish it would go away (Coutts, 2004). Teachers wish students would "just do it" (Cooper, Horn, & Strahan, 2005). Parents support it as long as it does not interfere with family life (Gill & Schlossman, 2004). Homework has long been a staple on the menu of educational practices used by teachers to attain curricular goals (Simplicio, 2005). Recent articles in the popular press and programming on visual media have once again brought the emotionally charged homework controversy to the forefront of public debate (Mathews, 2006; Van Voorhis, 2004). At the root of the current debate is the amount of homework that students are being asked to complete and its impact upon the family (Mathews, 2006; Loveless, 2003). Child advocates such as Kohn (2006) and parent activists such as Bennet and Kalish (2006) are among the most recent to add their opinions to the mix. Both hold positions that the amount of homework has increased dramatically and that this increase is damaging to children and their families. In order to provide meaningful input into this public discourse, I felt my faculty and I needed to better understand and explore the great homework debate and critically reflect on our current homework assignment practices at our school. Engagement in collaborative action research with my faculty seemed the perfect mechanism to foster our understanding and reflection.
>
> At the end of the 2005–2006 school year, a committee of faculty in my school had developed a research-based policy that had been approved by my entire faculty for implementation during the 2006–2007 school year. Upon review of the policy and the ways it was (and was not) working, it was the consensus of the committee that although the policy had some positive effect on homework completion rates, there was still much improvement required. It was determined that a data-based approach was needed to implement changes in the policy and determine the overall effects on homework completion rates and student achievement. It was also determined that the use of the targeted homework concept would be utilized via a professional development module for all instructional staff.
>
> The concept of "targeted homework," as developed by Heitzmann (2007), is rooted in the belief that homework can make a significant difference in student achievement. To accomplish this goal, Heitzmann (2007) groups homework assignments into four

categories: practice, preparation, extension, and creative. Homework assignments in each of these categories are designed, implemented and evaluated utilizing the following principles:

- Assignments are differentiated to meet individual student needs
- Assignments are linked to state and national standards
- A myriad of exigent assignments of various lengths should be utilized
- The teacher should provide a detailed explanation of the assignment and ensure the student has access to all required resources
- Sufficient time should be allowed for assignment completion
- Evaluate both assignment completion and performance
- Provide immediate feedback on collected assignments
- Hold all students accountable for completed assignments
- Honor the belief that homework deserves serious attention from all members of the school community and must play a significant role in instruction (Heitzmann, 2007, p. 11)

To gain insights into the ways our current school's homework policy might be improved with the incorporation of Heitzmann's targeted homework concept, a two-part inquiry was designed to gather information from members of the school community for use in developing policy revision and to collect data concerning the effectiveness of the policy revision. The specific questions we wished to address through this continuing inquiry were:

- What are students' perceptions concerning homework and school success?
- What are teachers' perceptions concerning the relationship of homework and student learning?
- What are parents' perceptions concerning homework?
- What is the relationship between the use of a targeted homework approach and increased homework completion by students?
- What is the relationship between the use of a targeted homework approach and the number of "F" grades received by students as a result of not completing homework?
- What is the relationship between the use of a targeted homework approach and student academic achievement as measured by the Florida Comprehensive Achievement Test (FCAT)? (Camp, 2007)

> ### PASSION 8 (SCHOOL PERFORMANCE) EXERCISE
>
> 1. Review data you have collected in the forms of test scores and progress monitoring assessments from across your school. Based on these data, name the subject area or skill within a subject area that you would like to see improvement in. Next, review any state curriculum guides or publications that related to your target area. Finally, peruse the Web sites of the national curriculum organization that corresponds to your target area (e.g., National Science Teachers Association, National Council for Teachers of Mathematics). In what ways can all of this information lead to an inquiry?

Passion 9: Social Justice

In the previous section, as principal Marion McCray developed her question based on the lowest quartile students at Lafayette Elementary, she noted that the vast majority of these students were economically disadvantaged. This finding led Marion to develop a passion for social justice and to focus inquiry work on moving herself and her faculty from an *understanding* of where the free-and-reduced-school-lunch students they served were "coming from" to *action* to help these learners succeed in life:

> I want to really make sure that we're not just going, "Oh, gee, now I know where they come from." I want us to say what we're doing about it. I read an article about a young black man that was a high school student and how he talked about how his school was the only stable place he had. And I want us to get to the point at our school where we see that we can be the stabilizing factor for these students, and, not only that but we can let them know that your expectations at school will have to be different than what they are at home if you want to be successful in life. I want us to see it, not just talk about it. I want us to see us doing it, and will utilize the process of inquiry with my faculty to frame a focus on taking action for these children. (Personal interview, 2007)

Promoting social justice is another ripe place for wondering development. According to Cochran-Smith and Lytle (1993), when educators research their own practice, "they begin to envision alternative configurations of human and material resources to meet the needs of culturally diverse groups of students, teachers, and administrators. And they are willing to invest more of their own resources and professional energy in larger efforts to reform classrooms and schools" (p. 80).

Your first administrator inquiry wondering may come from your desire to effect social change by exploring questions of race, class, gender, or ability. In fact, effecting social change in regard to issues of social justice may indeed become the focus for your entire administrative career. Inquiry can be a powerful vehicle that begins your journey toward this goal. Entire school districts have used the action research process to focus on equity, race, and closing gaps in opportunity and academic achievement between groups of students. For example, the Madison Metropolitan School District in Wisconsin has published a collection of research authored by teachers within its district focused on creating equitable classrooms through action research (Caro-Bruce, Flessner, Klehr, & Zeichner, 2007). These excellent examples range in scope "from a close study of one child and how his elementary teacher adapted instructional practices to ensure school success to a study of how a high school science department changed inclusive practices in an effort to eliminate tracking" (p. 3). I highly recommend this text for all principals interested in understanding how student and teacher learning can occur when administrators and teachers use action research to study issues of social and educational equity. Two examples of administrators who began their inquiry journeys by addressing the complex questions about equity that face our schools follow.

First, committed to providing meaningful and doable professional development for his teachers, veteran middle school administrator-inquirer Mark Bracewell (2006) became intrigued with the notion of book study. Knowing that his teachers already had tremendously full plates, he wanted to provide a flexible professional learning opportunity. He thus turned to on-line discussion to meet his faculty's wish for limiting additional meetings and to acknowledge their struggle to balance family and personal obligations with the ever-increasing demands for their professional time after school. With the blessing of his faculty, Mark implemented an on-line book study that teachers could participate in to earn professional development points, which were needed to keep their teaching certification. As they engaged in this new on-line experience together as a faculty, Mark simultaneously led his faculty in a schoolwide inquiry focused on the question: *In what ways does a whole-group book study on Ruby Payne's* A Framework for Understanding Poverty *contribute to how we, as a Lake Butler Middle School administration and faculty, might create change and work toward breaking the cycle of poverty?*

In the second example, Randy Scott (2006), an African American administrator leading an almost all white high school faculty in a school with a significant population of African American students, worked with several of his faculty to select a book to help them examine and improve their practices with the African American students they taught. The group settled on Lisa Delpit's 1995 book, *Other People's Children*. By reading this text together and meeting on a regular basis to discuss it, Randy had formed an inquiry-oriented learning community that explored the following questions together: *How can we help meet the needs of African American students? Do our instructional practices help or hinder these students? What role has our own heritage and upbringing played in the lives of these students?* and *What can we do to help close the achievement gap and improve our practice toward African American students?*

PASSION 9 (SOCIAL JUSTICE) EXERCISES

1. Look closely at the demographics of the students in your building. Pick a subset of them (e.g., gender, race, class, ability), and pay particular attention to them during the day. Record in a journal your general observations and emerging questions. Do these children all experience schooling in a similar way?

2. Brainstorm a list of units/topics that are taught in your school. Investigate the content of the resources you are using to teach these units. What perspectives seem to be present or missing (e.g., gender, race, class, ability)? Then analyze each unit by asking yourself how these resources and activities support diversity, democracy, and literacy opportunities for all students.

3. Write down your philosophy of how you prepare students in your building to become democratic citizens. What role does teaching children about democracy play in your school? To what extent does your school encourage the development of participation and character traits central to a democratic citizen?

SOME CAUTIONARY NOTES

In this chapter, we have explored nine passions that lead principals to articulate inquiry wonderings and the example questions that have emerged for principals within each of the nine categories. Table 2.1 summarizes the nine passions and sample questions presented. Yet, before concluding this chapter, it is important to note a few cautions as you begin the process of wondering development.

First, in the framing of your question, be careful not to focus your wondering on controlling or changing other people's practice. My good friend, colleague, and expert on classroom management, Jim Nolan, often shares with teachers that any classroom management system must emphasize that the teacher's influence on students stems from his/her

Table 2.1   Sample Inquiry Questions by Passion

Passion	Sample Question(s)
Staff development	• How does the process of peer coaching help veteran teachers continue to learn and grow, and what role can the principal play in facilitating this process? • In what ways can I as a principal help facilitate the professional growth of the teachers within my building through engagement in action research? • In what ways can I, as principal, best facilitate teacher professional development to aid in their integration of CTE and academic concepts throughout our high school curriculum?
Curriculum development	• In what ways has engagement in a cross-school curriculum project affected our school community? • How can I build my own knowledge of exemplary writing practice? • How do I use learning communities as a tool for teachers and myself in the transformation of the writing curriculum at our school? • In what ways can a career pathways curriculum be developed at my school to simultaneously satisfy our state's new requirement for career education, meet the developmental needs of our middle school students, and integrate seamlessly into our already established middle school curriculum?
Individual teacher(s)	• What types of support help my new teachers succeed? • How can I best help an out-of-field teacher succeed? • What is the relationship between changing a veteran teacher's grade-level assignment and getting her out of a rut?
Individual student(s)	• What happens to struggling readers in our school after they leave intervention programs? • What effect does the inclusion environment have on the reading achievement of eighth-grade language arts students at Lake Butler Middle School? • What is the relationship between students' participation in Williston High's SWAS (School Within a School) Credit Retrieval Program and their success in high school? • In what ways are out-of-school or in-school suspensions as a consequence for discipline referrals affecting student performance?
Community/culture building	• What role does a weekly schoolwide meeting play in creating a caring school culture? • In what ways can our school develop a collaborative culture characterized by teachers from different grade levels communicating, understanding, and sharing expectations for all our students?

(Continued)

Table 2.1 (Continued)

Passion	Sample Question(s)
Leadership skills	• What do I learn from comparing and contrasting my own perceptions, my teachers' perceptions, my leadership team's perceptions, and my supervisor's perceptions about my own instructional leadership as a principal? • How do I improve my ability to inspire others toward a common purpose? • How do I build a cohesive and spirited team? • How can I, as an administrator, promote teacher leadership in the elementary division at P. K. Yonge?
Management	• What are teachers' levels of satisfaction with the current block schedule? • How can we all work together (students, teachers, lunch paraprofessionals, kitchen workers, custodians, and principal) to make lunchtime a cooperative and pleasant time for everyone?
School performance	• In what ways will implementing the continuous improvement model help increase student achievement at Mellon Elementary? • What actions can our faculty take to improve the reading achievement of our lowest quartile students? • What is the relationship between the use of a targeted homework approach and student academic achievement as measured by the Florida Comprehensive Achievement Test (FCAT)?
Social justice	• In what ways does a whole-group book study on Ruby Payne's *A Framework for Understanding Poverty* contribute to how we, as a Lake Butler Middle School administration and faculty, might create change and work toward breaking the cycle of poverty? • What can we do to help close the achievement gap and improve our practice toward African American students?

own teaching behavior. Jim's philosophy for becoming a successful classroom manager is that the teacher's premise must be that the only person a teacher can control is himself (Levin & Nolan, 2004). Similarly, when dealing with the business of administration and inquiry, the emphasis must be that the principal's influence on teachers stems from his or her own administrator behavior, and an important premise for becoming a "head learner" and successful administrator is that the only person a principal can control is himself. Inquiry questions such as "How do I get the teachers in my building to comply with our school policy of submitting lesson plans each week?" and "How do I guarantee that every teacher in our building is implementing the state curriculum with fidelity?" rarely lead to the important self-discoveries about administrative practice that inquiry can reveal. If you find your wonderings beginning to focus on *controlling* or *changing* teacher behavior, try reframing them in ways that help you *understand* teacher behavior and allow you to discover what *you* can do as an administrator with those new understandings.

A second, important cautionary note is that it takes time to discover a true passion that will sustain you through the process. In our book on teacher research, my colleague Diane Yendol-Hoppey and I state, "Rarely does any teacher researcher eloquently state his or her wondering immediately. It takes time, brainstorming, and actually 'playing' with the question. . . . By playing with the wording of a wondering, teachers often fine-tune and discover more detail about the subject they are really passionate about understanding" (Dana & Yendol-Hoppey, 2009).

Similar to the teacher-researcher, as an administrator-researcher, allow yourself the time and space to carefully and thoughtfully select, articulate, and play with the wording of your wondering until you settle on a question that you first and foremost are passionate about exploring. In addition, be sure your question is:

- clear, concise, and specific;
- one whose answer you do not already know;
- free of judgmental language;
- phrased as an open-ended rather than dichotomous question; and
- "doable."

In addition to the bulleted list above, the most productive administrator inquiries focus in some way on the adult and/or student learning occurring in your building. Although a question such as "What is the most efficient fire-drill procedure to clear our building in the case of an emergency?" is certainly a critical and important question for an administrator to explore and answer, it focuses purely on a managerial safety issue unrelated to any of the significant learning occurring in the schoolhouse. Definitely seek answers to questions such as those, but reserve inquiry questions for topics and processes that will shed light on significant and substantial learning for you, your teachers, and/or the students in your building.

Because the initial articulation and fine-tuning of your wondering does take some time, it's important to seek help! The exercises at the end of this chapter will help you get started. In addition, you may be interested in exploring another related text to this book titled *The Reflective Educator's Guide to Professional Development: Coaching Inquiry-Oriented Learning Communities* (Dana & Yendol-Hoppey, 2008). In the third chapter of that book ("Helping PLC Members Locate a Wondering"), my colleague and I provide numerous stories and vignettes of teacher- and principal-inquirers as they are coached in the development of their wonderings. Finally, engage in conversations with teachers in your building, other administrators, and even family members, asking them to help you dream about potential inquiry questions and settle on one to focus your energies on during the upcoming school year (if you are a practicing principal) or the semester (if you are enrolled in coursework where you will propose and/or engage in action research).

Once your wondering is named and fine-tuned, a final cautionary note is to allow your wondering to change and evolve over time as you engage in inquiry. It is not unusual, as practitioner-inquirers collect data (a process discussed in detail in the next chapter), for them to gain insights into their initial wondering that leads them in a new direction midway through the inquiry. For example, principal Lynette Langford and her faculty began their inquiry exploring the question, *In what ways are out-of-school or in-school suspensions as a consequence for discipline referrals affecting student performance?* Over the course of their inquiry, Lynette and her faculty's wondering evolved into: *What are some alternative behavior management plans we could implement in our school, and in what ways are they effective for decreasing student tardiness, increasing student attendance in class, and, subsequently, increasing the chances of our students succeeding as learners at our school?* If sometime during the course of your inquiry journey you discover something that begs for you to "tweak" your initial wondering to better guide the remainder of your inquiry, or you learn something that makes your initial wondering "outdated" and you must move in a new direction—tweak or abandon away and chart a new course for your study! Just keep track of the decisions you make as an inquirer along the way, as articulating changes in course can also be an important piece of what you are learning. Remember Lynette's sharing about the wondering evolution process she and her faculty experienced: "Our wondering started out in one direction and actually took on another direction as well. That's what is so wonderful about the inquiry process—it keeps us constantly looking for better ways to serve our students and help them become successful" (Langford, 2008, p. 181).

CHAPTER 2 EXERCISES

1. *The Great Wondering Brainstorm.* Using Figure 2.3, list one or two wonderings you have about your administrative practice in relationship to each passion. Once your list is complete, review the entire list and place stars next to the three wonderings that you feel would be most important for you to explore through the process of inquiry this semester or school year. Finally, share your top three wonderings with trusted teachers in your school, members of your lead team or professional learning community, other principals, friends, family members, or members of your class. Discuss both the wondering itself and your reasons for selecting that wondering as one of your top three choices for exploration through the process of inquiry.

2. *Journal Writing.* Respond to one or more of the following prompts in your journal:

Prompt 1. What are some common real-world dilemmas administrators face each day? What types of questions do these dilemmas raise?

Prompt 2. Which of the nine passions (staff development, curriculum development, individual teacher(s), individual student(s), community/ culture building, leadership skills, management, school performance, social justice) do you feel is *most* important to explore at this time in your professional life? Why?

Prompt 3. Which of the nine passions (staff development, curriculum development, individual teacher(s), individual student(s), community/ culture building, leadership skills, management, school performance, social justice) do you feel is *least* important to explore at this time in your professional life? Why?

Figure 2.3   Principal as Inquirer: "The Great Wondering Brainstorm"

Brainstorm one to two "wonderings" you have in relation to each of the following areas:

Staff development:

Curriculum development:

Individual teacher(s):

Individual student(s):

Community/culture building:

Leadership skills:

Management:

School performance:

Social justice:

3

The Road Map

*Developing a Data
Collection Plan*

Once you have selected a focus for your inquiry and defined a wondering to pursue, the next step in the journey is learning about data collection and developing a plan for the study. Deciding on which of the many available alternative routes to take for this leg of your inquiry journey means exploring the many possibilities available for data collection and selecting those data collection strategies that give you the best insights into the wondering(s) you wish to pursue. As you explore and select data collection strategies to create the road map for your journey, it is important to keep in mind that meaningful administrator inquiry should not "depart from" the daily work of administrators but become "a part of" their daily practice. Creating the road map for your study thus means thinking about life in your school and the ways in which it can be naturally "captured" as data.

In the current era of accountability, perhaps the most prevalent and noticeable data in many schools are quantitative measures of student achievement. Given our immersion in high-stakes testing and accountability and the laserlike focus on student achievement, it is difficult for any principal *not* to consider performance on tests as a critical form of data. Hence, this chapter begins by discussing this most obvious type of data, as well as sharing some cautions for utilizing test data as a part of the administrator inquiry process. Next, I discuss eight additional forms of data collection that may not be as obvious as the quantitative measures of student achievement that abound in today's schools but are incredibly valuable for gaining insights into an inquiry question. These data collection strategies involve field notes, interviews, documents/artifacts/student work, digital pictures, video, reflective journals or Weblogs, surveys, and literature. Finally, this chapter ends with suggestions on how to take your knowledge of data collection strategies and apply them to the creation of a plan for your inquiry.

DATA COLLECTION STRATEGY 1: QUANTITATIVE MEASURES OF STUDENT ACHIEVEMENT (STANDARDIZED TEST SCORES, ASSESSMENT MEASURES, GRADES)

As previously stated, in this era of high-stakes testing and accountability, numerous quantitative measures of student performance abound, and these measures can be valuable sources of data for the principal inquirer. For example, when wondering about the ways regular education students at his middle school were being affected by the implementation of an inclusion model, principal Mark Bracewell collected his students' measures on the Scholastic Reading Inventory, as well as their performance on his state's annual achievement test. By looking at student performance on the Scholastic Reading Inventory (SRI), Mark was able to ascertain that his regular education students in the inclusion class for language arts were performing as well as or better than their counterparts in the traditional eighth-grade sections at his school. This data helped Mark allay the concerns of parents and some of his teachers, as well as his own personal worries, that regular education and high-achieving students at his school might not perform and achieve to their potential if placed in an inclusive environment.

Because standardized test scores and assessment measures take the form of "numbers," they are consonant with traditional notions of research and data held by many principals. In fact, one of the first images principals conjure up when they hear the word "research" is of number crunching and statistical analyses. Because of this image, as well as the prevalence and focus on these types of data in schools today, standardized test scores and assessment measures are sometimes the first and only type of data practitioner-researchers think about collecting (Dana & Yendol-Hoppey, 2008). Yet, Roland Barth (2001) reminds us that "good education is more than good scores and good leadership is more than generating good scores" (p. 156). Similarly, good principal action research is about more than generating good test scores or showing the relationship between one's administrative practice and student performance on state tests. When principals use standardized test scores or assessment measures as a form of data collection for their inquiries, they must delve deeply into the data and understand what the test/assessment data were designed to measure, thus being sure that they are utilizing the measure in the ways in which it was designed. Consider the following scenario depicted by Love (2004), which demonstrates a superficial use and reliance on standardized test score data:

> When educators in one Texas high school saw African-American students' performance drop slightly below 50% on their state mathematics test, putting the school on the state's list of low-performing schools, they reacted quickly. Decision makers immediately suggested that all African-American students, whether or not they failed the test, be assigned peer tutors (Olsen, 2003). Based on one piece of data and one way of looking at that data, these decision makers made assumptions and leapt to action before fully understanding the issue or verifying their assumptions with other data sources. They ignored past trends, which indicated that African-American students' scores were on an upward trajectory. They failed to consider that the decline was so small that it could better be explained by chance or measuring error than by their instructional program. They considered only the percent failing without digging deeper into the data to consider what students needed. Finally, their proposed intervention targeted only African-American students, while overlooking Hispanic and white students who also failed the test. (p. 22)

As this example shows, if you choose to utilize standardized test scores and/or other measures of student achievement, you must interpret that data carefully as well as consider other data sources that will create a richer picture of the complexity within the place we call school. Recall that one of the most critical reasons to engage in research on your practice as an administrator is to untangle some of the great complexities inherent in your work. Any one data source, whether student performance on standardized achievement measures or any of the data collection methods discussed in the remaining sections of this chapter, provides only one "take" of what is occurring in your school in relationship to your wondering. Good principal research invokes multiple sources of data to accomplish what qualitative researchers refer to as "triangulation" (Creswell, 1998; Patton, 2002). Using multiple sources of data can enhance your inquiry as you gain different perspectives from different strategies. For example, in Mark's study, he also observed and interviewed the two teachers trying out the inclusion model as well as created a survey that all students in the inclusion classroom completed. From that data, Mark learned about the unique ways coteaching by a special education and classroom teacher plays out. He was also able to ascertain the underlying tenets of the inclusion model that allowed it to work so well for all students in this particular language arts class. This knowledge prevented Mark from jumping to the conclusion that every teacher in his building ought to coteach in an inclusive setting based on the positive SRI data. Rather, through interview and observation data, Mark understood the uniqueness of these two teachers and what is needed for inclusion to work. His observations and interviews provided Mark, who had never experienced inclusion or coteaching himself, with valuable insights about the process and helped him support other teachers in his building interested in trying inclusion as well as to adjust his scheduling to allow more time for special education and regular education teachers to plan.

Besides creating a richer and more complete picture of what is occurring in your school by employing multiple data collection strategies, you will also be able to build a strong case for your findings by pointing out how different data sources led you to the same conclusions. Finally, multiple collection strategies will enhance your opportunity for learning when different data sources lead to discrepancies. It is often through posing explanations for these discrepancies that the most powerful learning during administrator inquiry occurs and that new wonderings for subsequent inquiries are generated. In Mark's case, he learned a valuable lesson when he discovered through his inquiry that the SRI data did not correlate with student performance on the state standardized test, which subsequently led him to wonder about his school's routine practice of using the SRI as a progress monitoring tool.

It is important to note that, although standardized test scores and other measures of student achievement are prevalent and readily available and can be a fine source of data for some administrator inquiry projects when carefully considered, not all principal wonderings lend themselves to this form of data. Do not feel compelled to use student achievement data if this form of data does not align with your wondering. For example, there was no need to view student achievement data to gain insights into principal Deirdre Bauer's inquiry question, *How does the process of peer coaching help veteran teachers continue to learn and grow, and what role can the principal play in facilitating the process?* Rather, two sources of insightful data Deirdre collected included field notes and interviews.

DATA COLLECTION
STRATEGY 2: FIELD NOTES

I opened Chapter 1 by describing some of the many staggering demands administrators face each school day. One reason the work of administration is so demanding is that schools and classrooms are busy places, jam-packed with "action." Administrators inter*act* with teachers, staff, parents, students, and central office administration each school day. As administrators inter*act* with the various constituencies they serve, teachers inter*act* with children, children inter*act* with each other, and teachers and children inter*act* with subject matter. All of these inter*actions* occur within a particular context that is mediated by values (e.g., all children can learn), norms (e.g., students must raise their hands and be called on before answering a question), and rituals (e.g., each morning, the principal leads the school in saluting the flag).

To capture the "action" in the school, many principal-researchers take field notes as they observe. Field notes are not interpretations; rather, they focus on capturing what is occurring without commenting on why the action is occurring or judging a particular act. Field notes can come in many shapes, forms, and varieties. Some practitioners script the dialogue and conversation, diagram a classroom or a particular part of the classroom, or note what a teacher or student is doing at particular time intervals (e.g., every two minutes). The form your field notes take depends on your wondering. For example, in Deirdre's case, she was interested in understanding how peer coaching could help two of her exemplary veteran teachers, Judi Kur and Marcia Heitzmann, learn and grow. One way she gained insights into this wondering was to observe the two teachers throughout one peer coaching cycle. Deirdre captured the preobservation and postobservation portions of the peer coaching cycle by scripting, to the best of her ability, everything Judi and Marcia said to one another at these critical junctures. Figure 3.1 provides an example of Deirdre's scripted field notes.

A great resource for learning more about the technique of field noting in educational research and ethnography is Bogdan and Biklen's *Qualitative Research for Education: An Introduction to Theory and Methods* (1992). This text and other resources on naturalistic research can help you develop your skills as a field note taker. In addition, you might consider some contexts in your own administrative practice that are natural iterations of field noting. For example, many administrators across the nation are currently instituting the Classroom Walk-Through (CWT) model, based on the principles of Management by Walking Around (MBWA) discussed in the 1985 book *A Passion for Excellence* (Peters & Austin, 1985). In this model, you conduct brief observations (as short as three minutes) of classrooms, writing down on index cards "only those most important things that will enable you to draw patterns over time and help you to home in on topics for a reflective dialogue that will be a meaningful growth opportunity for the teacher" (Downey, Steffy, English, Frase, & Poston, 2004, p. 106). Like field note taking (and consonant with the

Figure 3.1   Deirdre's Field Notes

> Post Conference
> 3/16/01
> Judi - Coach
> Marcia - Teacher

J— The Kiddos were engaged. I had trouble getting all you said.

m— We talked. It was stimulating + fun to do. It was fun.

J— I could tell you were having fun. The students were engaged.

m— Different. They were ready for it.

J— Ready for what?

m— To extend the book in a different way. Fluff?

J— It's not. Look at what you did. Comprehension, phonics, shared writing — they helped spell words.

m— Not my first intention. Have to engage first.

J— They knew the no excuse words and vowel sounds.

m— April did the /ed/ word. She didn't know vowels in the beginning of the year. She is blossoming.

m— At the end, they wanted to edit.

J— Trevor picked up the missing letter.

J— How did the edit it?

m— Keep pages and read through it. Makes sense. Left out words. Changed words. Ending not the way I wanted it.

J— Not the way you wanted it.

m— No, but that will do.

J— Didn't get as much there. Vocabulary different words.

m— Impressed with excitement. Would have started with that. I thought it was fun and they thought it was fun.

J— Lets kids have a plan, but kids directed where you went.

m— Engagement — different readiness than beginning books.

J— That's why we can only spend 2 days on beginning books, but these stories are meatier and kids really ready

J— Looking at the data - Kept going back to kids. Sometimes they did the word. You seemed excited + kept things moving.

Source: Deirdre Bauer, Principal, Radio Park Elementary School, State College, Pennsylvania.

administrative inquiry notion of *not* controlling another teacher's practice as discussed in Chapter 2), the CWT process does not judge or evaluate a teacher's effective use of a given teaching practice; rather, "it is about colleagues working together to help each other think about practice" (Downey et al., 2004, p. 4). Hence, "implementing this process requires a climate of trust between teachers and the principal" (p. 103). If you have established this important trust and are engaging in this model of collegial supervision, classroom walk-through notes, saved over time, can be wonderful, naturally occurring insights into a principal wondering. Two examples follow.

Principal Kathy Dixon (2008) and her elementary school faculty had been engaged in professional learning community work focused on increasing student engagement in their high-need, high-poverty elementary school for the past two years. As a part of this process, ten of her teachers had received training in some of Spencer Kagan's (1994) cooperative learning strategies, which can be utilized to organize interactions among students, and had been sharing what they had learned with others at faculty meetings. In addition, her faculty had engaged in a schoolwide book study of Robert Marzano and colleagues' popular text *Classroom Instruction That Works* (2001). Now, two years into engaging in this professional learning community work, Kathy wanted to understand how her school's implementation of Kagan's strategies and the nine Marzano strategies had affected student-engaged instruction. As one source of data, Kathy looked at the CWT notes she had collected over a two-year period, noting the instances on her note cards that indicated student engagement.

CWT notes become a natural choice for field note data when the topic of an administrator inquiry is related to this process. Principal Patrick Wnek utilized his CWT notes as a source of data to gain insights into a collaborative study he did with two of his newest secondary teachers at Hilltop Alternative School, exploring the question, *How does employment of a modified Classroom Walk-Through (CST) model influence a beginning teacher's self-directed growth and the development of reflective thinking/practice?* (Wnek, 2007).

DATA COLLECTION STRATEGY 3: INTERVIEWS

As principal, or in your observations of other administrators at work, you have probably witnessed no shortage of people asking for just a moment of the principal's time to explain how they think or feel about something. Of course, this explanation often actualizes itself as a complaint. Principals give people their "moment" to share how they feel, and then principals react to it. This cycle of administrative interaction is common and normal but can become draining; even the most energetic principals can fatigue quite quickly as they *react* to their many constituents' feelings and thinking, often needing to defend policy and decisions.

Now imagine this common scenario in reverse. You initiate a dialogue asking for a moment of someone's time. Your initiation of this meeting places you in the driver's seat. In this position, you can pose questions to gain an understanding of how someone feels or what he or she thinks. Their answers to these questions help you learn and subsequently take action for change and improvement in your practice as an administrator. This second scenario is actually energizing, as principals are proactive in understanding the thinking and feelings of the many constituents they serve, and the constituents feel honored to be asked to share their opinions and thoughts with the "Head Learner" in the building! When these sessions happen in relationship to a principal's inquiry, they take the form of interviews, a third powerful way principals can collect data to inform their research.

Although interviewing can be informal and spontaneous, often important data are revealed when they are more thoughtfully planned. For example, in her peer coaching inquiry, Deirdre Bauer developed an interview protocol to learn more about how peer coaching was working for Judi and Marcia, interviewing each of these two teachers individually about the process.

INTERVIEW PROTOCOL

- Talk about reflections thus far regarding peer coaching.
- Were inquiry and reflection fostered through this process? If so, how? What else could help?
- In pre- and postobservation conferences, what helped promote reflection and inquiry?
- Did questioning play a role? If so, how?
- As the coached teacher, what kinds of questions were helpful from your coach?
- How many cycles have you completed so far?
- Talk about the cycle—what worked, what didn't work, what helped? Any suggestions?
- What was the impact of the cycle process on your learning/teaching? How many cycles are needed to make an impact?
- Talk about the types of data collected and how they affected your inquiry, reflection, and teaching.
- What impact did peer coaching have on your reading instruction?
- You each tried different reading instructional practices. Imagine making the same changes to your reading instruction without peer coaching. Would there be a difference in what you did in your classroom and what you learned?

- Talk about your relationship with (Judi/Marcia) and how it affected your peer coaching relationship.
- If you peer-coached with someone else, what would be different given the newness of the relationship? Would you need to do anything differently? If so, what?
- What supports did/do you need to make peer coaching work?
- Would you recommend peer coaching to other teachers? If so, why and under what circumstances?
- Do you have any ideas about how to invite/encourage/support others engaging in peer coaching?

Source: Deirdre Bauer, Principal, Radio Park Elementary School, State College, Pennsylvania.

In addition to individual interviews, principals sometimes use focus group interviews as a form of data collection. For these interviews, a number of individuals gather at one time in one space as the interviewer poses questions. One example of how focus group interviews can be used as a data collection strategy is the follow-up inquiry Patrick Wnek conducted subsequent to his inquiry into facilitating new teacher reflection using a collaborative CWT model. In this second administrator inquiry, Patrick utilized the action research process to understand how well a schoolwide positive behavioral support (SWPBS) program was working to meet the needs of the students served at the second school in which he served as principal—Summit Academy, an exceptional student education (ESE) school.

At Summit Academy, students receive educational services designed to meet their individual needs in a more structured and therapeutic environment. Because Summit is an ESE school, the criteria for student placement in the school vary from having received a parent request, to the student's need for a therapeutic environment and small class size, to other, more specialized reasons dealing with behaviors, academic supports, and student IEPs. All decisions regarding ESE student placement require an IEP team recommendation.

Building on research conducted by several special education researchers (Walker, Cheney, Stage, & Blum, 2005; Nelson, Martella, & Marchand-Martella, 2002; Sailor, Zuna, Choi, Thomas, McCart, & Roger, 2006), Patrick had worked with his faculty to develop and institute a SWPBS with the goal of creating a consistent but flexible behavior management system responsive to the individual behavioral needs of the at-risk students. As one form of data to gain insights into his overarching wondering, *"In what ways does a Schoolwide Positive Behavioral Support (SWPBS) program meet the needs of students served at Summit Academy?"* as well as one of his subwonderings, *"What are students' perceptions of the effects of rewards and recognition in improving their behavior?"* Patrick conducted focus group interviews with students at his school. Through this data collection strategy, Patrick learned that there existed a strong connection between the SWPBS program and positive student perceptions of the school:

> One student reported, "The point system matters to me because it helps me stay on track in the three areas (respect, responsibility, and safety). I have never been this good in school." Another student said, "I know that if I keep my contract with the therapist and I earn my points I will be rewarded and it makes me feel like I am accomplishing something." Another student reported, "Staff and teachers find ways to help me achieve my goals. Even when I am not earning all my points they still find ways to reward me for something that I am doing right. This makes me want to try harder next time and not to give up on myself." (Wnek, 2008, p. 2)

Although focus groups can be a quick way to obtain information from a number of individuals, focus groups have some limitations. For example, they are more likely to capture a breadth of opinion, and therefore less detail about individuals' thoughts is obtained. In addition, due to the presence of diverging opinions, less-confident focus group members sometimes refrain from sharing their thoughts.

An important consideration in using individual or focus group interviews as a form of data collection is how to capture what is said during the interviews themselves. Some principals, like Deirdre, take notes as they conduct the interviews and, shortly after the interviewing is completed, expand and summarize their notes so that vital data aren't forgotten. Following are Deirdre's interview notes and summary.

INTERVIEW WITH MARCIA ABOUT THE IMPACT OF PEER COACHING ON HER READING INSTRUCTION (SUMMARY)

Talk about reflections thus far regarding peer coaching.

It was helpful. I trusted Judi's judgment. Judi has a degree in reading. We collaborate anyhow. There is no threat. I truly had a concern about my lower groups. I picked certain aspects and how to approach them. Teaching style. New ideas. It validated what I was doing. We were using terminology.

I loved watching her kids. The literature circle was fascinating.

Reflection

Were inquiry and reflection fostered through this process? If so, how? What else could help?

Given time to do it. Not during lunch or after school when it's a problem. We focused on planning—not about solving a problem. We remained focused on the specific areas of study. We were affirmed through conversations. I felt the pieces were in place, and we were affirmed.

In pre- and postobservation conferences, what helped promote reflection and inquiry?

Questioning. Have you looked at it this way? Encoding to decoding suggestion. Confirming comments and observations. Did kids get it?

Did questioning play a role? If so, how?

Explained what we're doing and helps think about it at a higher level. Articulated thoughts and brought them to the surface. Got me excited to do. Questioning helps with something new—helped me think through carefully and redefine what I was thinking.

As the coached teacher, what kinds of questions were helpful from your coach?

It confirmed for me that I was doing enough with comprehension. At what point do you focus on comprehension? Development of the kids is the focus. Talking through things. Confirmation makes decisions clear. Is it me not getting it? So talking with someone else helped.

Cycles

How many cycles have you completed so far?

Three, and we will do one more.

Talk about the cycle—what worked, what didn't work, what helped? Any suggestions?

Analysis and strategy parts we did at the same time together. We needed the other person's input to analyze the data. Preconference was a direct connection to the analysis and the postconference.

What was the impact of the cycle process on your learning/teaching? How many cycles are needed to make an impact?

We need more than one or two. It depends on the focus. If just confirming one aspect of teaching, then may not need as many. If making a real change, then need a lot more. Shouldn't really focus on something really big. It would be better to chunk it. More to do with time management. Stick with the focus you set. Teaching is more like a web—it is not linear, so you can get easily distracted and go on to other topics.

(Continued)

(Continued)

Data

Talk about the types of data collected and how they affected your inquiry, reflection, and teaching.

Arrows with names was very helpful. During the first observation, it was teacher question, then student answer. During the second observation after Judi had introduced literature circles it was more kid-kid-kid. The teacher's role is essential. The teacher needed to refocus. Kids spoke their feelings.

I would like to start it sooner, but they were not developmentally ready. They needed to have the foundation laid. They are readers now. Couldn't talk and respond to books that way in the beginning of the year.

Instructional Impact

What impact did peer coaching have on your reading instruction?

Answered above.

You each tried different reading instructional practices. Imagine making the same changes to your reading instruction without peer coaching. Would there be a difference in what you did in your classroom and what you learned?

It would be flat. I liked the confirmation. We each risked. Might not be as inclined to stick with something if we did not get the support through peer coaching. We have a tendency to focus on what's not working. The data confirmed there were differences from our perceptions. Peer coaching allowed us to try again. We also learned from being in each other's rooms. PC is like taking a step back for every 2 forward—reflection. Focus on the good things is a part of PC.

Relationship

Talk about your relationship with (Judi/Marcia) and how it affected your peer coaching relationship.

Trust is key. It won't work without it.

If you peer-coached with someone else, what would be different given the newness of the relationship? Would you need to do anything differently? If so, what?

Depends on style and personality. You need the relationship first without a critical lens. Relationship then peer coach, but need to have that personal relationship first. Egos are fragile. It is developmental. New teacher needs monitoring, so peer coaching in this way really would not work. Questioning could put a new teacher on the defensive rather than as a springboard for discussion.

Broader Impact

What supports did/do you need to make peer coaching work?

You covering, offering to support and cover, asking when we needed you. You supported meeting by giving us time. Talking helped focus on the process. You were the coach about peer coaching. The prior training helped. It sparked an interest.

Would you recommend peer coaching to other teachers? If so, why and under what circumstances?

Depends on the relationship factor.

Do you have any ideas about how to invite/encourage/support others engaging in peer coaching?

People not as collegial—development of collegial relationship to carry on in the other areas. Already so collegial. Could be threatening—the relationship is the sticky point. Mutual vulnerability—both in it to learn. No one is the expert.
   Avoid threatening.
   No right or wrong way.
   Stick to the point.
   Desire to change or look at something.
   Must be a perceived need and a desire to explore it.
   No expert!
   Need not be a deficit.
   Exciting, change, question something.
   Confidence in profession—not judgment.
   Nonjudgmental/trust/fair.
   Style is similar; it is easier to be nonjudgmental because of your own biases.

Source: Deirdre Bauer, Principal, Radio Park Elementary School, State College, Pennsylvania.

Other principals, such as Patrick, audiotaped the interviews and replayed the tape at a later time either to capture every word or transcribe pertinent and important parts of the interview. Most principals find that fully or partially transcribing an interview is insightful but time consuming and not necessarily worth the time it takes. Full transcriptions of interview data are usually reserved for principals engaging in action research to fulfill the dissertation component of their graduate degree work. In this case, full transcription is warranted as the process enables the more sophisticated data analysis that is an expectation for earning an advanced degree. The process of data analysis will be discussed in Chapter 4. In addition, you can learn more about the process of interviewing and can refine your interviewing technique by reviewing Patton's excellent chapter on the subject in his book *Qualitative Research and Evaluation Methods* (2002).

DATA COLLECTION STRATEGY 4: DOCUMENTS/ARTIFACTS/STUDENT WORK

As indicated, field notes and interview notes and their transcripts capture actions as data on *paper*. However, even without field notes and interview notes, schools and classrooms naturally generate a tremendous paper trail that captures much of the daily school activity. The paper trail includes student work, curriculum guides, textbooks, teacher manuals, children's literature, IEPs, district memos, parent newsletters, progress reports, teacher planning books, written lesson plans, and correspondence to and from parents, specialists, and yourself as the principal. The amount of paperwork that crosses a principal's desk can make any principal bleary-eyed. Often the papers principals view do not hold significant meaning in isolation or when read quickly so as to move on to the next item on the principal's "to do" list. In reality, principals need to "get through" paperwork to keep up with their work.

Yet, when administration and inquiry are intertwined, the papers become data and take on new meaning. When principal-inquirers select and collect the papers related to their research wonderings, we call these papers documents or artifacts. Systematically collecting papers allows you to look within and across these documents and analyze them in new and different ways. For example, as a method of tracking student productivity and developing understandings in relationship to a number of the state standards in science, environment, and ecology, principal Donnan Stoicovy and her team of coteacher-inquirers collected sample student work from five classrooms (one at each grade level) to gain insights into how a cross-school curriculum project was working in their building. By looking at student work over time, Donnan could make claims not possible by viewing a single piece of student work in isolation, perhaps hanging on the bulletin boards at school or noticed in brief snippets of time during her CWTs. A sample of student work collected by Donnan and her inquiry team appears in Figure 3.2.

DATA COLLECTION STRATEGY 5: DIGITAL PICTURES

Interviews, focus groups, and certain artifacts can capture words as data. A very old proverb you are likely familiar with is "A picture is worth a

Figure 3.2   Student Work Sample

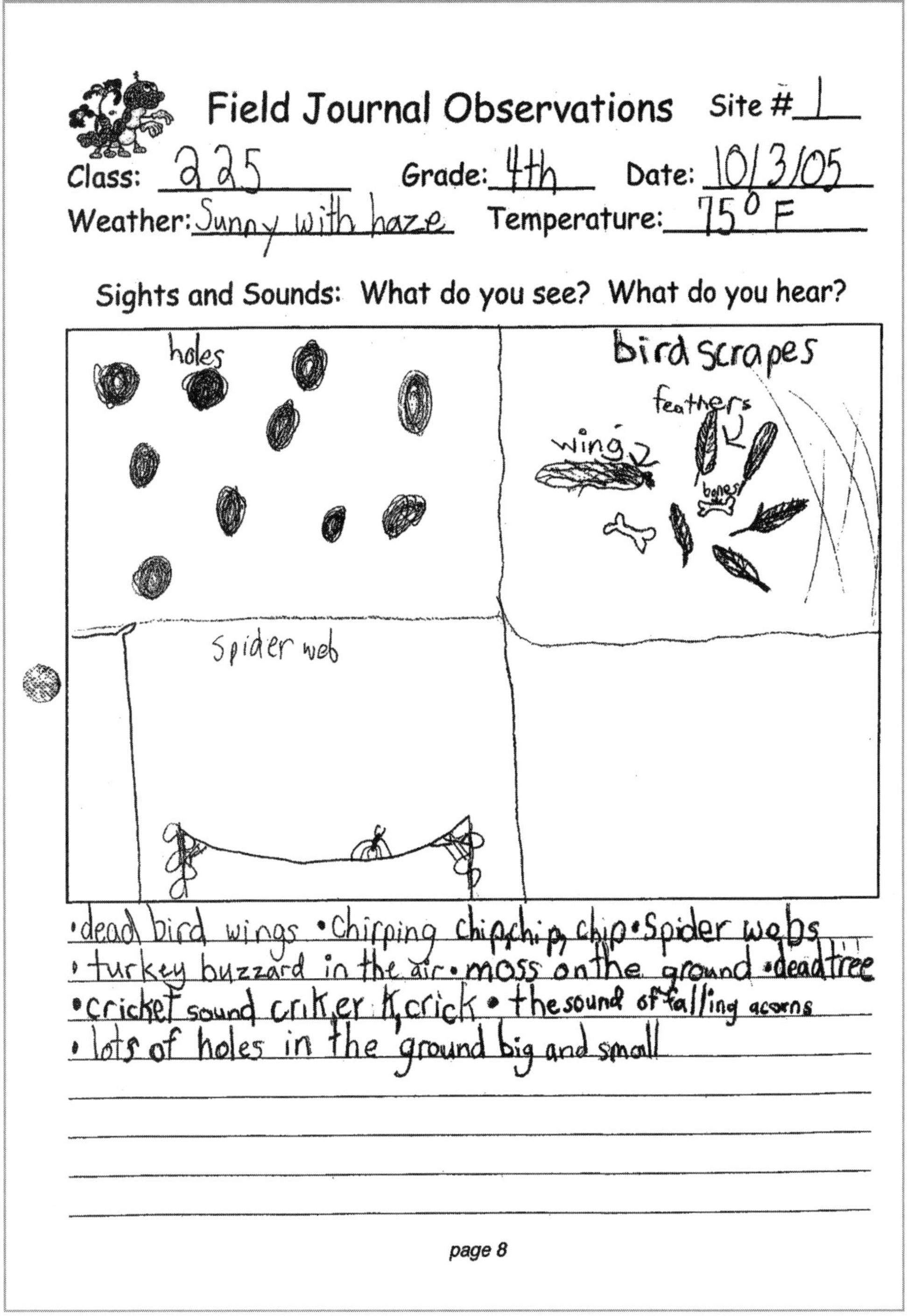

Field Journal Observations   Site #__1__

Class: _2 2 5_   Grade: _4th_   Date: _10/3/05_

Weather: _Sunny with haze_   Temperature: _75° F_

Sights and Sounds: What do you see? What do you hear?

holes

bird scrapes

feathers

wing

bones

Spider web

• dead bird wings • Chirping chip chip chip • Spider webs
• turkey buzzard in the air • moss on the ground • dead tree
• cricket sound crik er k crick • the sound of falling acorns
• lots of holes in the ground big and small

page 8

Source: Donnan Stoicovy, Principal, Park Forest Elementary, State College, Pennsylvania.

Figure 3.3 Observation Site

Source: Donnan Stoicovy, Principal, Park Forest Elementary, State College, Pennsylvania.

thousand words." Another wonderful way to capture action occurring in the school is through digital photography. In Donnan's curriculum inquiry, recall that students visited four different sites on the school grounds to make observations at eight different times over the course of the school year. To help make sense of the entire project and how it was playing out at her school, Donnan turned to her camera. One way digital pictures proved extremely useful was by capturing each of the four sites at the eight different observation times during the school year. Figure 3.3 shows one of the sites all the children in Park Forest Elementary School visited to conduct their observations during the winter months.

DATA COLLECTION STRATEGY 6: VIDEO

Digital pictures capture a single snippet of action at one point in time. Video as a form of data collection takes digital pictures one step further by capturing an entire segment of action in a classroom or school over a set time period. Given that educators often collect their best data by seeing and listening to the activities within their classroom and schools, video becomes a powerful form of data collection for the practitioner-researcher. Administrator and teacher researchers have found that using video can help them collect descriptive information, better understand an unfolding behavior, capture the process used, study the learning situation, and make visible products or outcomes. More specifically, through observing video of teaching, educators can observe attitudes, skill and knowledge levels, nature of interactions, nonverbal behavior, instructional clarity, and the influence of physical surroundings (Cloutier, Lilley, Phillips, Weber, & Sanderson, 1987).

DATA COLLECTION STRATEGY 7: REFLECTIVE JOURNALS AND/OR WEBLOGS

Thus far, we have discussed ways to make data collection a part of your administrative practice by capturing what is naturally produced in your school—student performance on achievement tests and other progress monitoring tools; action in the school, captured through field notes, digital pictures, and video; the work of students or teachers in your building, obtained through document analysis; and talk in the school through interviews and focus groups. One way interviewing and focus groups serve as powerful data collection strategies is through the *talk* of interviewing, because a principal-inquirer gains access into the *thinking* of the child or adult being interviewed.

Capturing "thinking" is a challenge for any researcher. One way a principal-researcher uncovers the thinking that occurs in the school and within his or her own mind is through journaling. Journals provide administrators with a tool for reflecting on their own thought processes. Similar to a journal, Weblogs are another excellent way principal-researchers can capture their thinking as an inquiry unfolds. Will Richardson (2006) defines a Weblog in its most general sense as "an easily created, easily updatable Web site that allows an author (or authors) to publish instantly to the Internet from any Internet connection" (p. 17). Because Weblogs consist of a series of entries arranged in reverse chronological order, they can serve as a sort of "online diary" where administrators can post commentary or news about the research they are currently engaged in. Unlike a journal as a form of data collection, the principal-researcher who blogs can combine text, images, and links to other blogs as well as post comments in an interactive format. The comment feature of blogs allows principal-researchers to receive feedback from anyone in the world (in an open blog community) or other practitioner-researchers (in a closed community).

Both journaling and blogging as a form of data collection can be very powerful tools, but sometimes it is difficult for the novice principal-researcher to view their own reflections as important data! Ironically, as educators in charge of facilitating the thinking and learning of others, we have not been socialized to think that our *own* thinking and learning matters! Yet, capturing your own thinking over time can lead to critical insights into your administrative practice, insights that may only occur when you revisit a thought or when you string a number of thoughts together that have come to you intermittently over a longer period of time. If you (or any of the students or teachers in your building) are Harry Potter fans, you will recall that the wise teacher and headmaster, Albus Dumbledore, has the ability to extract thoughts and recollections of events from his head and place them in a "pensieve." At critical times in the Harry Potter stories, Albus enters the pensieve, sometimes with Harry, to explore these old memories and thoughts and gains new insights with each visit. Journaling or blogging can serve as your personal pensieve to capture and store your thoughts and recollections safely so you can share them with teaching colleagues or other administrators and return to them at various times in the evolution of your inquiry, gaining new and deeper insights with each visit. Principal Mike Delucas (2008) discovered the power of journal writing to track and revisit his reflections over time as he studied the School-Within-a-School credit retrieval program put in place at his high school to assist students who had fallen behind in earning the necessary credits for graduation. An example of a journal entry from Mike's inquiry appears here.

JOURNAL ENTRY, JANUARY 8, 2008

A new semester has started today. For our School-Within-a-School [SWAS], we introduced two new students into the program today. They are both young ladies who seem to have matured recently. They are behind in school and don't want to face the prospect of being in school much past their traditional graduation date.

The four teachers in SWAS want me to remove two young men from the program. They explain that the young men have shut down and that they are making very little effort to retrieve credit or prepare for the FCAT or GED. Honestly, I don't want to take them out of SWAS and put them in regular classes. We put them in SWAS because they were without hope in our traditional curriculum. I can't imagine they would be much more hopeful now. At worst, I fear that they will be disruptive in classes of 20 or more (SWAS only has 13 students on our best day). What is a principal to do—go with instincts and risk offending four of my best teachers (each of whom volunteered for this duty) or go with the teacher's recommendation and risk dashing what little hope these young men have and risk offending the teachers who will inherit these two young men?

One of the young men is David Smith. My hope for David (and for several others) was for him to earn enough credits to become a sophomore so that he could take the sophomore FCAT and potentially graduate through the GED Exit Option. It does not appear that David has earned enough credits to become a sophomore. I will know for certain on Friday. I need to meet with each of the SWAS teachers and each of the SWAS students.

Source: Mike Delucas, Principal, Williston High School, Williston, Florida.

Besides using the journal or blog as a powerful data collection tool for the principal, as "Head Learners," principals can share their journal writing or blogging time with students to model a love of writing. One principal I worked with scheduled ten minutes of journal writing time into her schedule each week, coordinating this time with a writer's workshop in two of the fifth-grade classrooms in her building. The classroom teachers expected that she would show up once a week just as their own children were writing and that she would sit down at the front reading table and begin writing as well. In this way, this principal accomplished multiple goals simultaneously—she committed her reflections on practice to paper each week, she was visible to teachers and students in classrooms, she modeled writing for the young learners in her building, and she was making a subliminal statement that she supported these two teachers' commitment to implementing a writer's workshop in their classrooms. This example is yet another of the ways inquiry can become a part of, rather than apart from, the practice of an administrator.

DATA COLLECTION STRATEGY 8: SURVEYS

Some principal-inquirers employ more formal mechanisms to capture the action, talk, thinking, and productivity that are a part of every school day. The most common formal mechanism I have observed in my work with principals is surveys. Surveys give teachers, parents, and students a space to share their thoughts and opinions about any number of happenings in the school building. For example, principal Jim Brandenburg administered the survey termed "Druthers" shared in Chapter 1 to his teachers as he began exploring how he might better facilitate the professional growth of his teachers through action research (see Figure 1.1). Principal Mark

Bracewell utilized a survey to gather information about his eighth graders' experiences in a class cotaught by a regular and special education teacher. Donnan Stoicovy utilized both student and teacher surveys to ascertain the ways a schoolwide curriculum project designed to meet a number of state standards played out over the course of the school year. Donnan's student and teacher surveys appear in Figures 3.4 and 3.5.

Figure 3.4 Student Survey

PFE Schoolyard Project Student Survey

Name ▮▮▮▮▮▮▮▮▮ Grade 3 Room 218

1. What two or three things have you learned while doing our PFE Schoolyard Project?

1. Nature is wonderful and there is many wonderful things to see if you just stop to look.

2. When the seasons change alot besides the weather change like when it changes from winter to spring the animals that were hibernating would come out and plants grow green leaves and flowers sprout.

2. What have you liked about our PFE Schoolyard Project?

1 That we get a chance to go outside and get to enjoy the outdoors.

3. What would you change if you could about our the Schoolyard Project?

Nothing, I think it is perfect

4. Please share any other ideas to improve our PFE Schoolyard Project.

1. Rake the leaves! it is very hard to walk quietly through them.
2. I think we should go more places because we are very limited in space now.

Source: Donnan Stoicovy, Principal, Park Forest Elementary, State College, Pennsylvania.

You can learn more about the art and science of developing good questionnaires and surveys in one of the many outstanding introductory texts to survey development, such as Fowler's *Survey Research Methods* (2002) or Czaja and Blair's *Designing Surveys: A Guide to Decisions and Procedures* (2005).

Figure 3.5 Teacher Survey

PFE Schoolyard Project Teacher Survey

Name_____

1. Please share some strategies that your students used during their site visits that you found to be successful. *(of binoculars)*

* Providing a stencil shape to trace and then having kids pick one thing to look @ and sketch.
* Providing / *a focus* Narrowing the focus ... Find a bird today, look closely at a leaf

2. Which tools have you found to be most useful?

bird books   The wagons are full of so
bug boxes   many great things!
binoculars

3. What have you liked about our PFE Schoolyard Project?

* TIME to spend enjoying & discussing nature with kids.

* An opportunity for student interest to guide what we learn
(ie. - kids found insects and wanted to learn more -- this was an excellent spring board to other lessons.)

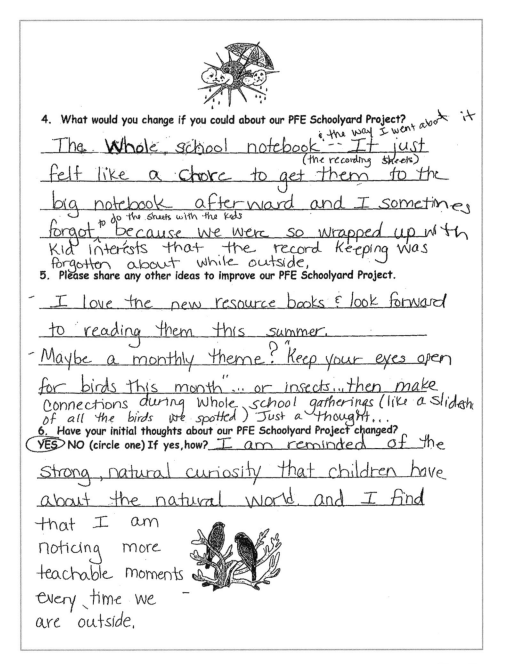

4. What would you change if you could about our PFE Schoolyard Project?

The Whole school notebook & the way I went about it -- It just felt like a chore to get them (the recording sheets) to the big notebook afterward and I sometimes forgot to do the sheets with the kids because we were so wrapped up with kid interests that the record keeping was forgotten about while outside.

5. Please share any other ideas to improve our PFE Schoolyard Project.

- I love the new resource books & look forward to reading them this summer.
- Maybe a monthly theme? "Keep your eyes open for birds this month"... or insects...then make connections during whole school gatherings (like a slideshow of all the birds we spotted) Just a thought...

6. Have your initial thoughts about our PFE Schoolyard Project changed? YES NO (circle one) If yes, how? I am reminded of the strong, natural curiosity that children have about the natural world. and I find that I am noticing more teachable moments every time we are outside.

Source: Donnan Stoicovy, Principal, Park Forest Elementary, State College, Pennsylvania.

DATA COLLECTION STRATEGY 9: LITERATURE

Although we often do not think of literature as "data," reading the literature stimulates you to think about how your work as a principal-inquirer is informed by and connected to the work of others. No principal conducts his/her administrative duties or inquiries in a vacuum. As educators, we are situated within a context (your school, district, state, country, etc.), and our context mediates much of what we do and understand as principals. Similarly, when administrators inquire, their work is situated within a large, rich, preexisting knowledge base that is captured in books, journal articles, newspaper articles, conference papers, and Web sites. Looking at this preexisting knowledge based on administration and teaching informs your study.

Further illustrating the importance of literature as an essential form of data, Matthews and Crow (2003) note:

> A common mistake that educators make is to claim that something is "research-based." For example, in supporting a block schedule for high schools, an educator may claim that longer class periods have been shown by research to be more effective for adolescent learners. Often the source is never cited. The study may have limitations as to how generalizable it is to other school settings. Likewise, educators read a lot of literature from journals that is only based on theory and not necessarily researched empirically. As a school leader, you need to understand the existing literature and be able to critique these sources. You also will need to explain to others what good research is and is not. (pp. 181–182)

To collect literature as a form of data for your inquiry, you will need to figure out which pieces of literature connect to your wonderings and will give you insights as your study is unfolding. Administrator-inquirers generally collect literature at two different times: (1) when they first define or are in the process of defining a wondering (as previously discussed in Chapter 2), and (2) as their studies lead them to new findings and new wonderings. In these cases, principals use the literature to become well informed about the current knowledge in the field on their topic. In fact, if you are engaging in action research for the purpose of earning an advanced degree at a university and will be producing a master's thesis or a dissertation, you will likely be expected to complete a thorough literature review on your topic, presented as its own section or chapter. Not all administrator action research culminates in a dissertation or thesis, but, nevertheless, literature is an essential form of data that every principal-inquirer should use to be connected to, informed by, and a contributor to the larger conversation about educational practice.

WHEN DO I COLLECT DATA, AND HOW MUCH DO I COLLECT?

Now that you have seen some examples of what data collection might look like, you are ready to think about your own wondering and which forms of data collection might work for you. As principal-inquirers ponder the "how" of data collection and select the strategies they wish to employ, they must also answer the related questions of how long they will collect the data and how much they will collect. The "when" and "how long" of data collection is often answered by natural constraints imposed by things such as the length of a unit if you are doing a curriculum inquiry like Donnan or the due date for your paper if engaging in inquiry as part of a graduate course. Optimally, data collection proceeds until you reach a state where you are no longer gaining insights into your wondering or question and no new information is emerging. This state is termed *saturation* by research methodologists (Creswell, 1998; Patton, 2002).

The complexities of administration and teaching are so great, however, that you could be collecting data and waiting for saturation to occur indefinitely. Drawing closure to an inquiry, however, allows you to experience one of the most rewarding and exhilarating components of practitioner inquiry—deeply immersing yourself in your data, articulating your findings, and allowing new wonderings to emerge. Therefore, it is important that you bind your study into a particular timeframe. Decisions about when and how long to collect data must be made as you balance what is feasible to do in the real world of your school and what is optimal for providing insights into your topic.

It is at this point that it is extremely valuable to develop a comprehensive plan for your inquiry. Hubbard and Power (1999) suggest that practitioner-inquirers write a research brief, defined as "a detailed outline completed before the research study begins" (p. 47). A research brief may cover aspects such as the purpose of your study, your wonderings, how you will collect data, how you will analyze data (which I explore in the next chapter), and a timeline for your study. Through the process of developing a brief, administrator-inquirers commit their energies to one idea. This commitment facilitates an inquirer's readiness to begin data collection. This chapter ends with three examples of original research briefs developed by an individual administrator-inquirer (Deirdre Bauer), a principal (Lynette Langford) engaging in collaborative inquiry with her faculty and lead team, and a group of principals who have formed an administrator professional learning community to conduct a collaborative inquiry (North East Florida Educational Consortium Administrators). These three different briefs provide examples of the different configurations principals might use to engage in the inquiry process (individual, collaborative with teachers in the building, and collaborative with other principals).

Note that, as with the development of your wondering, rarely does any practitioner-inquirer articulate a perfect plan on paper that is tightly constructed and plays out exactly as originally planned. The value of the inquiry brief is not to create a perfectly articulated document but to get something down on paper that others can provide feedback on and to get you started on this leg of your journey. If you are a master's or doctoral student, developing an inquiry brief and sharing it with your advisor is a great way to get feedback before you begin the often required task of writing a full-blown proposal for your study. If you are engaging in action research for your own professional development and to inform school improvement efforts at your school, developing an inquiry brief and sharing it with your lead team (or, if you are fortunate enough to be a part of a principal group, with your administrative colleagues) is a great way to get feedback to fine-tune your plan, make sure all components are tightly aligned (wonderings, data collection strategies, analysis, and timeline for completion), consider other forms of data collection that could be insightful, and troubleshoot potential problems or disconnects in your plan.

By invoking a feedback protocol, you can get valuable information from your colleagues in an efficient and powerful way. An example of such a protocol follows.

INQUIRY BRIEF DISCUSSION PROTOCOL:
SIX STEPS TO A FINE-TUNED PLAN FOR INQUIRY

Suggested Group Size: 3–4

Suggested Timeframe: 15–20 minutes per group member

1. Select a timekeeper.

2. Presenter hands out a hard copy of the inquiry brief to each member of the group.

3. Group members *silently* read the inquiry brief, making notes of issues/questions they might like to raise in discussion with the presenter (4 minutes). As group members read the brief, the presenter engages in a writing activity to complete the following sentences:

   Something I would like help with on my inquiry brief is . . .
   One thing this group needs to know about me or my proposed inquiry to better prepare them to assist me is . . .

4. At the end of 4 minutes (or when it is clear that every member of the group has completed reading and taking notes on the inquiry brief and the presenter has finished his/her response to the writing activity), the timekeeper invites the presenter to read his/her sentence completion activity out loud (no more than 1 minute).

5. Participants talk to each other as if the presenter was not in the room, while the presenter remains silent and takes notes (approximately 10 minutes). Participants focus on *each* of the following:

   • Provide "warm feedback" on the inquiry brief. This is feedback that is positive in nature and identifies areas of strength (1–2 minutes).

   • Address the area the presenter would like help with and discuss the following questions (8–10 minutes):

     o What match seems to exist (or not exist) between the proposed data collection plan and the inquiry question?

     o Are there additional types of data that would give the participant insights into his/her question?

     o Rate the "do-ability" of this plan for inquiry. In what ways does the participant's plan mesh with the everyday work of a teacher?

     o How does the participant's proposed timeline for study align with each step in the action research process?

     o What possible disconnects and problems do you see?

6. Timekeeper asks the presenter to summarize the key points made during the discussion that he/she wishes to consider in refining his/her plan for inquiry (1 minute).

When I facilitated principal-inquiry groups of administrators from different counties in north-central Florida, we had one meeting wherein the five members of the group arrived with enough copies of each of their inquiry briefs for each member of the group. One by one, each principal took a turn sharing the brief, and we used the protocol to guide our discussion and provide feedback to the administrator. Using the protocol guaranteed that every principal received valuable, focused feedback, helped us use time efficiently (each principal received 15–20 minutes of focused feedback, and we finished our session in 90 minutes) and assured that no one person dominated the group. I hope you will find this protocol helpful in whatever context you use to share your brief with others and that the exercises at the end of this chapter help you develop your own plan—and help you begin!

CHAPTER 3 EXERCISES

1. Individually, or with your leadership team (or other colleagues), brainstorm the types of data collection strategies you might employ by creating a data collection chart. Title your chart with your main inquiry question and generate two columns: (1) What information might help me answer my question? and (2) What data collection strategies would generate this information? An example based on one principal's inquiry into the value of peer coaching as a mechanism for staff development of her veteran teachers appears here.

Main Inquiry Question(s): *What can I learn about the process and implementation of peer coaching from two experienced teachers? What role can a principal play in supporting this work?*

Information That Would Help Me Answer My Question	Data Collection Strategies That Would Generate This Information
Knowing what the teachers discuss in their pre- and postobservation conferences	Field notes from observing the teachers Audiotapes of the teachers' dialogue
Knowing what the teachers think about the peer coaching process	Interviews with the teachers
Knowing what changes the teachers make in their practice based on engaging in the peer coaching process	Field notes from observing teachers
Knowing what the teachers expect from the principal to help facilitate peer coaching	Interviews with teachers Keeping a personal journal where I jot down ideas for how I can help facilitate the process and log my thinking about how some of my actions are working
My teachers' opinions about instituting peer coaching as part of their professional development plans	Surveys
Literature on peer coaching	Do a search for books/articles connected to peer coaching and staff development

After completing this brainstorming exercise, use your journal to write about your reflection on the process. What data collection strategies that appeared on your list surprised you? What data collection strategies would be great sources of data but impractical to obtain? What sources of data do you think would be most valuable and why?

2. Create your own inquiry brief, including all the aspects of conducting a teacher inquiry we have explored so far (wonderings and questions, collaborative support, data collection strategies). Begin your brief with a statement that summarizes the purpose of your inquiry. End your brief with a detailed timeline for completing your study.

3. Share your brief with others, using the protocol that appears on pages 96–97. Take notes as your colleagues discuss your brief as a part of the protocol process. Use the feedback you received through this process to improve your plan for study.

Sample Inquiry Brief 1: Individual Principal Inquiry (Deirdre Bauer)

RESEARCH DESIGN FOR INQUIRY PROJECT, DEIRDRE BAUER

Purpose

I have studied and practiced peer coaching techniques as a teacher and as an administrator since the beginning of my career in education. I found peer coaching to be a very satisfying professional growth activity because of the comfort I had in the relationship with my coach. In my previous school, I provided training for teachers to utilize peer coaching with another teacher as an alternative to the traditional teacher evaluation process. Many teachers utilized the process, but they completed only one cycle. In my research on peer coaching and in my own practice, I know that it is the ongoing cycle that makes peer coaching a powerful learning experience. I decided to start small this time by working with only two teachers who were already trusted colleagues. I thought that by starting small we could concentrate on the quality of the process by engaging in ongoing cycles rather than just one cycle. Marcia and Judi are in evaluation this year, and they requested to do an alternate project. I asked each of them if they would be interested in trying peer coaching as a professional growth activity. I knew they already had a strong professional and trusting relationship, which is the first step in developing a peer coaching partnership. Marcia and Judi agreed to try it out, and I agreed to offer the support needed to make it successful. My hope is to learn what is needed and then offer it to other teachers within the building.

Questions

What can I learn about the process and implementation of peer coaching from two experienced teachers? What role can a principal play in supporting this work?

(Continued)

(Continued)

Subquestions

- How are inquiry and reflection fostered by engaging in coaching? (Going beyond dialogue.)
- What kinds of questions do two experienced teachers ask during the pre- and postobservation conferences? How do they integrate reflective and inquiry-based questions in their dialogue?
- What supports are needed to help two teachers implement ongoing peer coaching?
- What kinds of questions do experienced teachers bring to the table about their practices?
- What kinds of data are experienced teachers interested in collecting and analyzing?
- How does the relationship between these two teachers affect the peer coaching process?
- What can I learn from their implementation that would help spread this work among other teachers?

Methods

- Participation in pre- and postobservation cycles when possible and taking notes during the conferences focused on the types of questions asked.
- Interviews with both Judi and Marcia throughout and at the conclusion of their last peer coaching cycle.
- Consider asking Marcia and Judi to keep a journal about the process that I could review and analyze or possibly co-journal with them.

Data Collection

- Analysis of questions Marcia and Judi ask.
- Analysis of their interviews and possibly journals.

Source: Deirdre Bauer, Principal, Radio Park Elementary School, State College, Pennsylvania.

Sample Inquiry Brief 2: Collaborative Inquiry (Principal Lynette Langford and Her Trenton Middle/High School Lead Team)

INQUIRY BRIEF, TRENTON MIDDLE/HIGH SCHOOL LEADERSHIP TEAM

How does behavior/office referral affect FCAT scores of ESE students?

Purpose

As an "A" school, we met AYP provisionally because our ESE students did not meet the required standard in learning gains. We have noticed an increased number of office referrals on ESE students. The consequence for the referral is usually in-school suspension or out-of-school suspension. It would appear that these students need to be spending more time in class with instruction than in suspension. As a result of this observation, we are interested in seeing whether, if different discipline procedures are used and students are in class, they will make better gains on FCAT.

Question

Can using alternatives to suspension for ESE student discipline help increase gains on FCAT?

Subquestions

- What relationship is there between ESE discipline procedures and FCAT scores?
- What alternatives to suspension can be used for ESE students?
- How can we progress-monitor ESE students to see if alternative discipline procedures are helping students make gains?
- How do teacher/student relationships affect student behavior?
- What role does the parent play in student behavior?

Method

We will work as a faculty on being proactive with behavior plans on ESE students. We will also search for alternatives to suspension. We will collect baseline data on ESE student FCAT scores and discipline records. We will track new discipline records and use ThinkLink and FCAT Test Maker to progress-monitor academic gains.

Data Collection

- Identify ESE students
- Chart discipline records
- Chart FCAT gains
- Collect new discipline reports
- Generate ThinkLink and FCAT Test Maker reports

Calendar

November
- Gather baseline data
- Administer ThinkLink
- Alternatives to suspension training

December
- Collect new discipline reports
- Give FCAT Test Maker assessments
- Administrators and teachers work together on behavior plans

(Continued)

(Continued)

January
- Collect new discipline reports
- Give FCAT Test Maker assessments
- Administrators and teachers work together on behavior plans
- Progress-monitor with ThinkLink

February
- Collect new discipline reports
- Give FCAT Test Maker assessments
- Administrators and teachers work together on behavior plans

March
- Collect new discipline reports
- Give FCAT Test Maker assessments
- Administrators and teachers work together on behavior plans
- Progress-monitor with ThinkLink

Data Analysis

- Ongoing

Source: Lynette Langford, Principal, Trenton Middle/High School, Trenton, Florida.

Sample Inquiry Brief 3: Principal Group Inquiry (North East Florida Educational Consortium Principal Inquiry Group)

PRINCIPAL INQUIRY BRIEF, THE NORTH EAST FLORIDA EDUCATIONAL CONSORTIUM'S FLORIDA READING INITIATIVE'S COHORT I PRINCIPALS

Fran Vandiver (facilitator), Michael Allan, Garry Durham, Lynette Langford, Jeffery Edison, Linda Johns, Mark Bracewell, Cheryl Beachamp

Purpose

There are many components to being a principal—management, budget, scheduling, dealing with parents, and so on. While the duties a principal must fulfill are great in number, one of the most important roles a principal can play is that of instructional leader in the school. Yet, in the business of each school day, it is often difficult to find the time to focus on the instructional leadership aspect of being a principal. Therefore, as a group of principals committed to helping each other reflect on and improve our own instructional leadership practices, we want to intentionally spend some time understanding and developing our individual instructional leadership through practitioner inquiry.

Wondering

What do we learn from comparing and contrasting our own perceptions, our teachers' perceptions, our leadership team's perceptions, and our supervisor's perceptions about our own instructional leadership as principals?

Data Collection

We plan to collect data in three ways. First, to deepen our own knowledge base about instructional leadership, we will continue to attend NEFEC meetings on leadership as well as read and discuss articles and books on principalship and instructional leadership with our fellow principals in Cohort I of the Florida Reading Initiative. We will gather materials and take notes at these meetings. Second, we will utilize Kouzes and Posner's Leadership Practices Self-Inventory. We will each fill it out for ourselves and discuss our responses within our principal study group. Finally, we will ask teachers, members of our leadership team, and our supervisors to complete Kouzes and Posner's Leadership Practices Observer Inventory.

Data Analysis

The self-survey and the observer surveys will be submitted to an outside consultant who will send us each individually a summary of all of the inventories received, including an item-by-item analysis of the responses. Once we receive this summary, we will compare the observer surveys with our own survey. We will note where there are similarities and where there are differences. As we are doing this, we will also return to our notes from our principal group meetings and the books we read for further insights into what we are learning about our individual practice as instructional leaders. We will make a plan for changes we will make in our practice based on what we learned through analyzing the data and share what we learned with each other so we can offer each other support as we set our individual goals for growth in our administrative work.

Timeline

October: Gather notes from readings and meetings with principal cohort group.

November 4: Take the self-inventory and complete item analysis at our monthly principal cohort meeting.

Rest of November: Decide whom we are going to ask to complete the observer inventory. Obtain the appropriate number of inventories from NEFEC. Hand out the inventories with information on where to send the completed form.

(Continued)

(Continued)

December/January: Continue to attend monthly principal study-group meetings. Receive data printout. Analyze the data.

February/March: Share the results at the principal study-group meeting and begin developing plans for changes in our practice based on the data analysis. Participate in the principal group's data analysis to discover themes across the group's aggregate data.

April: Participate in the inquiry conference and present our findings to other principals.

Source: North East Florida Educational Consortium, Palatka, Florida.

4

The Navigation of Uncertain Terrain

Analyzing Data

Congratulations! As you begin this chapter, you are well on your way to completing your first inquiry. With a wondering developed and data collected, you are ready to begin analyzing your data. While this is one of the most rewarding and exciting components of your inquiry journey, it can also be the most difficult to navigate, for you may be venturing into uncertain terrain. For many principals, this uncertainty results from not knowing exactly what data analysis entails—especially what to do with data that aren't quantifiable (i.e., field notes, interviews, artifacts, and journal entries). Some principals experience such a strong sense of trepidation as they approach data analysis that their journey is interrupted or even ends prematurely. If you find yourself at this point in your inquiry, lamenting, "Okay, I've collected all the *stuff*, but I have no clue what to do with it now!" you may be experiencing the first symptom of a common ailment: "Data Analysis Paralysis."

Data Analysis Paralysis manifests itself in two ways. First, principals engaging in action research as a professional development activity begin to avoid their data. Data gathers dust as an untouched pile on their desks as they continually forgo looking at it in favor of other tasks and duties (which, of course, is very easy to do given the busy work life of a principal!). Thoughts like "I just don't have the time right now" creep into the principal's head each time she glances at the looming pile of data on the desk. Eventually, the pile on the desk is moved to the top of a filing cabinet or shelf to make room for a new project or report that must be completed for the district office, and there the data sits, untouched, for months, until so much time has elapsed between data collection and analysis that it just doesn't seem worth continuing.

The second manifestation of Data Analysis Paralysis happens to current or future administrators engaged in action research as a meaningful way to satisfy the final requirement for their master's, specialist, or doctoral degrees—that is, the thesis or dissertation. These individuals have worked their way through the various components of their program—the courses, comprehensive exams, and research proposal—frequently interacting with faculty and other students in their program. Now they are being left relatively alone to carry out their thesis or dissertation study. At first excited about finally completing their degrees, they enthusiastically collect the data proposed in their studies. It piles up on their desks, and the same scenario unfolds—there the pile sits, untouched for months. The occasional e-mail message or phone call from the advisor to "check in" brings guilty feelings, coupled with the already prevalent feelings of trepidation at the data analysis and write-up tasks looming ahead. The result is that the student never returns to the data and, despite all the time invested in advanced study, never completes that final leg of the journey to earn his/her master's degree, become certified in educational administration, or become a "Dr."

Never completing your action research robs you of the opportunity to learn a great deal about practice and improve how you, the teachers you work with, and the students in your building experience schooling! There are four easy ways to be sure that Data Analysis Paralysis doesn't afflict you: (1) confront the data analysis task, (2) take control of the data analysis process by keeping it simple, (3) follow four steps to data analysis, and (4) have colleagues help in the process!

CONFRONT THE DATA ANALYSIS TASK

The famous line from Franklin D. Roosevelt's first inaugural address, "The only thing we have to fear is fear itself!" holds true for the data analysis process. In the process of inquiry, data analysis is nothing to fear and has actually been described by many practitioner-researchers as enlightening, interesting, insightful, and valuable. But to experience enlightenment, interest, insight, and value, one must first and foremost confront the task at hand.

The first step in confronting the task is to commit a block of time on your calendar to data analysis. Recall from Chapter 1 that a helpful hint to the principal for finding time to engage in inquiry is to schedule a planned, consistent time for reflection and inquiry each week. At this point in your research, this scheduled time can be devoted to the analysis process. As you block out this data analysis time in your calendar, keep in mind that many practitioner-researchers find one longer block of time more productive than a series of shorter ones each week at this point in their research. When engaging in collaborative inquiry with their lead team or faculty, some districts help principals find a longer block of time by reserving an inservice day toward the end of the school year for data analysis or by arranging for substitutes for a half or full day to free up lead team members who are classroom teachers. When individual principal inquiry is a part of the district's professional development program, some districts allow principals to take a "data analysis day" wherein the principal can stay at home to look at data and prepare conclusions to bring to the next district administrative meeting to share with and receive feedback from others. Still other principals decide to devote one full weekend day to the data analysis process to get it done.

Since you cannot confront what you don't know or understand, the second step in the data analysis task is to develop an understanding of what data analysis means and why it can *appear* to be difficult at the start. Simply put, data analysis can be defined as creating a picture of what you have learned based on a careful, thoughtful, and systemic look at your data. Research methodologists have developed, described, and named a long list of systematic processes that facilitate data analysis. Two of the processes most frequently discussed in the social sciences are coding and memoing. Schwandt's *Qualitative Inquiry: A Dictionary of Terms* (1997) provides brief, technical definitions of these concepts:

> *Coding:* To begin the process of analyzing the large volume of data generated in the form of transcripts, fieldnotes, photographs, and the like, the qualitative inquirer engages in the activity of coding. Coding is a procedure that disaggregates that data, breaks it down into manageable segments and identifies or names those segments. . . . Coding requires constantly comparing and contrasting various successive segments of the data and subsequently categorizing them. (p. 16)

> *Memoing:* A procedure suggested by Barney Glaser (*Theoretical Sensitivity, Advances in the Methodology of Grounded Theory*, Sociology Press, 1978) for explaining or elaborating on the coded categories that the fieldworker develops in analyzing data. Memos are conceptual in intent, vary in length, and are primarily written

to oneself. The content of memos can include commentary on the meaning of a coded category, explanation of a sense of pattern developing among categories, a *description* of some specific aspect of a setting or phenomenon, and so forth. Typically, the final analysis and interpretation is based on integration and analysis of memos. (pp. 89–90)

Although the data analysis work of a principal-inquirer does draw from the social sciences and borrows the processes described by these scholars, it is easy to get bogged down in the jargon or technical language in the definitions above. Phrases such as "disaggregating data," "coded categories," "phenomenon," and "final analysis and interpretation" may feel foreign to your administrative practice and set up a roadblock to data analysis. To help you around this roadblock, data analysis can be described using language, phrases, and metaphors more consonant with your life and work as an administrator. We will explore some of these descriptions later in this chapter.

In addition to the technical jargon used by researchers, the baggage we carry containing *our own prior conceptions* of what research is can make data analysis difficult. As previously stated, many of us conceptualize research and analysis as quantitative number crunching (Dana & Yendol-Hoppey, 2008). Although manipulating numbers may be a part of a principal-inquirer's work, particularly if you've utilized quantitative measures of student achievement or surveys as part of your study, the data analysis process I discuss in this chapter is much more inductive in nature. This method may be antithetical to how you've thought about research and what data are and how you've analyzed data in the past. Letting go of these prior conceptions is an essential part of beginning the data analysis process.

A final reason data analysis can appear difficult is that the inductive process you are about to enter into is *uncertain*. Many qualitative researchers I know have described such analyses as "murky," "messy," and "creative." It is easy for a process that isn't exactly clear-cut to feel like it is out of your control.

TAKE CONTROL OF THE DATA ANALYSIS TASK BY KEEPING IT SIMPLE

For you to take control of the process and jump the three hurdles to data analysis discussed in the previous section (technical jargon, prior conceptions of research, and uncertainty), it is helpful to explore data analysis by using language and images you are already familiar with. To do so, let's turn to metaphor. Over two decades ago, George Lakoff and Mark Johnson helped us begin thinking in a whole new way about language when they asserted in their book *Metaphors We Live By* (1980) that metaphor is much more than mere poetical and rhetorical embellishments. According to these authors, "Metaphor is pervasive in everyday life, not just in language but in thought and action. Our ordinary conceptual system, in terms of which we both think and act, is fundamentally metaphorical in nature" (p. 3).

Two metaphors that work well to exemplify the process of data analysis are the Jigsaw Puzzle Enthusiast and the Scrapbooker. Exploring data analysis through these metaphors will help you simplify the process, take control of it, and get it done!

The Jigsaw Puzzle Enthusiast

A useful way to understand data analysis is to imagine yourself putting together what might be touted in hobby stores across the nation as the "world's most challenging puzzle." One reason for this description is that the puzzle comes in a bag, not in the traditional box with a cover that pictures the completed puzzle. As you work, you know the pieces you are putting together will result in a picture, but you are uncertain what it will look like in the end. To top it off, the directions to completing this puzzle indicate that there are more pieces in your bag than you will need and that other pieces may still be at the store!

Anxious to begin the puzzle, you start the process by spreading all the jigsaw pieces out on your table, with no other objective than to just look at what you have. Next, you begin to assess the puzzle pieces that lie before you: "What do I notice about these pieces that might give me insights into what this puzzle is going to be?" Based on what you notice, you begin a process of grouping or sorting. Perhaps you group all the pieces by similar color (for example, blue), thinking that all these blue pieces might fit together to create a sky, or you group by straight edges, knowing that these will form the perimeter of the completed piece. As you actually begin fitting pieces together and the picture begins to take shape, you may realize that some of the ways you grouped the remaining puzzle pieces aren't correct (for example, "Some of these blue pieces I thought might be sky really belong as part of a blue boat that is taking shape in the bottom righthand corner of the puzzle"). You regroup as you continue your work on the puzzle, creating new, additional groupings or condensing two different groupings into one.

At times your work may feel overwhelming as you search for hours to find where one certain piece fits, only to conclude that it isn't even a part of the puzzle. Later, you realize you are missing two important pieces and must go back to the hobby store to find them. Although there are frustrations along the way, when you finally complete the puzzle, you take pride in your accomplishment and marvel at its beauty.

When doing practitioner inquiry and searching for what you have learned, the puzzle pieces are your data, and you are piecing your data together in different ways to create a picture of what you have learned for yourself and for others. The process is "messy," "murky," and "creative" because, like the puzzle enthusiast who proceeds without a box cover, at the start of the analysis, you are not quite sure what this picture of your learning will look like; you must be patient as you allow your data to "speak" for themselves and lead you to your findings.

The Scrapbooker

A second useful way to understand the data analysis process is to imagine yourself putting together a scrapbook to preserve memories of a significant event in your life. For example, in 1999, my husband and I were fortunate enough to spend two months traveling through Australia as part of a sabbatical during which I was committed to learning more about the action research process by visiting schools and universities in Australia considered to be "hotbeds" of practitioner research. At the time, our children, who accompanied us, were four and six years old, so we wove a good number of recreational and educational pit stops into our trip. When we returned to the United States, I rushed to develop the ten rolls of film we had shot during our travels (obviously, our trip occurred before the age of the digital camera). When the film was developed three days later, I whisked the almost 400 pictures out of the store and went straight to visit my parents. One by one, we went through each of the pictures in the order in which they were taken from the envelopes. After sitting at the kitchen table for two hours, we still had three envelopes yet to open and view. I sensed my parents' fatigue, and my heart grew heavy as I realized that laboring through every single picture did not convey to others the magnificence of our trip. The pictures were in no meaningful order, some were blurry, and in some cases, there were way too many photographs of the same things.

When I returned home, my husband eagerly greeted me at the door and queried, "Well, how did the pictures come out?" I sighed as I explained that the number of pictures was overwhelming me, and while many had come out great, there were some that were out of focus, and during some parts of our trip, we must have been too camera happy—there were way too many shots that were similar. I feared that the pictures that potentially held so much meaning for our family and our children's memories would become a meaningless pile placed in a box and stored away in the attic. I imagined our young children all grown up, telling others that once they had lived eight weeks in Australia but that they had been so young they hardly remembered a thing.

Disturbed by my disappointment in the pictures, my husband had an idea. He remembered that a new store had opened recently across town called Scrapbook Haven. He purchased a gift certificate and a series of classes for me in the hope that they would help me capture our travels in a way that was meaningful and memorable for our two children.

I was grateful. At my first class, I learned that the best scrapbook compilers begin by sorting through pictures. "There's no need to use every single picture you brought to this class," the teacher said. "Why don't you look through every picture that was developed first, just to get a sense of what you have." As I did so, I noticed I had some pictures from each stop on our itinerary. Some of the pictures were related to work. Many of the pictures were of our two children.

Next, the teacher shared,

It is often helpful to group your pictures in different ways to decide how you want to proceed with the organization of your scrapbook. You might organize your scrapbook chronologically, or maybe by key events that took place during your trip, or perhaps even group pictures by individual child. Try sorting and resorting your pictures into piles that have some sort of meaning until you feel a sense of orderliness, commonality, and comfort with your assemblage.

My first pass through our pictures was relatively easy. I sorted the pictures by stops on our travel itinerary, then put the piles in chronological order. Next, I sorted each one of these piles into two subcategories—quality and nonquality photos. Quality photos were in focus, had good lighting, and were framed nicely by the photographer. Nonquality photos were out of focus, had some part of the subject cut out of the picture, or were photos I considered to be "bad" pictures of myself, my husband, or our children.

After looking at the piles, I noticed that three of them were of different stops on our itinerary but were related in that they were all pictures of families we had stayed with at different times during our trip. I combined these three piles together and placed a Post-it note on the pile that read, "Family Stays." I also noticed other piles that could be further divided. For example, I had a pile of pictures I had named "Cairns, Australia," in the itinerary section. Within this pile, however, there were multiple pictures of our time snorkeling over the Great Barrier Reef, multiple photos of hiking in the Daintree Rainforest, and quite a few pictures of swimming in the Coral Sea. I subdivided the "Cairns" pile into three sub-piles and, in the process, realized that I had no photographs of our first stop in Cairns—a visit to the Tjapukai Aboriginal Cultural Park, where my son learned how to throw a boomerang. I would need to find the brochure from this park and add it to my Cairns pictures after I returned home. In addition, there were a couple of candid shots of our children at our hotel in Cairns. I decided to remove these from the "Cairns" sub-piles and started a new pile called "Assorted Candids." I also found a few pictures of my daughter's fourth birthday party that must have been at the start of the first roll of film we used in Australia. I placed these pictures aside and would not use them in the scrapbook.

After many iterations of the sorting process, the way my scrapbook might take form began to become apparent to me. At this point, the teacher said,

> It's time to create your first scrapbook page. Take one of your picture piles and arrange it on the page. Think about a statement you would like to write on this page that expresses the meaning this group of pictures holds for you. You also might want to add a title to your page. And remember, you don't have to use every single picture, and you might even use portions of a picture—it's OK to cut and paste.

My class ended. I excitedly burst into our home and shared my hard work with my husband. Over time, I created a complete scrapbook of our travels. The final page contained a picture of our children back home in the states on the night we returned. The page was titled "Home Sweet Home" and contained the following caption: "When we arrived home at 11:00 p.m., jet lag had already set in as we were ready for breakfast, not bed. It took a few weeks to fully recover and reestablish our routines. It was good to be home, yet we will always fondly remember our days down under."

After completing the scrapbook, I once again visited my parents' home to share my new creation. As they turned each page of the scrapbook, short stories, humorous moments, and key experiences seemed to jump out of the pages and fascinate them. The trip had been captured and conveyed to others in a way that never would have happened had the pictures stayed haphazardly thrown into a box labeled "Trip to Australia." I knew that the process of creating this book had enabled me to better understand the enormous implications this eight-week excursion had had for me, my husband, and, most important, my children. I knew that the scrapbook would serve as an important catalyst to triggering their memories as they grew into adulthood.

When searching for what you have learned during a practitioner inquiry, the Australian photographs are your metaphorical data that you must sort, label, and group into meaningful units. If you do not, your data are just like the pile of 400 pictures sitting in a shoebox labeled "Australia Trip"; what you have gathered remains an unsystematic piling up of events and happenings that have little meaning or value for yourself and others. Sorting through, grouping, labeling, and getting rid of some data will lead you to articulating and presenting your findings.

If you can put together a challenging jigsaw puzzle or create a scrapbook, you can analyze your data! When applying whichever metaphor for looking at the data works best for them, principal-inquirers follow four basic steps: description, sense-making, interpretation, and implication drawing.

FOLLOW FOUR STEPS TO DATA ANALYSIS

Data Analysis Step One: Description

In the description phase, principal-inquirers read and reread their entire data set with no other objective than to get a *descriptive* sense of what they have collected. In other words, the goal of this first step of analysis is to *describe* your inquiry data. Like the puzzle enthusiast who begins a new jigsaw puzzle by laying out all the pieces on the table, or like the scrapbook teacher who suggested, "Why don't you look through every picture that was developed first, just to get a sense of what you have?" begin your data analysis by gathering all the data you have collected into one place. Some practitioner-researchers find that it is helpful to place all their data into a large three-ring binder. After you have all of your data in one place, read through your entire data set. During your initial read of the data set, consider the following questions:

Why did I inquire?

What did I see as I inquired?

What was happening?

What are my initial insights into the data?

Data Analysis Step Two: Sense-Making

After you have read through your entire data set one time with no other goal than to get a sense of what you have, you begin the *sense-making* step by reading your data again and asking questions such as,

What sorts of things are happening in my data?

What do I notice?

How might different pieces of my data fit together?

What pieces of my data stand out from the rest?

You might take notes in the margins of your data or write down your answers to these questions on a separate sheet of paper. Organizing your data (like the puzzle enthusiast who groups same-colored pieces together or the scrapbooker who sorts pictures into different piles) is one of the most creative parts of the sense-making process. Sometimes inquirers get stuck at this stage and need some prompts to help with this sense-making process. The following organizing units can serve as helpful prompts for beginning your analysis:

Chronology	Key Events	Various Settings
People	Processes	Behaviors
Issues	Relationships	Groups
Styles	Changes	Meanings
Practices	Strategies	Episodes
Encounters	Roles	Feelings

For example, you might look at your data and see if a story emerges that takes a *chronological form*, you may notice that your data seems to be organizing itself around *key events*, or you may see some *combination* of organizing units that will be helpful. This chart is by no means exhaustive, and you should let the organizing units emerge from your own data rather than force an external set of units on them.

Based on your answers to the above questions and your emerging units of analysis, you will identify common themes or patterns and begin a process of grouping or sorting your data. One way to group data is to use a different colored marker for each theme or pattern you identify and highlight all excerpts from your data that fit this theme or pattern. Another way of grouping data might be to physically cut it apart and place the data in different piles. If you do decide to cut the data apart, you might want to consider keeping a complete set as a backup.

Just as the jigsaw puzzle enthusiast realizes that some of the puzzle pieces aren't necessary and just as I realized that some of my pictures were from my daughter's fourth birthday party and didn't belong in the scrapbook, you will notice as you engage in the sense-making process that not all the data you collected will be highlighted/coded or will fit into your developing patterns or themes. These diverging items should be acknowledged and explained if possible (for example, "Those pictures must have been at the start of our first roll of film and don't really belong"). Likewise, just as the jigsaw puzzle enthusiast realized that some pieces were still at the store and I realized I had no photographs of the Aboriginal Cultural Park, practitioner-researchers may find that they need to collect additional data to inform an emerging pattern. At this point, it is important to note that, while data collection and analysis are described as two different processes and I separate them into two chapters within this text, they are not actually discrete entities and often become intertwined with one another. Finally, like the puzzle enthusiast who discovered that some of the puzzle pieces grouped as blue sky really belonged to the blue boat, and just as I decided to regroup some pictures into new piles called "Family Stays" and "Assorted Candids," you might regroup, rename, expand, or condense the original ways you grouped your data as your findings emerge.

The process of sense-making may take many iterations. For example, you may make data categories, name the categories, combine the named categories, rename the categories, and eventually combine some of the combined renamed categories. As you move through this process, be sure to keep track of how you arrive at the final sense-making of your data. You may track it via a narrative form, or you may draw a concept map for each iteration of your analysis. No matter which method you choose to map out your sense-making process—do it! The documentation will really help as you begin the interpretive step of analysis, write up your inquiry, and discuss your findings with others.

Data Analysis Step Three: Interpretation

Just as the scrapbook teacher invited me to create my first page by writing a statement that expressed the meaning the group of pictures held for me, in this phase, patterns or themes yield statements about what a practitioner-researcher learned and what the learning means. Principal-inquirers often construct these statements by looking at the patterns that were coded and asking and answering questions such as,

What was my initial wondering, and how do these patterns inform it?

What is happening in each pattern and across patterns?

How are these happenings connected to . . .

> what I do as an administrator?
>
> the teachers in my building?
>
> the students in my building?
>
> the curriculum we teach?
>
> our school context?

The findings from this step can be illustrated by the administrator-inquirer in a number of ways, including but not limited to the following: themes, patterns, categories, metaphors, similes, claims/assertions, typologies, and vignettes. The following outlines possible illustrative techniques and provides examples.

STRATEGIES FOR ILLUSTRATING YOUR FINDINGS

Themes/Patterns/Categories/Labels/Naming: A composite of traits or features; a topic for discourse or discussion; a specifically defined division; a descriptive term, set apart from others.

Examples: Collaboration, Ownership, Growth, Care

Metaphors: A term that is transferred from the object it ordinarily represents to an object it represents only by implicit comparison or analogy.

Examples: "The Illustrator," "The Translator," "The Reporter," "The Guide," "Casting the Play"

Simile: Two unlike things are compared, often in a phrase introduced by "like" or "as."

Examples: "Principal as Coach," "Principal as Mediator," "Principal as Healer"

Claims/Assertions: A statement of fact or assertion of truth.

Examples: As a principal takes time to create time and space for teachers to engage in the peer coaching process, her time for other duties is stressed. Principals must utilize ingenuity to create time and space in their own calendars to assist teachers in the process of peer coaching.

Typologies: A systematic classification of types.

Example: Different uses for learning communities—building relationships, generating knowledge, attacking a problem

Vignettes: A brief, descriptive literary sketch

Example: "Reconceptualizing the Faculty Meeting"

The teachers entered the room and were surprised to find they would be sitting in assigned seats to create heterogeneous groups and break the norm of all teachers always sitting with their own grade level. There was nervous laughter, indicating a feeling of discomfort. As an opening to the meeting, the teachers were asked to each take a turn in their group, sharing their most memorable teaching moment from the previous month. Nervous laughter turned into a buzz of focused chatter, smiles, and genuine listening to each member of the group.

These strategies help illustrate, organize, and communicate inquiry findings to your audience. Once you have outlined your organizing strategy, you will need to identify the data that support each finding presented in your outline. Excerpts from these data sources can be used as evidence for your claims.

Data Analysis Step Four: Implications

Finally, upon completing each of the previous three steps, administrator-inquirers ask and answer one last set of *implication* questions, as follows:

What have I learned about myself as a principal?

What have I learned about teachers and students in my building?

What have I learned about the larger context of schools and schooling?

What are the implications of what I have learned for my work as a principal?

What changes might I make in my administrative practice?

What new wonderings do I have?

These questions call for principal-researchers to interpret what they have learned, to take action for change based on their study, and to generate new questions. Unlike the puzzle enthusiast who can marvel at the completed piece or the scrapbooker who has a final product to enjoy for years to come, the puzzle or scrapbook for the principal-inquirer is never quite finished, even after intensive analysis. Hubbard and Power (1999) note that "good research analyses raise more questions than they answer" (p. 117). While you may never be able to marvel at a perfected, polished, definitive set of findings based on the data analysis from one particular inquiry, you can marvel at the enormity of what you have learned through engaging in the process and the power it holds for transforming both your identity as a principal and your administrative practice. Through participating in inquiry as a principal, you are becoming the head learner at your school and engaging in a continuous cycle of self- and school improvement to help you and the teachers and students within your building truly become the best they can be!

HAVE COLLEAGUES HELP IN THE PROCESS

No one becomes the best he can be on his own. Principals who involve teaching colleagues or work with other principals in the process of data analysis have far richer inquiry experiences than do principals who try to go it alone. Asking others to help you think about your data has many benefits. First, having colleagues involved keeps you moving along. When you've scheduled a meeting or appointment with another person or people to talk about your data, you must prepare for that meeting, and it becomes much harder to put off the data analysis task. Second, having colleagues help you in data analysis contributes to your ability to self-reflect and make sense of your data. You already learned the importance of talking with others as you defined and refined your first questions and constructed a plan for your inquiry in Chapters 2 and 3. Similarly, as you continue on the practitioner research journey, discussions with other professionals as you analyze your data will help heighten your awareness of the knowledge you've generated about administration—knowledge that you have taken for granted—making what you know more visible to yourself and others. Making your tacit knowledge more visible can often lead to significant discoveries when you are individually or collaboratively analyzing and interpreting your data.

In addition, talking about your data with other professionals may help you call into question assumptions or "givens" about teaching and administrative practice, a process critical to your work. According to Cochran-Smith and Lytle (1993), "the givens of schooling compose a long list, including reading groups, rostering, inservicing, tracking, abilities, disabilities, mastery, retention, promotion, giftedness, disadvantage, special needs, departmentalization, 47-minute periods, coverage, standards, detention, teacher-proof materials, and homework" (p. 96). It is through talking with others about your data that you examine and critique the "givens" in education such as these. And, it is through talking with others about your data that you are able to generate possible alternatives to practice as well as consider different interpretations that help every administrator gain perspective as his/her inquiry unfolds.

Finally, involving others in the process of data analysis can lend credibility to your study. Of course, credibility is important for all practitioner inquiry, but it is heightened if your action research is a requirement for earning an advanced degree. Quality issues for all action research is discussed in the final chapter of this book, but if you are engaging in thesis or dissertation work, you may wish to familiarize yourself with two processes that research methodologists refer to as "peer debriefing" or "analyst triangulation," depending upon the system you follow. You can learn more about the data analysis process and enhancing the credibility of your study by reviewing some of the many wonderful resources on data analysis, peer debriefing, and analyst triangulation, some of which are listed below.

SOME ADDITIONAL REFERENCES ON DATA ANALYSIS

Creswell, J. W. (1998). *Qualitative inquiry and research design: Choosing among five traditions.* Thousand Oaks, CA: Sage.

Creswell, J. (2002). *Research design: Qualitative, quantitative, and mixed methods approaches* (2nd ed.). Thousand Oaks, CA: Sage.

Glanz, J. (1998). *Action research: An educational leader's guide to school improvement.* Norwood, MA: Christopher-Gordon.

Marshall, C., & Rossman, G. B. (2006). *Designing qualitative research* (4th ed.). Thousand Oaks, CA: Sage.

Patton, M. Q. (2002). *Qualitative researcher and evaluation methods* (3rd ed.). Thousand Oaks, CA: Sage.

Strauss, A., & Corbin, J. (1998). *Basics of qualitative research.* Thousand Oaks, CA: Sage.

Stringer, E. T. (1996). *Action research: A handbook for practitioners.* Thousand Oaks, CA: Sage.

Wolcott, H. F. (1994). *Transforming qualitative data: Description, analysis, and interpretation.* Thousand Oaks, CA: Sage.

If you are engaging in action research for your own professional development and school improvement efforts, invoking a protocol to get feedback from your colleagues can result in valuable and powerful results.

DATA ANALYSIS PROTOCOL: HELPING YOUR COLLEAGUES MAKE SENSE OF WHAT THEY LEARNED

Suggested Group Size: 4

Suggested Timeframe: 25–30 minutes per group member

1. *Presenter shares his/her inquiry* (4 minutes): Presenter briefly shares with his/her group members the focus/purpose of his/her inquiry, what his/her wondering(s) were, how data were collected, and the initial sense that the presenter has made of his/her data. Completing the following sentences prior to discussion may help the presenter organize his/her thoughts:

   • The issue/dilemma/problem/interest that led me to my inquiry was . . .
   • Therefore, the purpose of my inquiry was to . . .

(Continued)

(Continued)

- My wondering(s) was . . .
- I collected data by . . .
- So far, three discoveries I've made from reading through my data are . . .

2. *Group members ask clarifying questions* (3 minutes): Group members ask questions that have factual answers to clarify their understanding of the inquiry, such as, "How long did you collect data for?" "How many teachers did you work with?"

3. *Group members ask probing questions* (7–10 minutes): The group then asks probing questions of the presenter. These questions are worded so that they help the presenter clarify and expand his/her thinking about what he/she is learning from the data. During this 10-minute timeframe, the presenter may respond to the group's questions, **but there is no discussion by the group of the presenter's responses**. Every member of the group should pose at least one question to the presenter. Some examples of probing questions might include:

- What are some ways you might organize your data (see the earlier chart of organizing units)?
- What might be some powerful ways to present your data (see the previous Strategies for Illustrating Your Findings)?
- Do you have any data that doesn't seem to "fit"?
- Based on your data, what are you learning about yourself as a principal?
- What is your data telling you about the teachers and/or students in your building?
- What are the implications of your findings for your school?
- What have you learned about the larger context of schools and schooling?
- What are the implications of what you have learned for your administrative practice?
- What changes might you make in your own practice?
- What new wonderings do you have?

4. *Group members discuss the data analysis* (6 minutes): The group discusses the data analysis presented, asking questions such as,

What did we hear?
What didn't we hear that we think might be relevant?
What assumptions seem to be operating?
Does any data not seem to fit with the presenter's analysis?
What might be some additional ways to look at the presenter's data?

During this discussion, members of the group work to deepen the data analysis. The presenter doesn't speak during this discussion but instead listens and takes notes.

5. *Presenter reflection* (3 minutes): The presenter reflects on what she/he heard and what she/he is now thinking, sharing with the group anything that particularly resonated for him or her during any part of the group members' data analysis discussion.

6. *Reflection on the process* (2 minutes): Group shares thoughts about how the discussion worked for the group.

When I facilitated principal inquiry groups of administrators from different counties in north-central Florida, at one meeting toward the end of the school year the five members of the group arrived having each already completed steps one and two of the data analysis process (gathering their entire data set in one place and reading through it to get a sense of their data and, after subsequent readings, making a list of what they were noticing about their data). In addition, to help organize his/her thoughts, each principal completed the Sentence Completion Activity that appears in Figure 4.1 to prepare for the first step of the protocol.

One by one, each principal took a brief turn sharing a little background about his/her inquiry and the sense he/she was making of the collected data to date. The protocol guided the group's provision of feedback to the presenting administrator. Using the protocol guaranteed that every principal received valuable, focused feedback, helped us use time efficiently, and assured that no one person dominated the group. I hope you will find this protocol useful in whatever context you use to enlist the help of colleagues in analyzing your data.

Up to this point in this chapter, the data analysis process has been discussed in general terms. While a generic description of the data analysis process provides an overview and orientation to this stage of your inquiry, a glimpse into how the data analysis process might actually translate into practice can be tremendously helpful. For this reason, I end this chapter by illustrating the way the four-step process of data analysis might play out in practice, using the work of principal Deirdre Bauer. While reading Deirdre's story, you will become a "fly on the wall," observing the

Figure 4.1   Sentence Completion Activity

The issue/tension/dilemma/problem/interest that led me to my inquiry was:

Therefore, the purpose of my inquiry was to:

My wondering(s) was/were:

I collected data by:

So far, three discoveries I've made from reading through my data are:

1.

2.

3.

enactment of many of the concepts discussed in this chapter. As you reflect on Deirdre's work, remember the three words often used to describe the data analysis process—"messy," "murky," and "creative." With this in mind, realize that your particular data analysis experience might not proceed exactly as Deirdre's did. Every administrator is unique, every inquiry is unique, and, hence, every piecing together of the inquiry data to create a picture of the learning that has occurred is unique. Yet, as you finish this chapter, you now have knowledge of a common set of general procedures for analyzing data and a sense of how those general procedures may play out in a particular principal-inquirer's work. Finally, once again, a series of suggested exercises appears at the close of this chapter to help you enact your own data analysis component of the inquiry process.

AN ILLUSTRATION
OF THE DATA ANALYSIS PROCESS

Recall from Chapter 2 that Deirdre Bauer, in her second year as building principal at Radio Park Elementary School in State College, Pennsylvania, was remembering the experiences she had had in peer coaching as a teacher and administrator in her previous positions. She had found peer coaching to be a very satisfying professional growth activity and had witnessed its potential power as a trainer for teachers and an attractive alternative to the traditional teacher evaluation process. In her new position at Radio Park, she quickly noticed two exemplary first-grade veteran teachers—Marcia Heitzmann and Judi Kur. Their outstanding practices led Deirdre to wonder about the nature of professional development for accomplished veteran teachers and what role the principal could play in facilitating continued professional development for such consummate professionals. Deirdre decided to ask Marcia and Judi if they might be interested in trying peer coaching as a professional development activity. The two having already established a strong professional and trusting relationship, Marcia and Judi agreed, and Deirdre formulated her first inquiry wonderings: *How does the process of peer coaching help veteran teachers continue to learn and grow?* and *What role can the principal play in facilitating this process?* (Bauer, Kur, & Heitzmann, 2001).

To gain insights into her wonderings, Deirdre collected data in four ways over a two-month period. First, Deirdre collected literature on models of supervision and the peer coaching process. Deirdre's second form of data collection was field note taking. When she observed Judi and Marcia in the preconference and postconference segments of the peer coaching cycle, she did her best to script every word they said as well as note where they met to conference, how long these conferences took, and any nonverbal body language she observed between the two teachers as they engaged in these two facets of the peer coaching process. Deirdre's third mode of data collection was to keep a personal journal where she jotted down ideas for how she could help facilitate the process and logged her thinking about how her actions were working. The final mode of data collection was conducting an interview with Judi and Marcia after they had engaged in one peer coaching cycle.

After two months of collecting data in these forms, Deirdre approached the almost-filled box in which she was keeping all the data plus other articles and books she had found on peer coaching and instructional supervision. She set aside a few hours on a Saturday morning to begin creating a picture of what she had learned. To begin, she took each piece of data out of the box, organized it chronologically beginning with the first piece collected and ending with the latest, and read through every piece. By reading through her entire data set, Deirdre was reminded of incidents that had occurred throughout the duration of her inquiry (through her own field notes and interviews), as well as thoughts that had occurred to her about the peer coaching process as her inquiry unfolded (through her journal entries). In addition, reviewing readings that had appeared in publications such as the *Journal of Curriculum and Supervision, Journal of Staff Development, The Kappan,* and *Educational Leadership* contributed to Deirdre's developing understanding of her work in staff development as a principal. The process of reading the data set in its entirety "freshened up" all Deirdre had been thinking about and doing for the last two months.

With all she had collected fresh in her mind, Deirdre read through the entire data set a second time. On this second time through, as she read she asked herself, "What am I noticing about my data?" She constructed a list as she read titled "Data Notes" (see Figure 4.2).

After looking at this list, Deirdre decided that her next step was to read the data again, but this time to focus solely on her initial wonderings: *How does the process of peer coaching help veteran teachers continue to learn and grow?* and *What role can the principal play in facilitating this process?* She wrote these questions on an index card and laid it in front of her to remind her of what she was looking for in this third read of her entire data set. She decided to mark her data by highlighting any pieces that pertained to interactions between Judi and Marcia in pink and any pieces that pertained to her interactions with them in yellow.

Once this process was completed, Deirdre took a break for lunch and then returned to her data for a fourth reading. During this fourth sweep, however, Deirdre read only what had been highlighted in pink. While

Figure 4.2   Data Notes

● _Data Notes_ ●

• J&M joke frequently w/ each other —
 use humor as the talk abat their teaching

• Many higher level questions

• Data collected as part of coaching cycle.
 important to J&M

• Some stress in scheduling a time to
 have pre- + post- conferences

– J&M said my role in covering their
 classes was helpful and called
 me a "peer-coaching coach"

• Questions all over the place
 many —
 are they all the same?

Later in
my journal —
I like
doing but
causes me
stress to
find time.

Source: Deirdre Bauer, Principal, Radio Park Elementary School, State College, Pennsylvania.

reading only the pink data excerpts, she generated a list of five patterns that seemed to describe and capture the essence of what was occurring over and over again in the interactions between Marcia and Judi. She named each of these patterns as follows: (1) Questioning, (2) Relationship Building, (3) Humor, (4) Use of Data, and (5) Deviations From Peer Coaching Cycle. Again Deirdre read through her data, this time only reading what had been highlighted in yellow. While reading only the yellow excerpts, she generated a list of three patterns that seemed to describe and capture the essence of what was occurring over and over again in her own interactions with these two teachers. She named these patterns as follows: (1) Providing Support, (2) Providing Time, and (3) Issues Peer Coaching Created for Me.

Next, Deirdre created a coding mechanism for each of her named patterns, assigning a symbol to correspond to each pattern. For example, for the patterns she found in her pink-coded data, a question mark corresponded to pattern 1, two stick figures represented pattern 2, a "bubble" containing the word "HA" corresponded to pattern 3, a "D" was assigned to pattern 4, and a circular arrow represented pattern 5. She used the letters "P-S," "P-T," and "P-I" to correspond to the patterns she found in her yellow-coded data. Just as she had done previously when she wrote her wondering on an index card to remind her what she was looking for as she read, Deirdre noted each pattern and symbol on an index card and kept this card in front of her as she read through the entire data set a sixth time. This time through, she underlined and used her symbols to code the data. Deirdre's index card with the pattern symbols, as well as a sample of coded data from two different data-collection methods, appears in Figures 4.3 through 4.5.

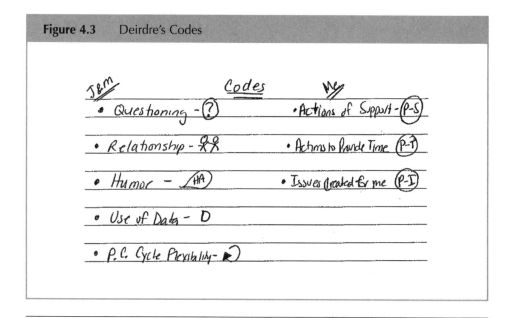

Figure 4.3   Deirdre's Codes

Source: Deirdre Bauer, Principal, Radio Park Elementary School, State College, Pennsylvania.

Figure 4.4   Deirdre's Field Notes

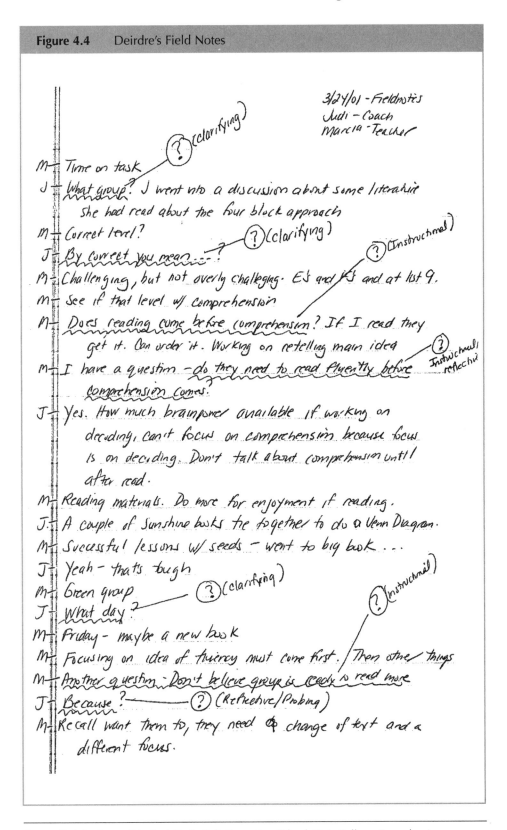

Figure 4.5   Deirdre's Journal Entry

Journal Entry 3/5

Today I observed peer coaching working at its best. Marcia served in the role of coach for Judi. Judi had shared with Marcia in the pre-conference that she felt like the discussions she was having about literature with her high-ability learners were like ping-pong matches. Judi would pose a question, a student in the group would respond. Judi would pose a second question, a different student would respond. Another questions from Judi, another student response and so on . . . Judi wanted to see if she could get her students to engage in true discussion with one another, rather than just respond to her questions, thinking this would be a much more valuable way for these high-ability learners to interact with literature. Marcia collected data for Judi by diagramming each learner in *D* this reading group, and drawing arrows between them every time there was an interaction about the book they were discussing. It was very cool to witness this form of data collection. As I watched Marcia collect data in this way, I was thinking I might be able to use this same strategy with other *(P-S)* teachers in the building when I am observing them so that I might help make explicit the nature of the interactions that are occurring in their classrooms -- who is participating more, who is participating less, etc. While this might be a good thought, I am continually struck when I observe Marcia and Judi in action by the unique, close relationship they share. I'm sure this is a critical ingredient in the coaching process. Even though I'm interested in helping teachers grow and develop, many of them view me as their evaluator, and don't trust me. I need to think about ways I can negotiate the role I play in teacher evaluation with the role I need to play in mentoring teacher *(P-I)* growth and development. Will I be able to rectify the tensions that exist between these two roles? And how? Maybe one answer to this lies in enacting some of what I'm learning from watching Judi and Marcia when they are in that coaching role. As I observe their pre- and post-conferencing behaviors (they are both great at making the other person feel at ease) and (posing questions to one another that are not evaluative, but help them reflect on their practice. I need to become more *(P-I)* cognizant of the separation of evaluation from my role in promoting teacher professional development. Easier said than done.

Source: Deirdre Bauer, Principal, Radio Park Elementary School, State College, Pennsylvania.

A few days later, Deirdre sorted her data by pattern, reading only the excerpts that pertained to each coded pattern. As she read through each coded excerpt, she asked herself, "What is happening in each pattern?" "How are the patterns connected to each other?" "What do these patterns mean in relation to my initial wonderings?" This time through, Deirdre noted the ways some patterns were connected to each other. For example, Deirdre saw connections between the two categories Relationship Building and Humor. She regrouped her data accordingly. In addition, Deirdre noted that one of her categories, Questioning, could be further sorted into questions the coach asked to clarify something and questions the coach posed that were reflective or probing. There were also questions that were instructional in nature. Deirdre regrouped her Questioning data to reflect this discovery.

That week, Deirdre talked about what she was seeing with a group of her peers at their district's administrator team meeting. As she talked about the patterns, Deirdre noted that the relationship between these two teachers was likely the most critical component contributing to the success of peer coaching. She also noted that there were a number of times that Judi and Marcia had deviated from the peer coaching cycle as it was discussed theoretically in the literature. Deirdre shared with her principal colleagues that this deviation concerned her, for she wasn't sure if the process of peer coaching was diluted when the cycle wasn't followed in a lockstep manner. Through discussion, her principal colleagues helped Deirdre focus on the data excerpt categorized as Deviations From Peer Coaching Cycle and determine what happened as a result of these deviations. Paying close attention to these excerpts revealed that, in the case of Judi and Marcia, deviations from the cycle were not inherently bad and often had positive outcomes that led the teachers to new insights about their teaching of reading. For example, there were a number of instances wherein Judi and Marcia deviated from the peer coaching cycle to give each other advice, an action the peer coaching literature suggests be done only sparingly. In one data excerpt from Deirdre's scripted field notes, Judi was recorded as saying: "Going beyond phonics skill work for poor readers is important because too much skill work does not work. If they don't get into deeper stuff they will stay poor readers." Marcia was grateful for this insight and shared that she felt it gave her "permission" to challenge her struggling readers, something she hadn't realized was as important for their growth and development as for her proficient readers.

As the group continued to discuss Deirdre's data, they drew a connection between the relationship Judi and Marcia had and the fact that deviating from the peer coaching cycle worked for them, although it wouldn't necessarily work for others. Because they had a strong, trusting relationship, Judi and Marcia were able to give frequent advice to one another without offending the other person or putting that person on the defensive. One principal in the group noticed in the data that Judi and Marcia had actually discussed the cycle at one point and the ways they thought it might be modified to work better for them. Agreeing on modifications in the cycle before beginning it appeared to be valuable.

As they discussed the data, all the principals were reminded of the importance of relationship building in their work as administrators, and they brainstormed some new wonderings that Deirdre and the group might explore together in the future. These new wonderings were related to the growing professional learning community work being done in the district and the tensions all the principals felt in negotiating their roles as evaluators with their roles in teacher professional development:

1. *What role does professional learning community work play in creating strong professional relationships between teachers (like that developed between Judi and Marcia) and between teachers and administrators that would enable all members of our school district to continually improve practice?*

2. *In what ways do we, as principals, develop nonthreatening relationships with all our teachers when we serve both in the role of evaluator and in the role of staff developer?*

Deirdre thanked the group for their insights and left the meeting with ideas for six assertions to present as findings, which she planned to discuss with Judi and Marcia and, if they felt comfortable, to present briefly at their next faculty meeting as a way to invite other teachers in the building to try peer coaching:

Assertion 1: Peer coaching can be a powerful alternative form of professional development for teachers at Radio Park Elementary School.

Assertion 2: To be successful, the relationship one develops with the peer coaching partner is of critical importance.

Assertion 3: To be successful, the peer coaching cycle needs to be flexible, but enacting the cycle differently than intended must be agreed upon between the two partners before beginning.

Assertion 4: When it comes to peer coaching, questions are where it's at! A coach must be a skilled questioner to help the coached teacher both clarify and reflect on practice.

Assertion 5: The principal can support the peer coaching process by covering classes, offering support, asking what is needed, giving time, and helping to focus the process.

Assertion 6: Ironically, as principals take the time to create time and space for teachers to engage in the peer coaching process, tensions arise for the principal in time management, and they must use ingenuity to create time and space in their own calendars.

The completed picture of Deirdre's learning and what that learning meant for her administrative practice was taking shape through data analysis. Her learning would be a springboard for spreading the power of peer coaching slowly within her school, and in so doing, she hoped that more teachers might be able to build the same strong relationship shared by Marcia and Judi. She also hoped that, by changing her administrative practice to provide support for the peer coaching process—as in offering to cover classes and other actions—she, herself, would also build stronger relationships with other faculty in the building. To successfully build these relationships, Deirdre knew she would have to negotiate tensions between serving as an evaluator and as a mentor and instructional leader to the teachers in her building, and a new wondering was born: *In what ways can I, as a principal, develop a nonthreatening relationship with the teachers at Radio Park to support and assist them in their continual professional growth and learning?* A new cycle of inquiry began.

CHAPTER 4 EXERCISES

1. The first step of analysis is to *describe* your inquiry. Read through your data carefully. Take notes as you read. Afterward, respond to the following questions:

- Why did you inquire?

- What did you see as you inquired?

- What was happening?

- What are your initial insights into the data?

2. The second step of analysis is to begin *making sense* of your data. The organizing units presented earlier can serve as prompts for helping you begin your analysis.

- Use the organizing units listed on page 114 to help you identify or construct possible categories for your data. Be sure to consider organizing units that emerge from within your inquiry.
- Now take a stab at organizing your data and identifying the units of analysis that emerge in your inquiry data. For example, maybe the important story in your data involves "changes," so you identify categories such as "changes for kids," "changes in content," and "changes in instruction."

3. Once you have a general idea of the important units of data and an idea of the emerging story, you need to decide how you will present the data. Read through the Strategies for Illustrating Your Findings on pages 116–117 to help you present your *interpretive* findings. Remember, this list is by no means an exhaustive one.

- Choose a strategy or strategies for illustrating and organizing your own findings for your audience. Once again, use your creativity to organize your thoughts.
- Outline the elements of your organizing strategy and identify the data you will use to support each component of your outline.

4. You probably thought the most difficult step of the analysis process was complete. However, the final *implications* step remains. Your remaining responsibility is to move from interpretation of the findings that you presented in step 3 to articulating the implications or *"so what?"* of your study. Some helpful questions follow that may prompt your thinking in this area:

- What have I learned about myself as a principal?

- What have I learned about teachers?

- What have I learned about the students in my building?

- What are the implications of my findings for the curriculum delivered at my school?

- What have I learned about the larger context of schools and schooling?

- What are the implications of what I have learned for my administrative practice?

- What changes might I make in my own practice?

- What new wonderings do I have?

5. Share your data analysis process with others using the Data Analysis Protocol presented in this chapter. Take notes as your colleagues discuss your data. Use the feedback you received through this process to improve your data analysis.

5 The Travelogue

*Sharing Your
Work With Others*

In Chapter 2, you began your inquiry journey by finding and defining your first wondering. Then you navigated different components of the inquiry process: developed a plan for your inquiry, collected data, and analyzed your data. You are nearing the end of your journey, but there are still a few last steps that must be taken to bring it full circle. These last steps involve making your inquiry public through the sharing of your work with others.

WHY IS IT IMPORTANT TO SHARE MY WORK WITH OTHERS?

Imagine that you notice a large pond that is stagnant and that you are enticed to create some type of movement or change in the water. As you near the edge, you notice that the pond is surrounded by numerous stones. You reach down, pick up a stone, and toss it as far out into the center of the pond as your strength allows. While lying beside the pond, the stone had no impact on the water, but once tossed in, it disturbs not only the stillness of the water where it lands but also emanates ripples from its landing place that eventually reach the perimeter of the pond.

An unshared practitioner inquiry is like the stone lying beside the pond. Unless that inquiry is tossed into the professional conversation that contributes to the knowledge base for teaching and administration, it has little chance of creating change. However, once tossed in, it disturbs the status quo of educational practices, creating a ripple effect that begins with the principal himself and his immediate vicinity (the teachers and students in the building) and emanates out to a district and a state, eventually reaching and contributing to a transformation at the perimeter of practice—in the education profession itself.

Hence, it is critical that you "get into the pond" and share your inquiry not only for yourself, your teachers, your students, and other administrators but for the profession as a whole as well! The added advantage for you is that the process of preparing your findings to share with others helps you clarify your own thinking about your work. Also, in the actual sharing of your work, you give other professionals access to your thinking so that they can question, discuss, debate, and relate. This process helps you and your colleagues push and extend your thinking about practice.

Clarifying, pushing, and extending thinking helps lead to informed, positive change in traditional school practices—the critical *action* part of action research and the reason you began this whole inquiry journey in the first place! Some inquiries inspire small, local change. Some inspire large, sweeping change. All change, large or small, is significant in that it is coming from those best positioned to make a difference in education and those that for years have been kept from making that difference— educators themselves.

Kincheloe (1991) writes about the ways educators have been kept from making a difference by drawing a comparison between teachers and peasants within a third world culture with hierarchical power structures, scarce resources, and traditional values:

> Like their third world counterparts, teachers are preoccupied with daily survival—time for reflection and analysis seems remote and even quite fatuous given the crisis management atmosphere and the immediate attention survival necessitates. In such a climate those who would suggest that more time and resources be delegated to reflective and growth-inducing pursuits are viewed as impractical visionaries devoid of common sense. Thus, the status quo is perpetuated, the endless cycle of underdevelopment rolls on with its peasant culture of low morale and teachers as "reactors" to daily emergencies. (p. 12)

The word *principal* can easily be substituted each time the word *teacher* appears in the quote above. As discussed in Chapter 1, principals, perhaps even to a greater extent than teachers, are preoccupied with daily survival and putting out fire after fire and have little time for reflection. By getting into the pond and sharing your inquiry, you contribute to breaking the cycle described above, and you contribute to educational reform: "The plethora of small changes made by critical [principal] researchers around the world in individual [schools] may bring about far more authentic educational reform than the grandiose policies formulated in state or national capitals" (Kincheloe, 1991, p. 14).

When you share your inquiry, you affect how people outside of education view educators and try to change education from the outside-in. And, by sharing your inquiry, you contribute to reforming the education profession . . . from the inside out!

WITH WHOM DO I SHARE MY WORK?

Recall that in the very opening to this book we discussed the complexity of the principalship due to the staggering demands from the many constituencies served simultaneously—teachers, students, parents, the superintendent and district office, the board of education, and the community at large. Because the principal serves so many different constituencies, he or she has many audiences with whom to share his/her research. In fact, depending on your wondering, any of the constituents you serve can become the audience for your inquiry. One example for each of the constituencies named above follows.

As Deirdre Bauer studied the ways peer coaching played out for two veteran teachers in her school, she documented the potential power of this process for teachers' professional development in her building as well as ascertained important factors for a successful peer coaching experience. Sharing her work with all of the *teachers* in her building gently encouraged more faculty to give the process a try.

When Donnan Stoicovy designed and implemented a whole-school curriculum project to help students in her building meet her state's academic standards in science (particularly the development of observational skills), Donnan used the process of inquiry to assess the learning and growth of the students and the success of the whole-school endeavor from the perspectives of the teachers and students in her building. Similar to how Donnan had introduced the unit at an all-school assembly, at the end of the year, Donnan once again shared with all the *students* at an assembly the ways she had collected data and observed them as they were studying the four schoolyard sites. Donnan concluded that all Park Forest Elementary School students should be congratulated as they had become keen observers of nature and learned a great deal! Sharing her inquiry with all the students in her building enabled Donnan to role-model the process of learning for all 400 plus students.

When Mike Delucas created a School-Within-a-School (SWAS) for students in his building who had fallen behind in the credits they needed for graduation, he turned to the process of inquiry to document how the program was working. Mike shared many of the findings from his research with *parents* of potential students for the SWAS credit retrieval program. By sharing his inquiry with parents, Mike helped them make an informed choice about enrolling their children in SWAS and provided hope that these at-risk learners could obtain a high school diploma.

Jim Brandenburg explored how he could facilitate the professional growth and learning of the teachers in his building using action research. His results revealed that it was important for him, as principal, to blend the action research process into already existing structures for professional development required by the district and the state. By presenting this inquiry to his *superintendent*, Jim was able to obtain permission to recast the traditional professional development plan form each teacher was required to complete each year to better align it with his teachers' engagement in researching their own practice. With his superintendent's support, Jim was thus able to make a routine district practice more meaningful for the teachers in his building.

When principal Lynette Langford, her lead team, and her entire school faculty studied how out-of-school and in-school suspensions were affecting student performance, their data convinced them that they must decrease student tardiness and encourage student attendance in class to increase the chances of their students succeeding as learners. They shared the results of the inquiry with the school board and members of the community, who were then driven to action. As one alternative discipline consequence, Lynette's district started a Neighborhood Accountability Board (NAB) where a group of eight community leaders sat and heard cases from students and their parents. Sanctions from the board include, but are not limited to, community service, anger management or other counseling, and/or letters of apology. Sharing their inquiry with the *school board* and *community* actually helped Lynette's school enlist the assistance of the community in creating an alternative to in-school suspension that kept students in class, made them accountable to the community, and got them services to get to the roots of their behavior (i.e., anger management; counseling).

Although each of these example inquiries matched one particular audience, any one inquiry can have more than one audience, and almost any inquiry will be of interest to other principals. For this reason, in addition to teachers, students, parents, the superintendent, the school board, and the community, it is important to share your inquiry with others who share your same role. These sharing sessions can happen informally or more formally at district administrative team meetings or state and national conferences. For example, an annual Teaching, Inquiry, and Innovation Showcase is held each year in Florida. Principal-inquirers appear on the program on a regular basis, and principals from across our state come to learn from one another. To share your work even more broadly with other principals, it is possible to publish your research in journals such as *Educational Administration Quarterly* (in the "From the Field" section), *Educational Leadership, Theory Into Practice,* and *Principal.* A number of state journals also publish practitioner research. By sharing your inquiry with other principals, you contribute to the professional learning and growth of your administrative colleagues. They will benefit from hearing about your research and can transfer what they've learned based on your inquiry experiences to their own administrative contexts.

Depending on the focus and the size of your inquiry, a final audience for your work may be policymakers. Through the work of the Teacher's Network Leadership Institute, many teachers across the nation are realizing the potential impact their action research can have on policy (Meyers & Rust, 2003). Principals' engagement in action research can thus raise the volume of administrator's voices in educational policy setting.

One cautionary note must be raised, however. Sometimes, the findings of your inquiry can create controversy or discomfort among the different constituencies you serve, and you will have to think carefully about navigating that controversy/discomfort when deciding whom you will share your work with, what exactly you will share, and how you will share it. For example, one principal shared with me the story of his tireless work with a team of teachers in his building to explore the question *What actions can we take as a faculty to align our current curriculum with the new state standards?* This principal and his team of teachers had collected data for an entire year, reading extensive literature, systematically reviewing their current text series and practices, reviewing numerous other textbook series, and listening to presentations by numerous textbook companies. Different teachers on the committee had piloted different texts and documented the results in their classrooms so they could compare and contrast different programs to find the one best suited to meet the learning needs of the students, align with the new standards, and enable students to perform well on the state exams. This principal and his team came to some dramatic conclusions that revealed that their current reading series did not align with the new standards, most notably being deficient in the development of student listening skills and writing. Based on their inquiry, the team recommended, with compelling evidence to back up each recommendation, three necessary actions to bring their school into alignment with the new standards and enable strong student performance on the test: (1) the adoption of a new textbook series, (2) the provision of afterschool tutorials for struggling readers, and (3) time for teachers to learn about the new standards and new practices to help students meet the standards. When this principal shared the results of the inquiry with his superintendent, the superintendent was impressed with the depth of research and knowledge the team had generated about the new standards and asked the principal to present their work to the school board, but with one caveat—focus only on what your inquiry revealed about the new state standards and provide the board with knowledge of these standards. The principal was not to share the recommendation of the team that a new textbook series was needed, as the superintendent did not wish the board to think that their current reading series, purchased only two years prior to this inquiry, would ill prepare students for the new standards.

After the principal presented to the board, he took questions. The first question from a board member was, "How do you think our new reading series will prepare students for the state test?" The superintendent, who was standing in the back of the room, nodded his head vigorously in encouragement that the principal remember their conversation and not share his finding that the series fell short in a number of areas. The principal faced a dilemma—honestly answer the school board member's question and risk upsetting the superintendent, who ultimately was in control of the resources that would enable his school to take action based on their inquiry, or dodge the question and continue to make the case with his superintendent for what was needed to align the curriculum with the new standards. This principal chose to dodge the question, and although his decision caused him a great deal of discomfort, eventually the superintendent did allocate funds to purchase the recommended series, to begin the afterschool reading program, and to send a number of teachers to conferences to learn about the standards and best practices for aligning with them. It is important as a principal-inquirer to be cognizant of the tensions that inquiry results can bring to your audiences and to navigate them thoughtfully and carefully, always keeping the best interests of the teachers and students at your school in mind.

HOW DO I SHARE MY WORK?

How you share your work is dependent on the audience(s) for which your inquiry is intended. Principals sometimes prepare different ways and forms of sharing the same inquiry, depending upon which audience he/she will share it with. However one prepares his/her inquiry, there are two basic forms of sharing—oral and written.

Oral Presentations

Oral presentations are the most common form of inquiry sharing. These presentations can be formal or informal. Some principal-inquirers organize informal gatherings outside the school structure (e.g., an after-school meeting at a coffee shop) to discuss their work. Or, if you are enrolled in a graduate class in which action research is a focus, you might have the semester culminate with a special meeting (perhaps a potluck dinner) where all share the results of their inquiry endeavors.

Within the school, formal sharing by principal-inquirers often happens within structures you already have in place as a principal. For example, like Deirdre, you might utilize ten minutes of your faculty meeting to share the results of your inquiry with the teachers in your building. Like Donnan, you might chat at an all-school assembly with your students in developmentally appropriate ways. You might present your research at a parent meeting, as Mike did, or, like Jim, you might share your work during a superintendent-principal appointment. Finally, like Lynette, you might share your work during a school board meeting.

In addition to these structures, districtwide structures can allow sharing your work with the audience who will *always* be interested in your inquiry, no matter what the question and focus—your principal colleagues. This sharing is often accomplished through dedicating special portions of district administrative meetings to inquiry or by totally reconceptualizing administrative team meetings to allow space for the ongoing sharing of inquiry. When action research is utilized as a professional development vehicle for administrators and teachers in a district, an entire inservice day can be devoted to inquiry, or a special evening inquiry celebration is planned wherein colleagues gather to share their work. For example, in the Pinellas County School District in Florida, teachers and administrators engage in practitioner inquiry as a regular form of professional learning districtwide. The district invites all inquirers (teachers and administrators) to share their learning with others at an evening celebration held in the large meeting room of their district's office building each year in May. Round tables are set up with numbered cards and balloons to create a celebratory feel. Participants arrive for a reception from 4:00–4:30, followed by a series of three thirty-minute roundtable sessions with two inquiry presentations of fifteen minutes each occurring at every table. All participants are provided with a program so they can choose which roundtable sessions to attend. One page of the May 2008 program appears in Figure 5.1

If district structures for the sharing of inquiry like those described above are not currently in place, you might begin building these structures simply by talking for a few minutes about your work at an administrative

---

Figure 5.1   Pinellas County Schools, Research Inquiry Celebration Program

Table 9   *RTI From a Principal Perspective*

Robert Ovalle, Principal, Belleair Elementary, ovaller@pcsb.org

As principal of an RTI pilot school, my inquiry looks at the development of processes within a school. How can a principal best support this initiative?

Inquiring Into a Culture of Inquiry: How Will Implementing Inquiry Into PLCs During Seminar Affect School Culture and Professional Development?

Kathy Rankin, Third-Grade Teacher, Rawlings, rankink@pcsb.org

How we can implement inquiry into the Rawlings seminar time, and what effect will this have on our school culture and professional development?

Table 10   *As the Principal of the School, What Action Can I Take That Will Improve the Effectiveness of the Teachers Conferencing With the Students in the Reading Workshop?*

Thea Saccasyn, Principal, Ponce de Leon Elementary, saccasynt@pcsb.org

How can a principal best help teachers increase the frequency of their student conferencing during Reader's Workshop?

What Does It Take to Retain Teachers?

Roslyn Walker, Speech Pathologist, Gulfport Elementary, walkerrose@pcsb.org

In the past eight years, there has been a revolving door of new teachers at my school. What is the relationship between school climate and teacher retention?

Source: Sylvia Boynton and Doug Tuthill, University of Florida Lastinger Center for Learning and Pinellas County Schools Partnership.

team meeting. Much of my own research has focused on building an inquiry culture (see, e.g., Dana, 1994, 1995, 2001; Dana & Silva, 2001, 2002; Silva & Dana, 1999; Dana & Yendol-Hoppey, 2008; 2009). As a result of this research, my colleagues and I have learned that building a culture of inquiry takes time and is best started slowly, as some of your current administrator colleagues may be reluctant to embrace inquiry and the changes it necessitates. Although building an inquiry culture is a slow process, it has to start somewhere, and it can start with you. Be patient, and persevere!

Oftentimes, principals create PowerPoint presentations to accompany the oral telling of their inquiry story. PowerPoint presentations can be very effectively used as an aid to help you communicate the essence of your inquiry experience. A number of wonderful Web sites exist that can help you think about the essentials of an effective PowerPoint presentation. The most important thing to remember about creating an effective presentation is to keep it simple! Remember, the PowerPoint is not the presenter—you are! The slides serve as a tool to enhance or emphasize points you wish to make about your inquiry, not to tell your entire inquiry story. Some of the most important aspects of keeping your PowerPoint simple appear here.

EFFECTIVE POWERPOINT PRESENTATIONS—KEEP IT SIMPLE!

Limit

- Information to the essentials
- Number of slides
- Special effects
- Fancy fonts

Use

- Key phrases
- Large font sizes (between eighteen and forty-eight points is the general range)
- Colors that contrast
- Clip art and graphics to balance the slide—not overwhelm it

---

The two most common mistakes I have witnessed when principals prepare PowerPoint slides to accompany their presentations are (1) having too much text on each individual slide in a font too small to read and (2) using too many "bells and whistles" in slide transitions or in building a slide that end up detracting from the presentation. In a witty Weblog titled "How to Change the World: The 10/20/30 Rule of PowerPoint," Guy Kawaski asserts that no PowerPoint presentation should be more than ten slides, last more than twenty minutes, or contain any font size smaller than thirty point:

> The majority of the presentations that I see have text in a ten point font. As much text as possible is jammed into the slide, and then the presenter reads it. However, as soon as the audience figures out that you're reading the text, it reads ahead of you because it can read faster than you can speak. The result is that you and the audience are out of synch.
>
> The reason people use a small font is twofold: first, that they don't know their material well enough; second, they think that more text is more convincing. Total bozosity. Force yourself to use no font smaller than thirty points. I guarantee it will make your presentations better because it requires you to find the most salient points and to know how to explain them well. If "thirty points," is too dogmatic, then I offer you an algorithm: find out the age of the oldest person in your audience and divide it by two. That's your optimal font size. (Kawaski, http://blog.guykawasaki.com/2005/12/the_102030_rule.html)

In *Giving Effective PowerPoint Presentations*, Scott Stratten echoes Kawaski's advice, with a particular focus on not falling into the "bells and whistles" trap:

> A common mistake is the overuse of PowerPoint animations and transitions during a slideshow. I'm sure you've seen what I'm talking about; the presenter that animates each sentence so it flies in, drops down, and explodes on the screen with an accompanying sound effect. What happens after that? Do you lose track of what the presenter is saying? Forget within three seconds what the point was because you were so focused on the effects that you missed the content?
>
> While the thought process behind these special effects is, "This highlights my point and emphasizes the importance," the outcome is often the opposite. People tend to get distracted by the effects. Especially with sounds, where the presenter can hear the whooshing noise, along with the few in the front of the room. The people in the middle think they heard something, but couldn't make it out and the people at the back are wondering why there is a fly somewhere in the meeting room. Laptops were not meant to project sound to fill a room, so don't use them to do that.

Want to emphasize a main point? Put it on the screen by itself and let people read it. A good rule for effective PowerPoint presentations is to put up only your main points and use the screen as a reference. If you run through your PowerPoint presentation (which you must do many times) and you see a slide with more than five points, start a new slide. Your slideshow is not the presentation, it is an aid.

If only the main points are on the screen, the audience will realize their importance. Don't overwhelm your audience with technofluff. The power of technology is neither the point of your PowerPoint presentation, nor the strength of it. The technology should be used only sparingly or to reinforce the information you have to share. (Stratten, http://sbinfocanada.about.com/cs/management/qt/powerptpres.htm)

If you plan to develop PowerPoint slides to aid in your oral presentation of your inquiry, keep in mind the clever advice from Guy Kawaski and Scott Stratten. To illustrate, a sample PowerPoint slide presentation of Lynette Langford's inquiry appears in Figure 5.2.

Write-Ups

You have just completed the process of data analysis during which time you sorted, resorted, and made sense of all you had collected throughout the duration of your inquiry project. You thought about your inquiry as a whole. You thought about what was happening in the data. You thought about what you learned. You thought about the implications of what you learned for your own administrative practice. In short, you did a lot of thinking!

A wonderful way to continue thinking about your inquiry is to *write*. Noted educational ethnographer Harry Wolcott (1990) goes as far as to state that writing and thinking are synonymous: "The conventional wisdom is that writing reflects thinking. I am drawn to a different position: Writing *is* thinking" (p. 21).

For this reason, I recommend writing as an extension of data analysis and as a wonderful way to expand your learning. Of course, if you are engaging in administrator action research as a meaningful way to fulfill your final degree requirements for an advanced degree, you are required to write up your work in the form of a master's thesis or dissertation. There are a number of good resources that can guide the writing of your thesis or dissertation such as Glatthorn and Joyner's *Writing the Winning Thesis or Dissertation: A Step by Step Guide*, 2nd edition (2005), Robert's *The*

Figure 5.2   Sample PowerPoint Presentation

DO STUDENTS NEED TO BE IN THE CLASSROOM TO LEARN?

Exploring Alternatives to Suspension as Disciplinary Consequences for
Middle and High School Students

Lynette Langford

The Journey

- Our school was an "A" school but made AYP only provisionally because we didn't have a large enough percentage increase in ESE students making gains.
- My basic wondering: Did the number of days ESE students were suspended for behavior cause this?

Analyzing the data:
34 ESE students did not make gains
10 had OSS/ISS days

Student	OSS 2006	ISS 2006	OSS 2007	ISS 2007	FCAT 2006	Thinklink 2007	2006 Tardies	2007 Tardies
1	13	1	4	1	1	2	98	15
2	10	6	0	1	1	2	84	15
3	9	7	5	0	1	2	51	15
4	9	2	1	7	1	1	18	4
5	8	5	5	3	1	1	30	12
6	7	9	0	1	1	2	23	6
7	5	4	2	2	1	1	20	12
8	5	2	1	4	1	1	20	8
9	3	5	0	4	1	2	8	3
10	3	2	0	0	1	1	8	7

- This data wasn't entirely conclusive, but we still believed that we needed to find other discipline alternatives.
- The excessive number of tardies seemed to be of even greater concern.
- Administrative team met and discussed that we needed to be creative and find other forms of consequences (instead of suspension) for misbehaviors.
- Formed a committee of teachers to discuss options.
- I started researching for what other schools were trying.

Alternative Consequences

- Ban from extracurricular activities
- Neighborhood Accountability Board
- Teen Court
- Parent come to class with student
- Partial days of ISS

Friday School

- Students and parents are notified when the student has three tardies, that they must serve Friday School.
- Students serve from 3:15–5:30 on Friday afternoon. They pick up trash around campus, clean teacher rooms, cafeteria, prepare fields for ball games, etc.
- If students do not attend or are late for Friday school, it becomes an office referral and they serve two days of ISS.
- Two teachers and one administrator monitor students. Teachers do this on a voluntary basis.

Saturday School

- Students may make up work for unexcused absences, but the grade remains "0" until they attend a Saturday school.
- Saturday school is 8:00–12:00 and students work on schoolwork or may read.
- If the parent attends with the student, they attend only from 8:00–10:00.
- Two teachers and one administrator monitor the students. Teachers do this on a voluntary basis.

Future Plans

- Training this summer on building better relationships between teachers and students.
- Behavior analyst will do a book study on adolescent behavior with the entire faculty.
- Analyze FCAT scores when they arrive.
- New Wondering: How are our alternatives to ISS working?

(Continued)

(Continued)

Inquiry

The best thing about inquiry is that it never stops; one wondering leads to another, and we are always finding ways to help our students.

Source: Lynette Langford, Principal, Trenton Middle/High School, Trenton, Florida.

Dissertation Journey: A Practical and Comprehensive Guide to Planning, Writing, and Defending Your Dissertation (2004), and Walliman and Buckler's *Your Dissertation in Education* (2008). Note that, although texts such as these can be extremely useful, some portions may not be applicable to your work due to the unique nature of practitioner inquiry. A great resource focusing specifically on this topic is *The Action Research Dissertation: A Guide for Students and Faculty* by Kathryn Herr and Gary Anderson (2005). Your advisor and committee members will help you navigate the requirements for the thesis and dissertation at your institution and the unique nature of action research to produce a dissertation study grounded in the everyday world of practice.

It is more difficult to make a case for writing up one's work for the principal who is not earning an advanced degree and is instead engaging in action research for his/her own professional development and/or to inform improvement efforts at his/her school. Of course, in this case, the principal's write-up would not resemble a dissertation or thesis in almost any way, shape, or form. Rather, the write-up would be much shorter and simpler, and the form it would take would once again depend on the audience for whom it is intended. Writing up your inquiry, even though it will be shorter and simpler than a dissertation or thesis, remains a wonderful way to clarify your thinking and make your inquiry tangible so that it can be shared with others.

Yet, unfortunately, writing about inquiry is not a routine part of an administrator's daily work, and it takes a great deal of time. Mills (2003) suggests challenging the time constraint by making writing a part of your professional life and responsibility and to capture minutes and hours for it—before school or after school, during cancelled faculty meetings, failed parent conferences, and professional development days, or, when all else fails, using personal time to get writing done.

If you can get past the time constraint and the resistance to engage in writing—which Wolcott (1990) describes at its best as "always challenging and sometimes satisfying" (p. 12)—I believe that the satisfying times will outweigh all the difficulty and frustration inherent in writing and that, through the writing process, you will take your own individual inquiry to a new level. Mills (2003) suggests sound reasons for writing (pp. 164–165):

1. *Clarification*: Writing your research requires clarity and accuracy of expression. Writing about your research activities encourages thought and reflection, and perhaps creates new questions that are resolved, which shape and complete your research.

2. *Empowerment:* Reflecting on your practices through writing will empower you to continue to challenge the status quo and be an advocate for your [school].

3. *Generative:* Writing is a generative activity that culminates in a product, something tangible that you can share with colleagues, supervisors, and parents.

4. *Accomplishment:* Writing up your research will provide you with a sense of accomplishment. It is both humbling and exciting when colleagues read your work and compliment you on your accomplishments!

Your first step to writing up your work (if a dissertation or thesis is not required) is to decide the audience you wish to share your writing with. This decision will help you decide on the form for your writing.

To share your inquiry outside your school or school district, you may wish to pursue publishing your writing. In this case, your writing will take the form of a manuscript and will likely be in the vicinity of five to twenty pages in length. Appropriate forums for administrator action research such as the *Educational Administration Quarterly, Principal,* and *Theory Into Practice* vary in the requested length, style, and tone of the inquiry write-up. If you are interested in writing up your inquiry to be published in a journal, you should review that journal's manuscript submission guidelines and read sample articles so you can write in a style and form that matches the targeted outlet for your work.

Another way to share your inquiry outside your school or district is blogging. Principal bloggers Steve Poling and Jan Borelli discuss the power of blogging for principals:

One of the most powerful practices in our professional development has been blogging about our thoughts and experiences being principals. . . . An educational blog is an online posting of your professional thoughts, questions, or experiences at a Website which others can read and leave a response. View our blogs as an example: Dr. Jan's Blog (http://drjansblog.blogspot.com/) and Mr. P's Blog (http://mr-ps-blog.blogspot.com/). . . . Through blogging, we developed collaboration and support for one another. Even though we have never met and our elementary schools are 1,000 miles apart, blogging has given us a chance to be close collaborators and supporters of each other. Blogging has given us a chance to share our insights, issues, and ideas in a forum that we and other principals can read and contribute to. Blogging also gives us an opportunity to reflect on our practice so that we become more intentional about what we do on a day to day basis. (Poling & Borelli, http://www.naesp.org/ContentLoad.do?contentId=2025&action=print)

Reflecting on practice to become more intentional about what principals do is the foundation of engagement in action research. Hence, blogging can be a wonderful way to share your research with colleagues that are 1,000 miles or more from your school. Principal blogger David Truss echoes the sentiments of Steve Poling and Jan Borelli regarding the benefits of blogging:

I call my blog my personal learning hub! From my blog, I can access my latest thoughts, others' thoughts with their comments, my recent comments, and my influence over others' writing. I also keep drafts of ideas on my blog that may or may not make it to the post stage. But more than anything, my blog permits me to "think big" for an extended period of time. If I were not a blogger, many of the ideas I've shared on my blog probably would not have been developed to the extent that they are. The act of writing for my blog encourages me to take ideas further, to explore concepts beyond a fleeting thought. For this reason, my blog is of great value to me both personally and professionally. . . . It forces me to play with, develop, and challenge ideas in a way that makes learning interesting and engaging for me. (Truss, personal communication, June 18, 2008)

Sharing your inquiry in the form of a blog will help you play with, develop, and challenge ideas that have developed about your administrative practice as a result of engaging in inquiry. Finally, sharing your inquiry in the form of a blog automatically connects you to a large audience of principals, as discussed by principal blogger Glenn Moses:

> Personally, my blog gives me a sense of satisfaction and, as vain as it may sound, a larger audience for my thoughts. Professionally it has connected me to people and schools that I do not believe would have happened otherwise. My blog is part of my personal learning community. I believe that this community has allowed me to grow at a pace that is much quicker than I would have been able to maintain on my own or with just the resources that are in my building. (Moses, personal communication, June 13, 2008)

If you are interested in blogging, you may wish to visit the Web sites of professional organizations, such as the National Association of Elementary School Principals, which are launching their own blog services exclusively for principals. In addition, you may wish to point your browser to http://supportblogging.com/Links+to+School+Bloggers (Blogs on Educational Blogging) for connections to principals' and other administrators' blogs.

In contrast to the write-up for the broad, large audiences of a journal or blog, a write-up to share internally with your school and/or district has a different purpose. In this case, the write-up is often intended to accompany an oral presentation or to capture your work for those not able to attend the presentation, as well as to document your inquiry for future reference. Depending on your purpose, you might construct a one-page bulleted summary of your work, complete a template that summarizes all the components of your inquiry (Figure 5.3), create a brochure that highlights the most salient aspects of your research, or write an "Executive Summary."

An example of an inquiry brochure appears in Figure 5.4. The brochure depicts a collaborative inquiry conducted by principal Kathleen Walts, assistant principal Sheila Walker, and school-based technology specialist Michelle Crabill from Fairfax County Public Schools in Virginia. These three women engaged in a collaborative inquiry to explore the ways Blackboard could facilitate communication among staff and administrators and provide a one-stop shopping location for teacher resources.

Executive summaries provide brief (three- to five-page) overviews of an administrator's inquiry, as well as provide contact information so more detail can be shared through personal contact with the author. Some districts collate executive summary write-ups into a monograph and distribute the monograph districtwide. An example of an executive summary write-up

Figure 5.3 Inquiry Template

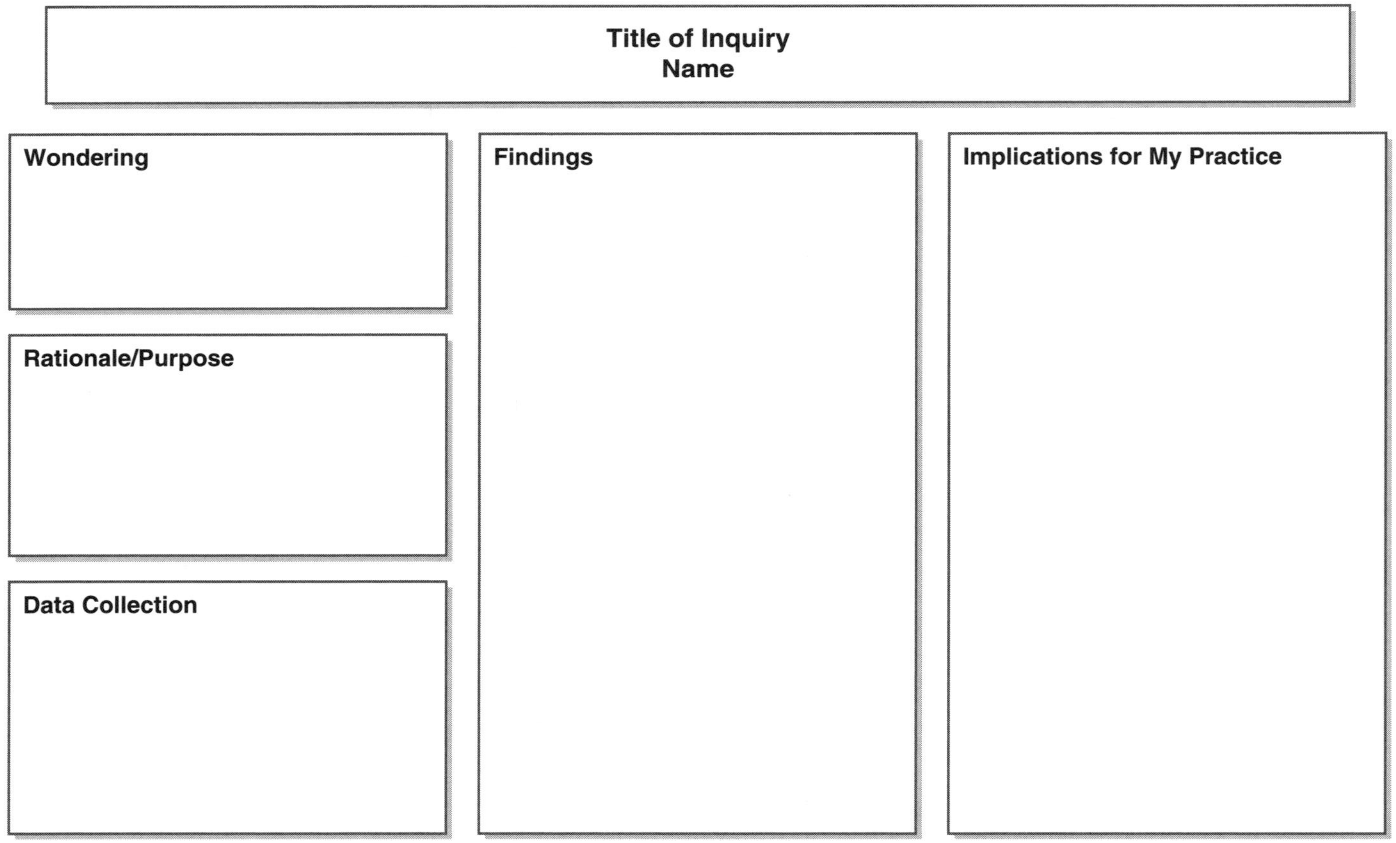

Title of Inquiry
Name

Implications for My Practice

Findings

Wondering

Rationale/Purpose

Data Collection

Figure 5.4   Sample Inquiry Brochure

What did we do?

- Established a Blackboard (FCPS 24-7 Learning) Plan for the school
- Established procedures for how FCPS 24-7 Learning is used
- Reviewed Blackboard plan with staff, encouraged feedback
- Trained teachers and staff on the use of FCPS 24-7 Learning
- Required all teachers to maintain a class site with specific areas that would be consistent from year to year
- Created and maintained a staff site to model the use of Blackboard and provide a teacher resource and online community for teacher collaboration
- Used the Discussion Board for all staff communication, including Staff News, Committee Minutes, and Office Communications
- Required staff to read Marzano's *Classroom Instruction that Works* and participate in an *On-line Discussion*
- Administered surveys and held a focus group discussion with teachers
- Reviewed course statistics to analyze use and trends

What did we find out?

- Establishing a "must use" policy encouraged teachers to go to Blackboard to access information
- Establishing an on-line discussion provided opportunities for teachers who would not normally collaborate with each other (vertical articulation)
- Accessing the staff site daily encourages teachers to begin using, maintaining, and promoting their own sites
- Making Blackboard useful to the teachers encourages them to access this resource. The design has to be clearly laid out and intuitive. If there is difficulty finding information teachers will discontinue use of the site
- Having the KP administrators model the use of Blackboard increased teachers' use of Blackboard for parent communication
- Administrators were instrumental in the transition from Outlook public folders to FCPS 24-7 Learning
- Not all students were able to access 24-7 Learning from home
- Next year, we will continue with our Staff Site and work toward having students access their class site from school

One-Stop Shopping for Resources and Communication

The use of Blackboard (FCPS 24-7 Learning) with teachers and parents

Fairfax County Public Schools

Fairfax, Virginia

To what extent does Blackboard (FCPS 24-7 Learning) create effective communication between staff and administrators and provide a one-step shopping location for teacher resources?

Kings Park Elementary School
Michelle Crabill, SBTS,
michelle.crabill@fcps.edu; Kathleen Walts,
Principal, kathleen.walts@fcps.edu; Sheila
Walker, Assistant Principal,
sheila.walker@fcps.edu 703-426-7000

FCPS 24-7 LEARNING

(Continued)

Figure 5.4 (Continued)

The First Steps

- Create a school Blackboard plan
- Create an online staff site
- Enroll all teachers and staff
- Have administrators move ALL communications to Blackboard (FCPS 24-7 Learning), posting important messages in the Announcements section of the site, etc.
- Organize the site to meet the needs of the school staff. Highlights of our site include:
  - *Instructional Resources—with online resources and lesson ideas*
  - *KP Documents*
  - *KP Forms*
  - *KP ROAR (our weekly newsletter)*
  - *Staff Directory*
  - *Links to the Instructional Gateways*

A Parent/Teacher Communication Tool

- Teachers attended trainings as needed to create Blackboard site (FCPS 24-7 Learning)
- Teacher created and maintained a classroom site for communication with parents and students
- Required areas on teacher sites:
  - *Teacher Contact Information*
  - *Weekly Announcements*
  - *Assignments Including Word Study, Homework, or Projects*
  - *Class Information Including Newsletter, Schedule, Calendars, etc.*
  - *Links to Web Sites Including School Site and Curriculum Resources*
- Teachers updated items on the class sites weekly, monthly, quarterly, and yearly according to the school plan
- At Back-to-School Night, teachers informed their parents how Blackboard would be used and how to log in
- Teachers monitored the use of their class sites through course statistics
- Teachers promoted the use of Blackboard throughout the year in newsletters or other communications
- Blackboard training was held for parents at a PTA meeting

An Online Community for Teachers

Quick access to:

- Administrators' Announcements
- Office Communications
- Staff News
- Memos
- Crisis Plan
- Committee Minutes
- Staff Directory
- Staff Weekly Newsletter
- Links to Instructional Resources
- The Instructional Gateways
- Subject Area Postings by Committees or Curriculum Leads
- Discussion Board Chat of Marzano Instructional Strategies

Teachers like:

- 24-7 access to information
- Collaboration with staff
- Password-protected staff information anytime, from anywhere
- "One-stop shopping" for centrally located school and staff resources
- Modeling provided by the administrators

Source: Fairfax County Public Schools, Fairfax, Virginia.

follows. It depicts the work of high school principal Chris Pryor from Flagler County Schools in Florida. In his inquiry, Chris wished to understand how one strategy for the teaching of reading that his high school teachers had been trained in, Reciprocal Teaching, was working in his building. Through analyzing his teachers' responses to a survey and e-mail artifacts received from his teachers, Chris was reminded that teachers need time to learn and understand new strategies and, as principal, he needed to remember to provide them that necessary time and support.

RECIPROCAL TEACHING: IMPLEMENTATION OF A NEW LEARNING STRATEGY

Background Information

Schools and school systems use different professional development models to improve schools, improve teaching, and therefore improve student performance. According to Darling-Hammond and McLaughlin (1995), the goals of professional development programs include changing teachers' practices, attitudes, and beliefs, and improving student outcomes. However, contrary to popular practice, effective professional development is not a single event but an ongoing and continuous process (Lieberman, 1995; Loucks-Horsley, Hewson, Love, & Stiles, 1998).

In the National Commission on Teaching and America's Future (NCTAF, 1996) report *What Matters Most: Teaching for America's Future*, the authors asserted that the quality of the teaching force needs to be improved to ensure that students meet high academic standards. "What teachers know and do is the most important influence on what students learn" (p. 6). In 2001, the National Staff Development Council (NSDC, 2001) established standards for professional development. They recommended that continuous professional development become the mechanism to help educators raise student achievement and that standards for quality professional development be established.

For the past eight years, in conjunction with P. K. Yonge Developmental Research School at the University of Florida, the North East Florida Educational Consortium (NEFEC) has conducted summer training academies in nearly 100 elementary, middle, and high schools on a schoolwide reform effort called the Florida Reading Initiative (FRI). Based on the Alabama Reading Initiative (ARI), the FRI model is designed to meet the National Staff Development Council (NSDC, 2001) standards and the Florida master inservice plan. Those standards include (a) a whole-school professional development approach, (b) continuous assessment of progress, (c) follow-up support, and (d) evaluation. Materials, personnel, and follow-up support for each participating school have been continuously provided by NEFEC and the P. K. Yonge Developmental Research School.

(Continued)

(Continued)

One of my main goals as principal and instructional leader is student achievement. One of the many indicators of student achievement is the Florida Comprehensive Achievement Test (FCAT). Since opening Matanzas High School in Flagler County in 2006, less than 50 percent of our lowest quartile of ninth- and tenth-grade students have failed to show adequate gains in reading as measured by the FCAT. This has resulted in the loss of one letter grade in our school score, bringing the 2007 score from a C to a D. Because of our students' poor reading achievement and because of my personal involvement with and dissertation research on FRI, our school participated in the Florida Reading Initiative in the summer of 2007. Participation in FRI requires that 85 percent of each school's teachers participate. We were able to train 85 percent of our 2006–2007 teacher population during the 2007 summer academy. However, because we are a new school and added another grade level for the 2007–2008 school year, we added an additional twenty-five teachers to our staff who did not participate in FRI.

During the weeklong FRI training, participants are introduced to dozens of reading strategies. Over the past few years, the most important strategies have been grouped into "The Essential Six" strategies; Pre-Reading strategies, Question-Answer Relationships, Summary Frames, Concept Maps, Column Notes, and Reciprocal Teaching.

Reciprocal Teaching (RT) allows students to gradually learn to assume the role of teacher in helping their peers construct meaning from text. It consists of four reading comprehension strategies: predicting, questioning, clarifying, and summarizing. Because RT has been found to be a very powerful set of strategies (Rosenshine & Meister, 1994; Alverman & Phelps, 1998) and because we felt that concentrating on one strategy schoolwide might help our teachers and students find a common focus, we asked all of our teachers to utilize RT during the year. Teachers received training in RT in several ways: during FRI, modeling and instruction via the reading coach, or a combination of the two; in some cases, teachers had prior experience and training in FRI at other schools.

Because the goal of professional development includes changing teachers' practice and beliefs, I began my inquiry project by seeking to answer several questions. To what extent was RT being implemented at Matanzas High School? How confident do teachers feel about implementing RT? Are there possible relationships between teachers' experience with RT and their implementation of the strategy? Is there a connection between teachers' level of confidence and the implementation of RT? Does the method of training affect the implementation of RT? Does the method of training have a connection with the teachers' confidence level?

Design of My Inquiry

Matanzas High School is located in northeast central Florida. Our student population for 2006–2007 was 1,056, and the teacher population was 63. During 2007–2008, our student population reached 1,452, and our teacher population was 88. Student demographics were as follows: white, 71.3 percent; African American, 11.6 percent; Asian, 3.6 percent; Hispanic, 10.5 percent; Native American, 0.1 percent. The percentage of students on free/reduced lunch was 31.5, and we had 71 ELL students.

All teachers were asked to complete a paper and pencil survey that included questions about subject area, type of training, years of experience with RT, their confidence with using RT, and the number of times they had used RT in the current year. The surveys were distributed to teachers in their mailboxes and were completed at the end of February. There were sixty-two respondents.

I also e-mailed all teachers and asked them to share with me via e-mail their thoughts on the usefulness of RT, how they liked it, and whether they believed their students found it useful. There were seven respondents.

What I Have Learned

Survey Data

After totaling the surveys, it was found that teachers reported four different methods in which they received training in RT:

- Prior training in locations other than MHS—8.9 percent
- Training only at the FRI summer academy—33.9 percent
- Training only with our reading coach—10.7 percent
- Training at FRI supplemented with modeling by the reading coach—46.4 percent

Most teachers reported that they had implemented the strategy five or more times:

- 0 times—16.1 percent
- 1–2 times—26.8 percent
- 3–4 times—19.6 percent
- 5 or more times—37.5 percent

More than half of my teachers reported that they had less than one year of experience with RT:

- No experience (excluded from the study)
- Less than one year experience (those trained during the 2007–2008 year)—53.6 percent
- One year (those trained during the 2006–2007 year or during FRI)—25 percent
- Two or more years experience—21.4 percent

(Continued)

(Continued)

Nearly two-thirds of our teachers were somewhat confident in the use of RT:

- No confidence—7.1 percent
- Somewhat confident—64.3 percent
- Very confident—28.6 percent

When comparing the rate of implementation with the training method (Figure 5.5), there seemed to be more teachers implementing the strategy three to five times or more when FRI was supplemented with modeling by the reading coach. A comparison between training method and teacher confidence (Figure 5.6) showed that more teachers were very confident when FRI training was paired with modeling by the reading coach.

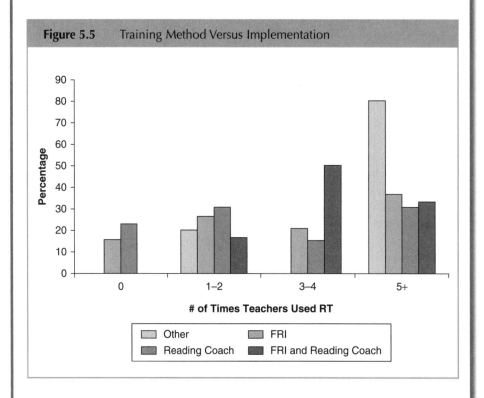

Figure 5.5   Training Method Versus Implementation

Teachers appeared to use RT more often (Figure 5.7) and to be more confident (Figure 5.8) when they had more experience with RT. In Figure 5.9, it can be seen that, the more confident teachers are, the more likely they are to consider using the strategy.

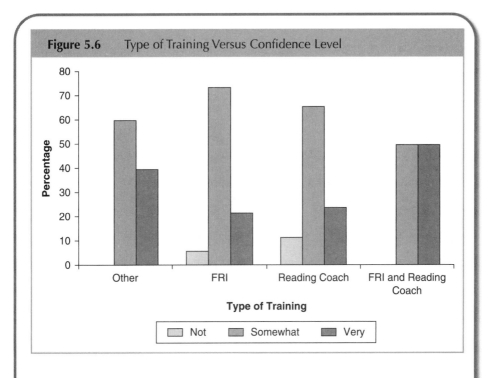

Figure 5.6 Type of Training Versus Confidence Level

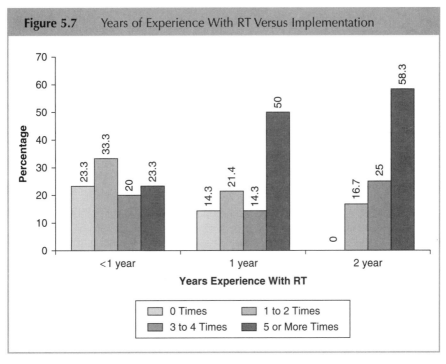

Figure 5.7 Years of Experience With RT Versus Implementation

(Continued)

(Continued)

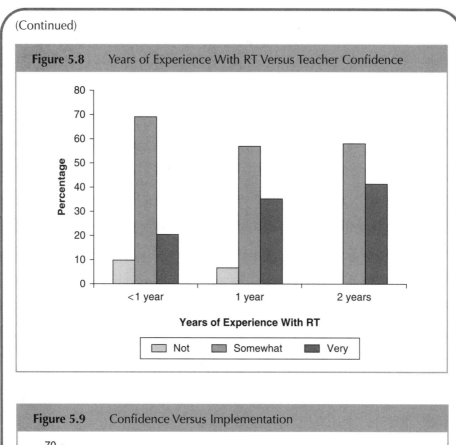

Figure 5.8 Years of Experience With RT Versus Teacher Confidence

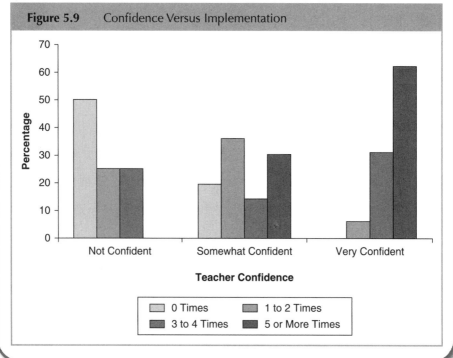

Figure 5.9 Confidence Versus Implementation

What Teachers Had to Say About RT

Only seven teachers responded to my e-mail request about how they were doing with RT. However, their comments were encouraging. The comments indicated that they felt that the strategy has merit but will take time to master.

- RT is still a work in progress for me. My students and I are learning it together. I've accepted that sometimes students get off task and start talking about what happened yesterday during lunch. However, as long as they are consistently regrouping and connecting to the text, I'm ok with the occasional side conversation. I feel if RT is relaxed and enjoyable, they will be more willing to participate in it.
- I've found that clarifying is an excellent, indirect way to teach vocabulary, and force students to use their context clues. Many abhor the labor of opening a dictionary, so they'll scrutinize the word as best they can to come up with the meaning. They are usually right!
- The strategy has a lot of merit if you can get the student to buy into it. . . . When it works, it's a beautiful thing.
- Even though I have known about this strategy for a long time, it really takes a good while to teach the students all of the parts. I have used prediction and questioning, but that is really as far as we have gone.
- Predicting works very well with ESE students, especially when it comes to handouts. Kids want to know if they were right.
- I had [our reading coach] come in a few weeks ago to demonstrate it to me and my 4A class. I will preface this by saying that my 4A class is a challenge. Well, they were engaged and enjoying it. I will be trying it on my own for the first time tomorrow.
- I have this student who NEVER talks, and I am floored, because I just heard him volunteer to READ ALOUD in his group. Apparently RT is worth doing, because this student would absolutely never volunteer to read aloud for the entire class.

Using the descriptive evidence, I believe that teachers are using Reciprocal Teaching at Matanzas High School. Most of my teachers have confidence in their ability to use RT. The data also indicates that the higher the level of confidence and more experience a teacher has the more likely he or she is to implement RT. Also, the type of training and follow-up seems to increase the use of RT and teachers' confidence in their ability.

Concluding Thoughts

As a principal, I am responsible for providing structure for teacher collaboration and learning. This means that somehow I need to provide for opportunities for ongoing, content-specific professional development. We do this by allowing and encouraging our master teachers and reading coach time to work

(Continued)

(Continued)

with our teachers to do demonstrations and modeling of best practice. The data here indicate the importance of follow-up training after professional development. This would not take place without the support of the school's leadership.

It is very easy to forget that change is difficult and takes time. Many times we send teachers to a one-shot type training and expect them to come back completely inoculated and ready to implement the change. It is not that easy. The challenge of changing teacher instructional practice is difficult because innovations require investments of effort over long periods with uncertain results. Teachers do not want to change their practice if they are unsure of the results. The uncertainty of success and criteria exacerbate teachers' investment in change. Most individuals want to know exactly what skills and practice are required for success beforehand (Fullan, 1985). It takes patience and perseverance!

Teacher attitudes and beliefs have a strong effect on whether new strategies will be used. This data seems to support this. Guskey's (2002) model of teacher change shows that changes in teacher beliefs and attitudes come after they see evidence that the instructional innovation produces changes in student learning outcomes. When teachers find that elements of a change initiative work and that they help students, they will use them again. They will believe strategies work when they have seen them work.

There are other things that I need to remember. Teachers need time to learn and understand new strategies. I need to understand this and remember to provide time and support. Also, Fullan (2001) reminds us that after the initial surge of enthusiasm there will be a loss of momentum and a dip in implementation. This is normal during a change effort, but I need to be ready for it and encourage my teachers to stay the course.

References

Alverman, D., & Phelps, S. (1998). *Content reading and literacy* (2nd ed.). Needham Heights, MA: Allyn & Bacon.

Darling-Hammond, L., & McLaughlin, M. W. (1995). Policies that promote professional development in an era of reform, *Phi Delta Kappan, 78*, 597–604.

Fullan, M. (1985). Change forces and strategies at the local level. *Elementary School Journal, 85*, 391–421.

Fullan, M. (2001). *Leading in a culture of change.* San Francisco: Jossey-Bass.

Guskey, T. R. (2002). Professional development and teacher change. *Teachers and Teaching: Theory and Practice, 8*, 382–391.

Loucks-Horsley, S., Hewson, P. W., Love, N., & Stiles, K. E. (1998). Designing professional development for teachers of science and mathematics. Thousand Oaks, CA: Corwin.

National Commission on Teaching and America's Future. (1996). *What matters most: Teaching for America's future.* New York: Teachers College Press.

National Staff Development Council. (2001). *NSDC standards for staff development* [Electronic version]. Retrieved November 15, 2004, from http://www.nsdc.org/standards/index.cfm

Rosenshine, B., & Meister, C. (1994). Reciprocal teaching: A review of the research. *Review of Educational Research, 64*, 479–530.

Source: Chris Pryor, Principal, Matanzas High School, Palm Coast, Florida.

However you choose to share your inquiry with others—whether orally; in writing as a manuscript submitted to a journal, a blog, a one-page bulleted summary, a template, a brochure, or an executive summary; or in some combination of oral and written presentation—in general, there are four important aspects of your work that you will want to consider as you plan to share, which I describe in the next section.

WHAT'S IMPORTANT TO SHARE?

The four critical tasks you must perform when you share your inquiry include (1) providing background information, (2) sharing the design of the inquiry (procedures, data collection, and data analysis), (3) stating the learning and supporting the statements with data, and (4) providing concluding thoughts.

Providing Background Information

A strong way to begin your sharing is to provide background information. Sharing your context, what led you to this particular study, how it is connected to others' thinking about the topic, and what processes you utilized to gain insights into a particular wondering provide your audience a foundation for understanding your work and making judgments as to its transferability to their own administrative situation (a concept I'll discuss in Chapter 6).

Sharing the Design of the Inquiry (Procedures, Data Collection, and Data Analysis)

A key feature that sets inquiry apart from the daily reflection administrators engage in is that it is conducted in a systematic, intentional way. Hence, sharing your system (what you did) as well as your intentions (how you did what you did—data collection and analysis) is important.

Stating the Learning and Supporting the Statements With Data

With detailed knowledge of the "how" of the inquiry, the audience is now ready to understand your findings, which, as discussed in Chapter 4, you can represent as themes, metaphors, similes, claims or assertions, typologies, or vignettes. However you present your findings in this section, it is important to build an argument to support your findings through providing evidence from your data. When you share your inquiry, in essence you are building an argument not unlike a district attorney building a case to prosecute a defendant. A judge would never let a case go to trial that was built on only one piece of evidence. The attorney must piece together a string of evidence to create a strong case. The same is true for a principal-inquirer. In presenting and sharing findings, the principal-inquirer pieces together a string of evidence to support statements of his/her learning. The case is stronger when evidence is provided from multiple sources (referred to by research methodologists as triangulation, as mentioned in Chapter 4).

The most popular way I have seen principals present their work is by using claims or assertions. To illustrate how principal-inquirers might support their findings by providing evidence from their data, I turn to the work of Donnan Stoicovy (2008). When Donnan and some of her teachers prepared a paper to present at a conference about her inquiry into holding schoolwide meetings to help create a caring school culture, she reported the following claims with supporting evidence from her data.

Claim 1: The all-school gatherings were viewed positively by parents, and many parents enjoyed attending on a weekly basis. Parents perceived that the all-school gatherings were having a positive impact on their children.

To provide evidence to support this claim, we have selected two excerpts (one from a parent survey and one from an e-mail artifact) that are representative of all comments received:

- Many of us parents really value the all-school assembly. The assembly builds school community, helps everyone to shine, and creates a sense of belonging that can disappear when you have a big school and no time for anything. Besides building community between kiddos, it also builds it between grown-ups. It is great to be recognized in front of your peers and teachers. My children like to get the citizenship awards and like it to be in front of everyone. The opportunity to put on a skit, do a dance, or even read a poem about Halloween safety is immeasurable. . . . I am glad that parents are welcome and that it is always at the same time, same day. I can plan ahead, and I do take the afternoon off to go and attend the assembly. . . . I'm sure that teachers may have gotten their time usurped, but I sure do appreciate it!
- I had the opportunity to attend the all-school assembly. . . . I was so impressed with what I observed that I felt you should know about it. Today's assembly was a little different than the weekly assemblies because it was held in the lobby. I admit I expected chaos and was quite surprised when

students knew exactly how to adapt to the unusual setting and were able to arrive in an orderly and considerate, yet not restrictive, way. . . . So many students were individually honored and recognized. . . . Every contribution to the school community builds the school population into a true community. . . . It was clear that the students themselves knew that their efforts were welcome and appreciated. . . . The public recognition they receive can only serve to reinforce the fact that their contributions are valuable to the community. . . . The lessons the students learn regarding the importance of contributing to the community will serve them, and the communities they live in, well when they are adults.

Claim 2: Students want and yearn for community. All-school gatherings were an enjoyable weekly event for kindergarten through fifth-grade students at Park Forest Elementary.

Evidence to support this claim comes from two data sources: a lunchtime poll and interviews with selected kindergarten and fifth-grade students. One hundred percent of the 401 students polled during lunchtime indicated that they liked all-school gatherings and that they would miss them if we did not have them. They indicated that the aspects they liked best were:

- Skits/movies (165)
- Citizenship and Community Service awards (101)
- Penguin Awards (75)
- Music (27)
- Everything (15)
- Miscellaneous (Pledge, seeing other people, being involved, announcements, jokes, and guests) (16)

Further evidence to support this claim comes from student interview data. The most salient quotes from fifth-grade students and kindergarten students are shared below. Especially for the youngest learners in our building, music was a valued component of the all-school gatherings and for building school community.

Fifth Grade Quotes

- I like them because they are different every week and they bring our school together.
- I think they are really good and helpful. They help us know what is going on in our school. Everyone can help improve something at our school when they know what is going on.
- I like them because I think it is helpful to get the school together.
- It is good to see what everyone is doing. We learn a lot about what we are all learning.

(Continued)

(Continued)

Kindergarten Quotes

- I like to hear and sing music. Having the whole school sing together is fun.
- We like the music, especially when the fifth graders play their instruments for us.
- It is something that I look forward to each week. We get to see the older students who are not in our hall.
- I like them a lot!

Claim 3: Teachers perceived numerous benefits of holding a weekly all-school gathering, including, but not limited to, behavior improvement, opportunities to present in front of peers, being recognized for achievements, connections to the language arts curriculum, building confidence, and building community schoolwide.

A sampling of teacher comments collected on an open-ended survey include:

- I really do think that improvements in behavior have been a huge success. Teachers and students have been given many opportunities to try new things and take risks.
- I think it is a strong motivator to be able to get up in front of everyone and be recognized.
- I love the learning that happens when the audience watches, but even more so, I think, the value of preparing a presentation is even greater.
- The gatherings unite the whole school rather than having the grades totally separate. Also, it promotes positive competition, which makes the kids strive to work harder.
- When the students actively participate in presenting citizenship skills, the skills have more meaning to them as well as providing them with an opportunity to address LAC [Language Arts Continuum] outcomes of speaking and listening.
- I have enjoyed watching students that I never dreamed would stand up in front of hundreds of people get up and do a nice job presenting something to the school. It helps build confidence.
- It's a nice way to see former students. It's one of the few times I get to see many faculty members. I love the idea of taking time to build community building wide.

Yet, not all data fit the "perceived benefits" pattern. Some data indicated that teachers have mixed feelings about weekly all-school gatherings due to the academic pressures of No Child Left Behind and testing. According to the information gathered on the surveys, these teachers value the all-school gatherings but question the time "sacrificed" weekly (thirty to thirty-five minutes) to building whole-school community:

> With all the demands of curriculum on us, it is challenging to have a thirty- to forty-minute assembly every week. I am not sure what the solution to the problem is. I do believe that learning does take place outside of the class-room doors and that our children can learn a lot from experiences like this. However, I do feel a lot of pressure with all of the curriculum demands and responsibilities we have put on us.

It is clear from this data excerpt that teachers have academic pressures on them; they need the principal's reassurance that building community is important and promotes achievement. The support and involvement of the principal are key, and I need to continue to search for ways to alleviate the stress on my teachers produced by the era of high-stakes testing and accountability and help them navigate and balance the competing demands for achieving academic, social, and emotional goals for all learners at Park Forest Elementary.

Source: Donnan Stoicovy, Principal, Park Forest Elementary, State College, Pennsylvania.

Besides Donnan's method of building a case for each of her three claims through stringing together pieces of evidence from multiple data sources, there are two additional noteworthy points to highlight from her inquiry write-up. First, under Claim 3 where Donnan discusses the pattern of "perceived benefits," note that she ends by discussing how some data did not fit with this pattern:

> Yet, not all data fit the "perceived benefits" pattern. Some data indicated that teachers have mixed feelings about weekly all-school gatherings due to the academic pressures of No Child Left Behind and testing. According to the information gathered on the surveys, these teachers value the all-school gatherings but question the time "sacrificed" weekly (thirty to thirty-five minutes) to build-ing whole-school community.

While principal-inquirers are often quite excited about finding patterns in their data and are most apt to report those patterns when sharing their work with others, it is also insightful to look at data that doesn't fit and include explanations for that inconsistency as well. Research methodologists refer to such data as "negative cases." It is often through looking critically at data that does not fit and adding it to your report that you learn more about the patterns themselves. In addition, reporting about data that does not fit enhances the credibility of your inquiry. By not sharing negative data, you risk painting an unrealistic portrait of your school that can be met with skepticism by your audience, who knows well that nothing within the vast complexities of administration is simple. Reporting your negative data contributes to a picture of your learning that rings true to life.

Second, note that each of Donnan's three claims were supported with multiple sources of data but not nearly all the data Donnan had collected over the course of her inquiry or that she had sorted into categories during data analysis. For sharing purposes, Donnan selected the most powerful pieces of data to represent the patterns she found and the statements of her learning. As you construct your case to support statements of your learning through inquiry, you may experience difficulty selecting which data excerpts to use. Wolcott (1990) notes:

> The major problem we face . . . is not to get data, but to get rid of it! With writing comes the always painful task (at least from the standpoint of the person who gathered it) of winnowing material to a manageable length, communicating only the essence rather than exhibiting the bulky catalogues that testify to one's painstaking thoroughness. (p. 18)

Once the winnowing down is completed and your arguments clearly articulated, the last step in sharing your inquiry is to provide conclusions.

Providing Concluding Thoughts

When you read a good mystery, you expect that the conclusion of the book will provide answers to solve the mystery. Similarly, concluding thoughts are often thought of as the answers to the initial questions posed by the inquiry study. Sometimes, they are. However, just as often, concluding thoughts do not answer the initial research question but generate additional questions and further areas for inquiry.

Recall from Chapter 4 on data analysis that the work of a practitioner-researcher is never quite finished because good data analyses will generate more questions than answers. It is difficult to conceive of how to finish a piece of writing or a presentation when the work of a principal-inquirer is never done. Many administrators finish their presentations or writing by reflecting in general on the specific inquiry just completed, generating directions for the future, and stating further wonderings. By doing so, they begin the cycle of inquiry anew.

As you continue to spiral through the process of inquiry throughout your professional lifetime, it is important to pause at the end of each cycle and reflect on the quality of the research you have just completed. If you do so, you continually improve not only as a principal but as a researcher as well. The better researcher you become, the better-informed decisions you will make as a principal. The better-informed decisions you make as a principal, the deeper and more interesting the inquiry you can engage in becomes. In sum, you just keep getting better and better as an administrator and make life and learning better and better for the teachers and students in your building. For this reason, in the next chapter, we tackle one final task—assessing the quality of your own and others' research.

CHAPTER 5 EXERCISES

1. Outline an inquiry oral presentation and/or write-up for your study utilizing the general four components of sharing an inquiry discussed in this chapter: (1) providing background information, (2) sharing the design of the inquiry (procedures, data collection, and data analysis), (3) stating the learning and supporting the statements with data, and (4) providing concluding thoughts. Share your outline with another principal, classmate, teachers, or other colleagues to receive feedback.

2. Peruse the administration journals mentioned in this chapter as well as others that could be an outlet for sharing your work more broadly with other principals in written form. Note the style, tone, and manuscript submission guidelines. Prepare a manuscript for submission.

6

The Continuing Journey as "Head Learner"

Assessing the Quality of Inquiry

Chapter 5 discussed the importance of sharing your work with others, the different audiences with whom your inquiry might be shared, and tips on sharing your work in both oral and written forms. While sharing your practitioner research is an important part of the inquiry process, there is one danger inherent in sharing your work. After you've completed an oral presentation or write-up of your inquiry, it feels final, like the end of a long journey; therefore, you may begin to view practitioner inquiry as a linear process and focus on the outcome, the end of the project, the exploration, the wondering, . . . and then go back to your everyday work as a principal and "business as usual." If treated as a linear *project*, practitioner inquiry is not a part of administration but, rather, apart from it. When you complete a presentation or write-up of your work, it's important to remember that administrator inquiry is not about completing an action research project at any given point in time. Rather, administrator inquiry is a continual cycle that all educators spiral through throughout their professional lifetimes. It is a professional *positioning* or *stance* where questioning, systematic study, and, subsequently, improving one's practice becomes a natural part of an administrator's work, necessary because of the inherent complexity of the principal's job. *Doing* action research, presenting, and/or writing up your work is just one powerful way to actualize this stance. Although a particular action research project might *appear* to culminate with sharing the research, one's inquiry stance must continue to be a powerful force and source of knowledge for self and others throughout a professional lifetime—just like a circle, it has no end. Picking up on the journey metaphor we have used throughout this book, principals with an inquiry stance toward their administrative practice often adopt the old inspirational adage, "It's the journey, not the destination," to describe their work as administrators, researchers, and agents of change.

By adopting an inquiry stance toward administration and continuing your inquiry journey indefinitely, you provide a living example and inspiration for others in your building, demonstrating that inquiry is less about what one does (presenting one action research project) and more about who one is (an educator who positions himself or herself professionally, not as an implementer of rigid, unchanging routines year after year but as a constant and continuous questioner, wonderer, and explorer). You understand that engaging in inquiry is not about solving every educational problem that exists; rather, it's about finding new and better problems to study and, in so doing, leading a continuous cycle of self and school improvement . . . truly becoming the best that you can be. Indeed, through engagement in practitioner research, you become the "head learner" in your school.

Engaging in practitioner research might help you become the best you can be as a principal, but what about becoming the best you can be as a researcher? If, through inquiry, you can find a way to enhance and build your research skills in addition to the ways you are improving your administrative practice, the power of your inquiry magnifies exponentially with each cycle you complete. The purpose of this chapter is to help you find that way!

WHY IS IT IMPORTANT TO ASSESS THE QUALITY OF MY WORK?

When practitioners complete their first inquiry projects, it is often the presentation of that work that gets all the attention. Certainly the completion of one cycle through the inquiry process should be noted, celebrated, and shared with others, similar to how the Pinellas County School District and other districts across the country organize sharing celebrations of practitioner research each school year. Yet, the spotlight on one particular inquiry project potentially overshadows the importance of the inquiry stance. Remember, it is because practitioner research actualizes an inquiry stance toward administration and positions you as the head learner in your building that you engage in it in the first place!

That being said, it is still natural, necessary, and important to focus on each single cycle through inquiry, as we have done in this text. It is through focusing intently on each individual cycle that administrators take charge of their own professional development and continually improve their practice. With each individual cycle of inquiry, the quality of your work as a principal and your attempts at school improvement efforts are enhanced. And the extent of the enhancement of your administrative practice and school improvement efforts is directly related to the quality of the inquiry. For this reason, it is important for principal-inquirers to commit both to quality administrative practice *and* to quality administrative research.

One gets better as a principal and researcher not only by engaging in practitioner research but through the research of colleagues as well. As you hear about and read the action research of other principals and teachers, it is important for you to assess the quality of their work, not to find fault or become judgmental but to understand and assess the ways a colleague's action research might inform your own administrative practice, a quality researchers refer to as "transferability."

WHAT IS THE DIFFERENCE BETWEEN GENERALIZABILITY AND TRANSFERABILITY?

In Chapter 1, I explained that the reason I prefer the generic term *inquiry* to *action research* or *practitioner research* is that the word *research* often conjures up images antithetical to practitioner practices (that is, extensive number crunching and statistical analyses, white lab coats, experimental designs with control and treatment groups, and long hours in the library). A finding often associated with good research is generalizability, or the extent to which the answers from a research study will hold true and should be applied to other populations. But just as practitioner research is not consonant with extensive number crunching and statistical analyses, white lab coats, experimental designs, and long hours in the library, it is not meant to be generalizable to *all* practitioners *everywhere*.

For example, recall Deirdre Bauer's inquiry into how peer coaching was playing out for two veteran teachers in her building. Through this inquiry, Deirdre learned that peer coaching was a powerful mechanism for these two teachers in examining and enhancing their teaching of reading. Because peer coaching was successful for Marcia and Judi, however, Deirdre should not necessarily mandate that all teachers at Radio Park Elementary engage in peer coaching, as one might believe if the purpose of practitioner research was to be generalizable. In addition, Deirdre should not suggest that all principals everywhere institute peer coaching as a form of staff development in their buildings. To do so would be a mistake. To begin with, Deirdre's sample size (two teachers) was small. Deirdre did not select these two teachers because she wished to have an adequate sample size so that her findings could be applied to other classroom teachers in all schools everywhere. Instead, Deirdre selected Marcia and Judi because they were both accomplished teachers, and Deirdre cared deeply about finding ways not only to help new teachers learn and grow but also to keep her most experienced teachers excited about teaching and learning so they would remain fresh and enthusiastic and could work alongside Deirdre as colleagues to provide leadership for the school. In addition, Deirdre did not consciously and deliberatively isolate what might be considered her "treatment variable" (engaging in the peer coaching cycle) from all other intervening variables that might play a role in Marcia and Judi's continued development as reading teachers (such as working with the district's curriculum resource teacher to learn about the latest practice and research in the teaching of reading). Deirdre didn't remove herself from the "intervention" (peer coaching) so as not to "contaminate" the process but, instead, integrated everything she knew about peer coaching from her prior positions in other districts and her reading on the subject and purposefully intervened to cover classes, offer suggestions, and help with Marcia and Judi's success. Deirdre approached her research not as a scientist who wished to discover the best form of teacher professional development but as a principal who cared passionately for all teachers in her building, with the hope of discovering insights to help her keep veteran teachers vibrant in their teaching. Deirdre's research, like all practitioner research, was designed to focus *inward*—on informing her own administrative practice—rather than *outward*—on proving that a particular strategy will be effective for others!

Lawrence Stenhouse noted that the difference between the practitioner-researcher and the large-scale education researcher is like that between a farmer with a huge agricultural business to maintain and the "careful gardener" tending a backyard plot:

> In agriculture the equation of invested input against gross yield is all: it does not matter if individual plants fail to thrive or die so long as the cost of saving them is greater than the cost of losing

them. . . . This does not apply to the careful gardener whose labour is not costed, but a labour of love. He wants each of his plants to thrive, and he can treat each one individually. Indeed he can grow a hundred different plants in his garden and differentiate his treatment of each, pruning his roses, but not his sweet peas. Gardening rather than agriculture is the analogy for education (Rudduck & Hopkins, 1985, 26). (Stenhouse cited in Hubbard & Power, 1999, p. 4)

Like the careful gardener, the principal-inquirer is constantly reflecting on her practice, looking closely and systematically at individual teachers and students in her building, and using the process of inquiry to attend to the unique teaching and learning styles of all members of the schoolhouse. A principal as an inquirer is not a scientist in a lab coat, removed from his "research subjects," but a human being in the midst of what we call school, carefully weighing the value of different methods of teaching and learning and doing what he can as an administrator to make the teaching and learning process better for all! (Hubbard & Power, 1999).

The notion of the *inward* versus the *outward* significance of practitioner research brings forth an important question: Is there any worth in Deirdre's research for other teachers and principals? The answer to this question is a resounding "Yes!" The worth of Deirdre's finding (or any individual's practitioner research) for others is in its transferability to other schools and classrooms. According to Jeffrey Barnes and his colleagues (2007), qualitative researchers define transferability as

a process performed by readers of research. Readers note the specifics of the research situation and compare them to the specifics of an environment or situation with which they are familiar. If there are enough similarities between the two situations, readers may be able to infer that the results of the research would be the same or similar in their own situation. In other words, they "transfer" the results of a study to another context. To do this effectively, readers need to know as much as possible about the original research situation in order to determine whether it is similar to their own. Therefore, researchers must supply a highly detailed description of their research situation and methods. (n.p.)

Another important component of assessing the transferability of another's action research to your own school and other classrooms is considering the quality of that research, a process that is easier said than done. Administrator-researchers, however, must know the quality of the study to determine whether the knowledge shared in the form of findings could be useful in their own schools.

HOW DO I GO ABOUT ASSESSING PRACTITIONER RESEARCH QUALITY, AND WHY IS IT SO DIFFICULT TO DO?

Although it is easy to make a case for assessing practitioner research quality, it is a much more difficult task to discuss how to do it! One reason it is hard to assess practitioner research quality is that traditional notions of what constitutes quality research (such as generalizability) might creep into the discussions, even though they are not applicable to practitioner research studies. This is especially likely to occur when the assessment is done by those with limited understanding of practitioner research and how it differs from other research traditions as discussed in Chapter 1. If discussions of quality become biting critiques or attacks on the validity, generalizability, or reliability of an individual's research, the field of educational administration risks deterring current and future administrators from engaging in research to begin with. Such critiques, steeped in traditional notions of research and the process-product paradigm, would be erroneous and nonsensical. You cannot assess research produced in one research paradigm from the viewpoint of a different paradigm. To do so would be like assessing the play of a football player using the criteria a professional dancer invokes to assess the performance of a ballerina. For a principal-researcher to become discouraged due to assessments of his/her work that use nonsensical criteria would be a travesty!

Another complication in determining the quality of action research is due to the different purposes for engaging in the process as an administrator and the multiple audiences for which principal action research may be intended. If you are engaging in action research as the final requirement for earning an advanced degree at a university, contributing to the knowledge base becomes your primary goal, and your audience is your dissertation advisor, committee members, and other scholars in the field of administration. If, on the other hand, you are engaging in action research as a principal in order to learn and grow in your work as an administrator and make informed, thoughtful improvements at your school, your primary purpose for engaging in action research is for your own professional development and school improvement, and your audience can be any one of the many constituencies you serve. While the two purposes for engaging in principal action research (contributing to the knowledge base for administration and principal professional development/school improvement efforts) are not mutually exclusive, nor are the audiences for an administrator's research totally independent of one another, the amount of time and energy a principal can put into the inquiry process is dependent on which of the two purposes for engagement in the process is their primary goal. For example, if you are a graduate student, you have enrolled or will likely enroll in at least one three-credit-hour research course that links you with other professionals and experts in educational administration to focus on the development of your research. In addition, you likely meet regularly with your advisor, an experienced researcher. In contrast, the principal-inquirer engaged in action research primarily for his own professional development has a different support structure. He shares the inquiry process with teaching colleagues and other principals at administrative team meetings, leadership team meetings, and/or as a part of his school's learning community work. No administrative team, lead team, or learning community I have ever seen has the luxury of meeting for three hours each week, and when they do meet, often other items and issues on the meeting agenda compete for time with the inquiry work in progress. Hence, when assessing the quality of administrator action research, it is important to match your expectations with the primary purpose and reason for engaging in the process and the audience for whom it was intended in the first place.

A third reason it is difficult to assess the quality of principal research is the relationship that exists between inquiry stance (one's mode of being as an educator) and the products resulting from actualizing that stance (a piece of action research). As previously mentioned, more important than any one action research product is the inquiry stance. It is the cultivation of such a stance in every educator that will improve our profession. Although you can't assess stance (you either have it or you don't), you can assess a piece of action research produced because of that stance. In fact, given the definition of inquiry stance, an administrator who possesses it would logically invite reflection on the quality of her individual pieces of action research.

But which comes first—the adoption of an inquiry stance toward administration or the production of action research projects? Posing this question resembles the old chicken-and-egg adage, "Which comes first, the chicken or the egg?" It might be logical to think that stance comes first, but I have seen many practitioner-researchers approach the inquiry process first as a requirement to complete professional development points for state licensure, as a new professional development initiative by their school or district, or as an assignment in a college course. Although they initially approached their work as a *project*, it was through completing the project that they developed a *stance*. If engagement in projects can lead to stance, once again, it would be a travesty if any principal-researcher became discouraged by quality assessment and, subsequently, abandoned action research.

A fourth reason that assessing the quality of principal research is difficult is that the methods administrators use to encapsulate what they did and what they have learned for sharing purposes come in many shapes and sizes. As discussed in Chapter 5, some principals share their work orally with different audiences, whereas others write detailed accounts of their work in a dissertation or master's thesis, write an article for publication, create bulleted one-page handouts, complete a template, create a brochure, or write an executive summary. No matter how principal-researchers encapsulate and report on their learning, there are always limitations in time and space. Principal-researchers make decisions about which portions of their inquiry journey they will emphasize and, sometimes, which portions they won't even mention in a written account or an oral presentation. Therefore, assessments might be made about the quality of a teacher research based on the absence of particular components of the inquiry journey that may have been present but are just not a part of the written or oral report.

A final reason it is difficult to assess the quality of an inquiry is that, in any discussion of practitioner research quality, it is important to consider where administrators are developmentally as researchers and principals. One cannot assess quality for every project using criteria that would apply for an experienced practitioner-researcher's work. After all, just as one's teaching and administrative practice develops over the years through experience, so do one's research skills. As a principal, when you enter classrooms to observe teachers for their annual evaluation, you would not hold the same expectations for a novice teacher as you would for a twenty-five-year veteran. Likewise, it is unrealistic to think that the first time you engage in research you will excel at every aspect of the inquiry process. Not excelling at every aspect of the process, however, is not a reason to negate the value of a piece of administrator research or, more important, not a reason *not* to engage in research as a principal!

Everyone has to start somewhere, and if you take the time to assess the quality of your research, you will grow as a researcher with each cycle of the inquiry process. Furthermore, if you engage in careful, thoughtful assessment of others' action research, you can make more informed decisions about the transferability of your colleagues' research to your own administrative practice. Participating in careful discussions of quality—what it is and how to achieve it—helps us all improve both administrative practice and administrator research, as well as further understand the intimate connection between the two. In turn, these discussions move the profession of administration forward.

In the next section of this chapter, then, I offer five quality indicators that you can utilize to consider the quality of your own and others' research, as well as spark a discussion among you and your colleagues about what constitutes quality. Definitions of each quality indicator are followed by two separate lists of questions that you can use as a "mental checklist." The first list of questions are about what you can ask yourself as you reflect on and assess your own inquiry work. The second are questions you can ask yourself as you reflect on and assess the quality of work done by other administrator- and teacher-researchers and the ways their work might be transferable to your own school context. This list of quality indicators and questions is by no means definitive or exhaustive but serves as a starting point for reflecting on research quality. As you read these indicators, keep in mind that one develops as a practitioner-researcher over many years and many cycles of inquiry. Rarely is any principal-researcher outstanding in all aspects of the inquiry process all the time. Rather than using these indicators to scrutinize and "grade" every aspect of your own and others' work, use them as a tool to gain insights that you can apply to your next research cycle.

WHAT ARE SOME QUALITY INDICATORS FOR PRACTITIONER RESEARCH?

Quality Indicator 1: Context of Study

Principal-researchers provide complete information about the context in which their research took place. This may include but not be limited to information about the school, district, teachers, students, content, and curriculum. Questions you might ask yourself when you consider the context of your study include:

- Have I considered all aspects of my administrative context in the design of my study?
- Did I situate my principal research for others such that they understand my context?

Questions you might ask yourself when assessing the quality and transferability of others' inquiry context to your own school include:

- In what ways are my administrative context and this principal-researcher's context similar and different?
- Did the principal-researcher describe his/her context in enough detail so that I can understand the context in which his wonderings emerged and the decisions he made throughout his research?

- Did the principal-researcher thoughtfully consider her context in the design of the inquiry?
- To what extent did this principal-researcher's work stimulate my thinking about teaching and learning in my own context (even if the other context was dramatically different from my own)?

Quality Indicator 2: Wondering(s) and Purpose

Principal-researchers explain the root of their question(s)/wondering(s) in detail. The explanation makes a convincing case for the wondering's personal importance to the researcher. The stated wondering(s) are connected to appropriate and pertinent literature from the field. The purpose and question(s)/wondering(s) are clearly articulated, free of educational jargon, focused inward (on the administrator's own practice), and open-ended (i.e., the principal-researcher did not pose a question for which the answer was already known). Questions you might ask yourself when you consider your wondering(s) and purpose include:

- Did I describe the dilemma or tension in my administrative practice that led to the formation of my wondering?
- Did I connect my own personal wondering(s) with existing knowledge about my topic by mentioning related literature?
- Is my wondering clearly articulated (free of educational jargon)?
- Did my wondering focus on me, on my personal administrative practice, and on something that *I* can affect rather than on trying to "fix," "change," or "prove something" to others through my research?
- Did I ask something I really didn't know?
- Did I *not* frame my wondering as a simple, dichotomous (yes/no) question and thus honor the complexity that the job of a principal entails?

Questions you might ask yourself when assessing the quality and transferability of others' inquiry wonderings and purpose to your own school include:

- Did the wondering emerge from a real tension, dilemma, issue, or problem of practice the principal-researcher faced?
- How does the principal-researcher's tension, dilemma, issue, or problem resonate with my own felt difficulties and real-world dilemmas?
- Did the principal-researcher share how the tension, dilemma, issue, or problem her wondering addresses resonates with broader discussions of related issues by addressing literature from the field?

- Were the principal-researcher's wonderings clearly articulated, free of educational jargon, and open-ended?
- Did the principal-researcher's wondering focus *inward* on the principal's own practice?
- Did the principal-researcher convince me of his/her passion for the topic?

Quality Indicator 3: Principal Research Design (Data Collection and Data Analysis)

Principal-researchers collect data from multiple sources (i.e., test scores, surveys, field notes, student work, interviews, journal entries, etc.). Each data collection strategy employed is clearly explained and is a logical choice in relation to the principal-researcher's posed question(s)/wondering(s). Principal-researchers include detailed explanations of all procedures and a timeline for data collection, as well as an explanation of how data were analyzed. Questions you might ask yourself when you consider the design of your inquiry include:

- Did I carefully consider all the sources of data that could potentially give me insights into my wondering when I designed my inquiry (see Chapter 3 Exercises)?
- Did I use three or more data sources to gain insights into my wondering (i.e., quantitative measures of student achievement, field notes, interviews, documents/artifacts/student work, digital pictures, video, journals, blogs, surveys)?
- Did I collect literature related to my topic as a form of data?
- Did I explain all procedures associated with my inquiry, including a timeline for my work and how I analyzed data?
- Was my timeline consonant with the nature of my wondering (that is, did I spend too much or too little time collecting data)?
- Was I flexible in implementing my plan for inquiry (for example, did I adjust my wondering(s)/data collection strategies along the way if I found such adjustments were important for my learning)?

Questions to ask yourself when assessing the quality and transferability of others' inquiry design to your own school include:

- Did the principal-researcher employ multiple forms of data to gain insights into his wondering (i.e., quantitative measures of student achievement, field notes, interviews, documents/artifacts/student work, digital pictures, video, journals, blogs, surveys)?

- Given the principal-researcher's wondering, were the data collection strategies the principal selected logical choices?
- Did the principal-researcher collect literature related to her topic as a form of data?
- Did the principal-researcher collect data for a sufficient amount of time to gain credible insights into his wondering? (If the data collection period was one week in length, did that timeframe make sense for this wondering? Conversely, if the data collection period was an entire school year, did that timeframe make sense for this wondering?)
- Did the principal-researcher explain all procedures associated with the conduct of the inquiry?
- Did the principal-researcher describe changes or adjustments she made in her inquiry procedures that were warranted based on what she was learning while engaging in the process?

Quality Indicator 4: Principal-Researcher Learning

Principal-researchers articulate clear, thoughtful statements about what they learned through the process. Each statement is supported, in detail, by data. If relevant, data may also be included that did not appear to fit with what the principal is claiming, with possible explanations for the discrepant data. Principal-researchers weave readings and other relevant experiences into the discussion about their findings if the readings and experiences relate to what was learned. Principal-researchers not only discuss what was learned about their topic of study but also include a personal reflection on what was learned about the process of inquiry. Questions to ask yourself when you consider the learning that resulted from your inquiry include:

- Did I select a strategy for illustrating my findings to others (i.e., themes, patterns, categories, metaphors, claims, vignettes) that best captures what I learned through the inquiry (see Chapter 4, Strategies for Illustrating Your Findings, on pages 116–117)?
- Did I support every statement of learning with excerpts from my data?
- Am I confident that my findings, as well as my selection of a strategy to illustrate my findings, emerged from my data and my learning and that I did not force my data to fit the opinions and values I had in place before beginning the inquiry?
- Did I carefully consider data that didn't fit with the themes/ patterns/claims I am making as a result of my research?
- Can I explain data that didn't fit?

- Did I weave what I know about administration and the topic of my inquiry from my prior experiences and readings into my analysis and interpretation of data?
- Did I reflect on what I learned about the practitioner research process in addition to thinking about what I learned for my administrative practice?

Questions to ask yourself when assessing the quality and transferability of the learning reported by others as a result of engagement in inquiry include:

- Did the principal-researcher select a powerful way to illustrate his findings to me (i.e., themes, patterns, categories, metaphors, similes, claims, assertions, typologies, vignettes)?
- Did the principal-researcher support every statement of learning with excerpts from her data?
- Are the learning statements made by this principal directly related to the principal's data, or is there a disconnect between the principal's learning statements and the data he shared?
- Does the principal-researcher share and explain data that doesn't seem to fit with her learning?
- Did the principal-researcher integrate knowledge from his own prior experiences and educational readings into his analysis and interpretation of the data?
- Does the integration of these experiences and readings enhance the learning that emerged for this principal-researcher as a result of her data and analysis, or did she force the data to fit into learning statements it appears the principal held prior to beginning her research?
- Does the principal-researcher reflect on what he learned about his administrative practice as well as what he learned about the process of practitioner inquiry?
- To what extent do this researcher's reflections resonate with my own administrative experience?
- To what extent do this principal-researcher's reflections inspire me as a principal and inquirer?

Quality Indicator 5: Implications for Practice

Practitioner-researchers detail examples of change they have made or will consider making based on what they learned through their research. Changes in practice flow logically from the researcher's statements of learning. In addition, practitioner-researchers discuss wonderings that might be pursued in the future based on what was learned from their current research. Questions to ask yourself when you consider the implications your inquiry holds for your practice include:

- Did my inquiry result in action (changes I have made or plan to make in my practice based on what I learned through this inquiry)?
- Are the actions I've taken or plan to take logical outgrowths of what I've learned through my inquiry?
- Do I have a plan for further assessing, reflecting on, and/or studying the changes in practice that have resulted from my inquiry?
- Did I share new wonderings that emerged for me as a result of my inquiry?

Questions to ask yourself when assessing the quality and transferability of the implications for practice reported by others as result of inquiry include:

- Did the principal-researcher address action he has taken or will take to change and improve practice based on what he has learned?
- Are the stated actions informed by the principal's learning through this cycle of inquiry?
- In what ways do this principal-researcher's actions resonate with my own administrative experience?
- How might what this principal has learned and done throughout her inquiry apply to my own school?
- What actions might I take in my own administrative practices based on what I learned from this principal-inquirer?

WHAT ARE SOME WAYS OF ENHANCING INQUIRY QUALITY?

As previously mentioned, the quality of administrator inquiry, or any practitioner research for that matter, can be enhanced simply by taking the time to reflect on and discuss the quality of your work with others and apply what you learn through these discussions to your next cycle as a principal-inquirer. The questions provided in the previous section are designed to get you started on these reflections and discussions. In addition to engaging in collaborative reflections on the quality of your inquiry with colleagues, you may wish to heighten the visibility of inquiry as professional development for all adult learners in your building. If you wish to embark on the inquiry journey together with teachers in your building, a parallel text to this book titled *The Reflective Educator's Guide to Classroom Research: Learning to Teach and Teaching to Learn Through Practitioner Inquiry* (Dana & Yendol-Hoppey, 2009) follows the same step-by-step process outlined in this book but focuses on teachers' passions for inquiry and examples of research conducted by teacher-inquirers in their own classrooms. A final way to enhance the quality of all practitioner inquiry occurring in your building (both your own and your classroom teachers' research) is to focus on the coaching practitioner-inquirers should receive throughout the process. Because the quality of coaching that a practitioner-researcher receives is directly related to the quality of his work (Dana & Yendol-Hoppey, 2006; Drennon & Cervero, 2002), it will be helpful to focus on and improve your own ability to coach inquiry as well as to cultivate the coaching skills of some of the teacher-leaders in your building. These coaches might be teachers with many years of inquiry experience or National Board Teachers in your district who have made inquiry a central piece of their teaching practice. Alternatively, you might solicit help from university partners who specialize in coaching the teacher research process. Whomever you select, involving an experienced coach can greatly enhance the quality of inquiry since engaging in conversation with a critical friend about your wondering will deepen both the process and the knowledge constructed. If you are interested in paying careful and thoughtful attention to the development of quality coaching, you might enjoy a companion book to this text, *The Reflective Educator's Guide to Professional Development: Coaching Inquiry-Oriented Learning Communities* (Dana & Yendol-Hoppey, 2008).

As you near the end of this text, congratulations are in order. You have completed one cycle through the inquiry process! I hope you have enjoyed each step of the way, the ultimate goal being not to produce a project but to adopt a stance toward your practice as an administrator that is characterized by continuous problematizing of practice and by study leading to change and school improvement. This is the ultimate journey on which I hope you will embark.

I believe no other author captures the nature of this journey as eloquently as Roland Barth (1990) in the following quote I used at the very opening of this book. Coming full circle, I close this book as I began it:

> Sustaining the development of school leaders is crucial to the quality of life and to the best interests of all who inhabit the schoolhouse—and to their development as a community of learners. Principals, no less than teachers, need replenishment and invigoration and an expanded repertoire of ideas and practices with which to respond to staggering demands. . . . The principal need no

longer be the "headmaster" or "instructional leader," pretending to know all. The more crucial role of the principal is as head learner, engaging in the most important enterprise of the schoolhouse— experiencing, displaying, modeling, and celebrating what it is hoped and expected that teachers and pupils will do. (pp. 46, 73)

Through engagement in principal inquiry, you replenish and invigorate your work as an educator. Through engagement in principal inquiry, you expand your repertoire of ideas and practices with which to respond to the staggering demands of your work. Through engagement in principal inquiry, you experience, display, model, and celebrate what is hoped for every adult and student in your school. Through engagement in principal inquiry, you become head learner, the most important role any principal could ever play. . . . Happy Inquiring!

CHAPTER 6 EXERCISES

1. Table 6.1 summarizes the five quality indicators in this chapter and the corresponding questions you can use to reflect on and assess the quality of your own work. Use this table to review your most recent piece of principal research. What do you consider to be your strengths as a principal-inquirer? What are some areas you wish to improve upon in your next pass though the inquiry cycle?

Table 6.1 Quality Indicators for Assessing Your Own Inquiry

Quality Indicator	Description	Questions to Ask Myself When Self-Assessing the Quality of My Inquiry
Context of Study	Principal-researchers provide complete information about the context in which the action research took place. This may include, but not be limited to, information about the school, district, teachers, students, content, and curriculum.	• Have I considered all aspects of my administrative context in the design of my study? • Did I situate my principal research for others such that they understand my context?
Wondering(s) and Purpose	Principal-researchers explain the root of their wondering(s) in detail. The explanation makes a convincing case for the wondering's personal importance to the researcher. The stated wondering(s) are connected to appropriate and pertinent literature from the field. The purpose and question(s)/wondering(s) are clearly articulated, free of educational jargon, focused inward (on the principal's own practice), and open-ended (i.e., the principal researcher did not pose a question for which the answer was already known).	• Did I describe the dilemma or tension in my administrative practice that led to the formation of my wondering? • Did I connect my own personal wondering(s) with existing knowledge about my topic by mentioning related literature? • Is my wondering clearly articulated (free of educational jargon)? • Did my wondering focus on me, on my personal administrative practice, and on something that I can affect rather than on trying to "fix," "change," or "prove something" to others through my research? • Did I ask something I really didn't know? • Did I not frame my wondering as a simple, dichotomous (yes/no) question and thus honor the complexity that the job of a principal entails?

(Continued)

Table 6.1 (Continued)

Quality Indicator	Description	Questions to Ask Myself When Self-Assessing the Quality of My Inquiry
Principal Research Design (Data Collection and Data Analysis)	Principal-researchers collect data from multiple sources (i.e., test scores, surveys, field notes, student work, interviews, journal entries, etc.). Each data collection strategy employed is clearly explained and is a logical choice in relationship to the principal-researcher's posed question(s)/wondering(s). Principal-researchers include detailed explanations of all procedures and a timeline for data collection, as well as an explanation of how data were analyzed.	• Did I carefully consider all the sources of data that could potentially give me insights into my wondering when I designed my inquiry (see Chapter 3 Exercises)? • Did I use three or more data sources to gain insights into my wondering (i.e., quantitative measures of student achievement, field notes, interviews, focus groups, digital pictures, journals, blogs, documents/artifacts/student work, surveys)? • Did I collect literature related to my topic as a form of data? • Did I explain all procedures associated with my inquiry, including a timeline for my work and how I analyzed data? • Was my timeline consonant with the nature of my wondering (that is, did I spend too much or too little time collecting data)? • Was I flexible in implementing my plan for inquiry (for example, did I adjust my wondering(s)/data collection strategies along the way if I found such adjustments were important for my learning)?
Principal-Researcher Learning	Principal-researchers articulate clear, thoughtful statements about what they learned through the process. Each statement is supported, in detail, by data. If relevant, data may also be included that did not appear to fit with what the principal-researcher is claiming, with possible explanations for the discrepant data. Principal-researchers weave readings and other relevant experiences into the discussion about their	• Did I select a strategy for illustrating my findings to others (i.e., themes, patterns, categories, metaphors, claims, vignettes) that best captures what I learned through the inquiry (see Chapter 4, Strategies for Illustrating Your Findings, on pages 116–117)? • Did I support every statement of learning with excerpts from my data? • Am I confident that my findings, as well as my selection of a strategy to illustrate my findings, emerged from my data and my learning and that I did not force my data to fit the opinions and values I had in place before beginning the inquiry?

Quality Indicator	Description	Questions to Ask Myself When Self-Assessing the Quality of My Inquiry
	findings if the readings and experiences relate to what was learned. Principal-researchers not only discuss what was learned about their topic of study but also include a personal reflection on what was learned about the process of principal research.	• Did I carefully consider data that didn't fit with the themes/patterns/claims I am making as a result of my research? • Can I explain data that didn't fit? • Did I weave what I know about administration and the topic of my inquiry from my prior experiences and readings into my analysis and interpretation of data? • Did I reflect on what I learned about the principal research process in addition to thinking about what I learned for my administrative practice?
Implications for Practice	Principal-researchers detail examples of instructional change they have made or will consider making based on what they learned through their research. Changes in practice flow logically from the principal-researcher's statements of learning. In addition, principal-researchers discuss action that might be pursued in the future based on what was learned from their current principal research.	• Did my inquiry result in action (changes I have made or plan to make in my practice based on what I learned through this inquiry)? • Are the actions I've taken or plan to take logical outgrowths of what I've learned through my inquiry? • Do I have a plan for further assessing, reflecting upon, and/or studying the changes in practice that have resulted from my inquiry? • Did I share new wonderings that emerged for me as a result of my inquiry?

2. Table 6.2 summarizes the five quality indicators in this chapter and the corresponding questions you can use to reflect on and assess the quality and transferability of others' principal research to your own school. Use this table to review a piece of principal research that you have recently read or heard presented at an administrative team meeting, as a class presentation, at a conference, or at any other venue where you had the opportunity to hear principal-researchers share their work.

Table 6.2   Quality Indicators for Assessing Others' Inquiries

Quality Indicator	Description	Questions to Ask When Assessing the Quality and Transferability of Principal Research to My Own School
Context of Study	Principal-researchers provide complete information about the context in which the action research took place. This may include, but not be limited to, information about the school, district, classroom, students, content, and curriculum.	• In what ways are my administrative context and this principal-researcher's context similar and different? • Did the principal-researcher describe his context in enough detail so that I can understand the context in which his wonderings emerged and the decisions he made throughout his research? • Did the principal-researcher thoughtfully consider her context in the design of the study? • To what extent did this principal-researcher's work stimulate my thinking about teaching and learning in my own context (even if the other context was dramatically different from my own)?
Wondering(s) and Purpose	Principal-researchers explain the root of their wondering(s) in detail. The explanation makes a convincing case for the wondering's personal importance to the researcher. The stated wondering(s) are connected to appropriate and pertinent literature from the field. The purpose and question(s)/wondering(s) are clearly articulated, free of educational jargon, focused inward (on the principal's own practice), and open-ended (i.e., the principal-researcher did not pose a question for which the answer was already known).	• Did the wondering emerge from a real tension, dilemma, issue, or problem of practice the principal-researcher faced? • How does the principal-researcher's tension, dilemma, issue, or problem resonate with my own felt difficulties and real-world dilemmas? • Did the principal-researcher share how the tension, dilemma, issue, or problem her wondering addresses resonates with broader discussions of related issues by addressing literature from the field? • Were the principal-researcher's wonderings clearly articulated, free of educational jargon, and open-ended? • Did the principal-researcher's wondering focus *inward* on the principal's own practice? • Did the principal-researcher convince me of his/her passion for the topic?

Quality Indicator	Description	Questions to Ask When Assessing the Quality and Transferability of Principal Research to My Own School
Principal Research Design (Data Collection and Data Analysis)	Principal researchers collect data from multiple sources (i.e., test scores, surveys, field notes, student work, interviews, journal entries, etc.). Each data collection strategy employed is clearly explained and is a logical choice in relationship to the principal-researcher's posed question(s)/ wondering(s). Principal-researchers include detailed explanations of all procedures and a timeline for data collection, as well as an explanation of how data were analyzed.	• Did the principal-researcher employ multiple forms of data to gain insights into his wondering (i.e., quantitative measures of student achievement, field notes, interviews, focus groups, digital pictures, journals, blogs, documents/ artifacts/student work, surveys)? • Given the principal-researcher's wondering, were the data collection strategies the principal-researcher selected logical choices? • Did the principal-researcher collect literature related to her topic as a form of data? • Did the principal-researcher collect data for a sufficient amount of time to gain credible insights into his wondering? (If the data collection period was one week in length, did that timeframe make sense for this wondering? Conversely, if the data collection period was an entire school year, did that timeframe make sense for this wondering?) • Did the principal-researcher explain all procedures associated with the conduct of the inquiry? • Did the principal-researcher describe changes or adjustments she made in her inquiry procedures that were warranted based on what she was learning while engaging in the process?
Principal-Researcher Learning	Principal-researchers articulate clear, thoughtful statements about what they learned through the process. Each statement is supported, in detail, by data. If relevant, data may also be included that did not appear to fit with what the principal-researcher is claiming, with possible explanations for the discrepant data. Principal-researchers weave	• Did the principal-researcher select a powerful way to illustrate his findings to me (i.e., themes, patterns, categories, metaphors, similes, claims, assertions, typologies, vignettes)? • Did the principal-researcher support every statement of learning with excerpts from her data? • Are the learning statements made by this principal-researcher directly related to the principal-researcher's data, or is there a disconnect between the principal's learning statements and the data he shared?

(Continued)

Table 6.2 (Continued)

Quality Indicator	Description	Questions to Ask When Assessing the Quality and Transferability of Principal Research to My Own School
	readings and other relevant experiences into the discussion about their findings if the readings and experiences relate to what was learned. Principal-researchers not only discuss what was learned about their topic of study but also include a personal reflection on what was learned about the process of practitioner research.	• Does the principal-researcher share and explain data that doesn't seem to fit with her learning? • Did the principal-researcher integrate knowledge from his own prior experiences and educational readings into his analysis and interpretation of the data? • Does the integration of these experiences and readings enhance the learning that emerged for this principal-researcher as a result of her data and analysis, or did she force the data to fit into learning statements it appears the principal held prior to beginning her research? • Does the principal-researcher reflect on what he learned about his administrative practice as well as what he learned about the process of principal inquiry? • To what extent do this principal-researcher's reflections resonate with my own administrative experience? • To what extent do this principal-researcher's reflections inspire me as a principal and inquirer?
Implications for Practice	Principal-researchers detail examples of change they have made or will consider making based on what they learned through their research. Changes in practice flow logically from the principal-researcher's statements of learning. In addition, principal-researchers discuss action that might be pursued in the future based on what was learned from their current research.	• Did the principal-researcher address action he has taken or will take to change and improve administrative practice based on what he has learned? • Are the stated actions informed by the principal-researcher's learning through this cycle of inquiry? • In what ways do this principal-researcher's actions resonate with my own experience as a principal? • How might what this principal-researcher has learned and done throughout her inquiry apply to my school? • What actions might I take in my own administrative practice based on what I learned from this principal-researcher?

3. Discuss the five quality indicators presented in this chapter with principal-inquirer colleagues. Which of the quality indicators do you agree and disagree with, and why? What are some additional quality indicators you would add to this list? How can you create a mechanism for providing honest feedback to colleagues on their inquiries that both honors and celebrates the principal's work to date and provides areas for future growth and development as a principal-researcher? How can you ensure that discussions with colleagues about enhancing the quality of their own as well as your own principal inquiry in future cycles will not negate the value of the research you all have produced to date?

References

Adelman, C. (1993). Kurt Lewin and the origins of action research. *Educational Action Research, 1*(1), 7–24.

Barnes, J., Conrad, K., Demont-Heinrich, C., Graziano, M., Kowalski, D., & Neufeld, J. (2007). *Generalizability and transferability*. Fort Collins: Colorado State University, Department of English. Retrieved April 30, 2007, from http:// writing.colostate.edu/guides/research/gentrans/

Barth, R. (1981). The principal as staff developer. *Journal of Education, 163*(2), 144–162.

Barth, R. (1990). *Improving schools from within: Teachers, parents, and principals can make the difference*. San Francisco: Jossey-Bass.

Barth, R. (2001). Principal centered professional development. *Theory Into Practice, 25*(3), 156–160.

Bauer, D., Kur, J., & Heitzmann, M. (2001, April). *Peer coaching—A road to deeper understanding*. Presentation at the annual Pennsylvania State University–State College Area School District Teacher Inquiry Conference, State College, Pennsylvania.

Bogdan, R. C., & Biklen, S. K. (1992). *Qualitative research for education: An introduction to theory and methods*. Boston: Allyn and Bacon.

Boyd, T. A. (1961). *Prophet of progress: Selections from the speeches of Charles F. Kettering*. New York: E. P. Dutton.

Bracewell, M. (2006, April). *A principal reflects on Ruby Payne's* A Framework for Understanding Poverty. Presentation at the second annual University of Florida Center for School Improvement Teaching, Inquiry, and Innovation Showcase. Gainesville, Florida.

Bracewell, M. (2008). The "Forgotten Factor" in the inclusion equation: What effect does the inclusion environment have on the reading achievement of eighth grade language arts students? In D. C. Delane & S. B. Hayes (Eds.), *Improving Florida schools through teacher inquiry: Selections from the 2007 Teaching, Inquiry, and Innovation Showcase* (pp. 239–240). Gainesville, FL: Center for School Improvement and North East Florida Educational Consortium.

Buckles, T. (2008). Monitoring what goes on in the school building: A closer inspection of classroom instruction and student learning through implementation of the continuous improvement model. In D. C. Delane & S. B. Hayes (Eds.), *Improving Florida schools through teacher inquiry: Selections from the 2007 Teaching, Inquiry, and Innovation Showcase* (pp. 229–238). Gainesville, FL: Center for School Improvement and North East Florida Educational Consortium.

Byrne-Jimenez, M., & Orr, M. T. (2007). *Developing effective principals through collaborative inquiry*. New York: Teachers College Press.

Camp, J. L. (2007). The use of targeted homework to increase homework completion and academic achievement of high school students. Paper submitted to University of Florida for coursework, EDA 7206: Organizational Leadership, Gainesville, Florida.

Caro-Bruce, C., Flessner, R., Klehr, M., & Zeichner, K. M. (2007). *Creating equitable classrooms through action research*. Thousand Oaks, CA: Corwin.

Caro-Bruce, C., & McCreadie, J. (1994). Establishing action research in one school district. In S. Noffke (Ed.), *Practically critical: An invitation to action research in education* (pp. 33–40). New York: Teachers College Press.

Carr, W., & Kemmis, S. (1986). *Becoming critical: Knowing through action research*. Geelong, Australia: Deakin University Press.

Chapko, M. A. (2006). A principal's job is never done. *Principal, 86*(2), 28–32.

Clark, C. (1995). *Thoughtful teaching*. New York: Teachers College Press.

Cloutier, D., Lilley, B., Phillips, D., Weber, B., & Sanderson, D. (1987). *A guide to program evaluation and reporting*. Orono, ME: University of Maine Cooperative Extension Service.

Cochran-Smith, M., & Lytle, S. L. (1993). *Inside/outside: Teacher research and knowledge*. New York: Teachers College Press.

Cochran-Smith, M., & Lytle, S. L. (1999). The teacher research movement: A decade later. *Educational Researcher, 28*(7), 15–25.

Cochran-Smith, M., & Lytle, S. L. (2001). Beyond certainty: Taking an inquiry stance on practice. In A. Lieberman & L. Miller (Eds.), *Teachers caught in the action: Professional development that matters* (pp. 45–58). New York: Teachers College Press.

Cochran-Smith, M., & Lytle, S. L. (2006). Troubling images of teaching in No Child Left Behind. *Harvard Educational Review, 76*(4), 668–697.

Connolly, M. (2007). Harried principals aren't helpful principals. *Principal, 86*, 32–35.

Copland, M. A. (2003). Leadership of inquiry: Building and sustaining capacity for school improvement. *Educational Evaluation and Policy Analysis, 25*(4), 375–395.

Cory, S. M. (1953). *Action research to improve school practice*. New York: Teachers College Press.

Creswell, J. W. (1998). *Qualitative inquiry and research design*. Thousand Oaks, CA: Sage.

Czaja, R., & Blair, J. (2005). *Designing surveys: A guide to decisions and procedures*. Thousand Oaks, CA: Pine Forge Press.

Dana, N. F. (1994). Building partnerships to effect educational change: School culture and the finding of teacher voice. In M. J. O'Hair & S. J. Odell (Eds.), *Partnerships in education: Teacher education yearbook II* (pp. 11–26). New York: Harcourt Brace College Publishers.

Dana, N. F. (1995). Action research, school change, and the silencing of teacher voice. *Action in Teacher Education, 16*(4) 59–70.

Dana, N. F. (2001, April). Inquiry in the PDS: The thread that ties the content areas together. Paper presented at the annual meeting of the American Educational Research Association, Seattle, Washington.

Dana, N. F., & Silva, D. Y. (2001). Student teachers as researchers: Developing an inquiry stance towards teaching. In J. D. Rainer & E. M. Guyton (Eds.), *Research on the effects of teacher education on teacher performance* (pp. 91–104). Dubuque, IA: Kendall/Hunt Publishing Company.

Dana, N. F., & Silva, D. Y. (2002). Building an inquiry oriented PDS: The journey toward making inquiry a central part of mentor teachers' work. In I. N. Guadarrama, J. Nath, & J. Ramsey (Eds.), *Research in professional development schools* (pp. 87–104). Greenwich, CT: Information Age Publishing.

Dana, N. F., Tricarico, K., Quinn, D., & Wnek, P. (2008, March). *The administrator as action researcher: A case study of five principals and their engagement in systematic, intentional study of their own practice.* Paper presented at the annual meeting of the American Educational Research Association, New York, New York.

Dana, N. F., & Yendol-Hoppey, D. (2006, April). *Facilitating the inquiry of others.* Paper presented at the second annual Teaching, Inquiry, and Innovation Showcase, Gainesville, Florida.

Dana, N. F., & Yendol-Hoppey, D. (2008). *The reflective educator's guide to professional development: Coaching inquiry-oriented learning communities.* Thousand Oaks, CA: Corwin.

Dana, N. F., & Yendol-Hoppey, D. (2009). *The reflective educator's guide to classroom research: Learning to teach and teaching to learn through practitioner inquiry* (2nd ed). Thousand Oaks, CA: Corwin.

Darling-Hammond, L. (1994). Developing professional development schools: Early lessons, challenge, and promise. In L. Darling-Hammond (Ed.), *Professional development schools: Schools for developing a profession* (pp. 1–27). New York: Teachers College Press.

Darling-Hammond, L. (2007). The story of Gloria is a future vision of the new teacher. *Journal of Staff Development, 28*(3), 25–26.

Darling-Hammond, L., LaPointe, M., Meyerson, D., Orr, M. T., & Cohen, C. (2007). *Preparing school leaders for a changing world: Lessons from exemplary leadership development programs.* Stanford, CA: Stanford University, Stanford Educational Leadership Institute.

Darling-Hammond, L., & McLaughlin, M. W. (1995). Policies that support professional development in an era of reform. *Phi Delta Kappan, 76*(8), 597–604.

Deal, T. E., & Peterson, K. D. (1990). *The principal's role in shaping school culture.* Washington, DC: U.S. Department of Education.

Delpit, L. (1995). *Other people's children.* New York: W.W. Norton and Company.

Delucas, M. (2008, April). *Chasing high school credits—A school-within-a-school approach.* Paper presented at the fourth annual University of Florida Center for School Improvement Teaching, Inquiry, and Innovation Showcase, Gainesville, Florida.

Dewey, J. (1933). *Democracy and education.* New York: The Free Company.

Dixon, K. (2008, April). *Increasing student engaged instruction: What works?* Paper presented at the fourth annual University of Florida Center for School Improvement Teaching, Inquiry, and Innovation Showcase, Gainesville, Florida.

Downey, C. J., Steffy, B. E., English, F. W., Frase, L. E., & Poston, W. K. (2004). *The three-minute classroom walk-through: Changing school supervisory practice one teacher at a time.* Thousand Oaks, CA: Corwin.

Drennon, C. E., & Cervero, R. M. (2002). The politics of facilitation: Negotiating power and politics in practitioner inquiry groups. *Adult Education Quarterly, 52,* 193–209.

DuFour, R. (1991). *The principal as staff developer.* Bloomington, IN: National Educational Service.

DuFour, R., & DuFour, B. (2007). What might be: Open the door to a better future. *Journal of Staff Development, 28*(3), 27–28.

DuFour, R., & Eaker, R. (1998). *Professional learning communities at work: Best practices for enhancing student achievement.* Bloomington, IN: National Educational Service.

Dussault, M. (1997). *Professional isolation and stress in teachers.* Paper presented at the annual meeting of the American Education Research Association, Chicago, Illinois.

Easton, L. B. (2004). *Powerful designs for professional learning.* Oxford, OH: National Staff Development Council.

Educational Research Service. (1999). *Professional development for school principals.* The Informed Educator Series. Arlington, VA: Author.

Elliot, J. (1988). Educational research and outsider-insider relations. *Qualitative Studies in Education, 1*(2), 155–166.

Flinder, D. J. (1988). Teacher isolation and the new reform. *Journal of Curriculum and Supervision, 4*(1), 17–29.

Fowler, F. J., Jr. (2002). *Survey research methods.* Thousand Oaks, CA: Sage.

Fullan, M. (2001). *Leading in a culture of change.* San Francisco: Jossey-Bass.

Fullan, M. (2008). *What's worth fighting for in the principalship?* New York: Teachers College Press.

Glanz, J. (1998). *Action research: An educational leaders' guide to school improvement.* Norwood, MA: Christopher-Gordon Publishers, Inc.

Glatthorn, A. A. (2000). *The principal as curriculum leader* (2nd ed). Thousand Oaks, CA: Corwin.

Glatthorn, A. A., & Joyner, R. L. (2005). *Writing the winning thesis or dissertation: A step by step guide* (2nd ed.). Thousand Oaks, CA: Sage.

Hargreaves, A. (1994). *Changing teachers, changing times: Teachers' work and culture in the postmodern age.* New York: Teachers College Press.

Hargreaves, A., & Fullan, M. (1998). *What's worth fighting for out there?* New York: Teachers College Press.

Hart, A. W. (1993). Reflection: An instructional strategy in educational administration. *Educational Administration Quarterly, 29*(3), 339–363.

Herr, K. G., & Anderson, G. L. (2005). *The action research dissertation: A guide for students and faculty.* Thousand Oaks, CA: Sage.

Hollinger, A. (2007, April). *One administrator's quest to promote teacher leadership.* Paper presented at the University of Florida Center for School Improvement's third annual Teaching, Inquiry, and Innovation Showcase, Gainesville, Florida.

Hubbard, R. S., & Power, B. M. (1993). *The art of classroom inquiry: A handbook for teacher researchers.* Portsmouth, NH: Heinemann.

Hubbard, R. S., & Power, B. M. (1999). *Living the questions: A guide for teacher researchers.* York, ME: Stenhouse.

Hurst, D. (2007). How long do we continue reading remediation? In N. F. Dana & D. C. Delane (Eds.), *Improving Florida schools through teacher inquiry: Selections from the 2006 Teaching, Inquiry, and Innovation Showcase* (pp. 142–144). Gainesville, FL: Center for School Improvement and North East Florida Educational Consortium.

Johnson, J. L. (2007). *The intersection of academic and career and technical education (CTE): An inquiry.* Paper submitted to University of Florida for EDA 7206: Organizational Leadership, Gainesville, Florida.

Kagan, S. (1994). *Cooperative learning.* San Clemente, CA: Resources for Teachers. www.KaganOnline.com/

Kawaski, G. (2005, December). How to change the world: The 10/20/30 rule of PowerPoint. Retrieved June 2008 from http://blog.guykawasaki.com/2005/12/the_102030_rule.html

Kincheloe, J. L. (1991). *Teachers as researchers: Qualitative inquiry as a path to empowerment*. New York: Falmer Press.

Kouzes, J. M., & Posner, B. Z. (2002). *The leadership challenge* (3rd ed). San Francisco, CA: Jossey-Bass.

Kriete, R. (2002). *The morning meeting book* (2nd ed.). Greenfield, MA: Northeast Foundation for Children.

Lakoff, G., & Johnson, M. (1980). *Metaphors we live by*. Chicago: University of Chicago Press.

Langford, L. (2008). Do students have to be in class to learn? Exploring alternatives to suspension as disciplinary consequences for middle and high school students. In D. C. Delane & S. B. Hayes (Eds.), *Improving Florida schools through teacher inquiry: Selections from the 2007 Teaching, Inquiry, and Innovation Showcase* (pp. 180–182). Gainesville, FL: Center for School Improvement and North East Florida Educational Consortium.

Leithwood, K. A., & Riehl, C. (2003). *What we know about successful school leaders*. A report by Division A of the American Educational Research Association.

Levin, J., & Nolan, J. F. (2004). *Principals of classroom management: A professional decision-making model*. Upper Saddle River, NJ: Pearson Education, Inc.

Lieberman, A., & Miller, L. (1990). Teacher development in professional practice schools. *Teachers College Record, 92*(1), 105–122.

Lieberman, A., & Miller, L. (1992). *Teachers—Their world and their work: Implications for school improvement*. New York: Teachers College Press.

Lortie, D. C. (1975). *Schoolteacher: A sociological study*. Chicago: University of Chicago Press.

Love, N. (2004). Taking data to new depths. *Journal of Staff Development, 25*(4), 22–26.

Luekens, M. T., Lyter, D. M., Fox, E. E., & Chandler, K. (2004). *Teacher attrition and mobility: Results from the teacher follow-up survey, 2000–01* (NCES 2004–301). Washington, DC: National Center for Educational Statistics, U.S. Department of Education.

Mangin, M. (2007). Facilitating elementary principals' support for instructional teacher leadership. *Educational Administration Quarterly, 43*(3), 319–357.

Marchman, B. (2006, April). *Learning "Round the Block"—P. K. Yonge D.R.S. implemented an alternating day, 100-minute black schedule five years ago*. Presentation at the University of Florida Center for School Improvement second annual Teaching, Inquiry, and Innovation Showcase, Gainesville, Florida.

Marzano, R. J., Pickering, D. J., & Pollock, J. E. (2001). *Classroom instruction that works: Research-based strategies for increasing student achievement*. Alexandria, VA: Association for Supervision and Curriculum Development.

Matthews, L. J., & Crow, G. M. (2003). *Being and becoming a principal: Role conceptions for contemporary principals and assistant principals*. Upper Saddle River, NJ: Pearson Education, Inc.

McCray, M. (2007). Student goal setting: How effective is it? In D. C. Delane & S. B. Hayes (Eds.), *Improving Florida schools through teacher inquiry: Selections from the 2007 Teaching, Inquiry, and Innovation Showcase*. Gainesville, FL: Center for School Improvement, University of Florida.

Meyers, E., & Rust, F. (Eds.). (2003). *Taking action with teacher research*. Portsmouth, NH: Heinemann.

Miller, J. L. (1990). *Creating spaces and finding voices: Teachers collaborating for empowerment.* Albany: State University of New York Press.

Mills, G. E. (2003). *Action research: A guide for the teacher researcher.* Upper Saddle River, NJ: Pearson Education.

National Commission on Teaching and America's Future. (2003). *No dream denied: A pledge to America's children.* New York: Author.

Nino, J. G. (2008). Improving communication systems to better support students as they transition between grade levels. Unpublished paper, Texas State University.

Nelson, R., Martella, R., & Marchand-Martella, K. (2002). Maximizing student learning: The effects of a comprehensive school-based program for preventing problem behaviors. *Journal of Emotional and Behavioral Disorders, 10,* 136–149.

Oberg, A. (1990). Methods and meanings in action research: The action research journal. *Theory Into Practice, 29*(3), 214–221.

Osterman, D. (1991). *Reflective practice: Linking professional development and school reform.* Paper presented at the annual meeting of the National Council of Professors of Educational Administration, Fargo, ND.

Patton, M. Q. (2002). *Qualitative research and evaluation methods* (3rd ed.). Thousand Oaks, CA: Sage.

Payne, R. (1995). *A framework for understanding poverty.* Highlands, TX: aha! Process, Inc.

Peters, T., & Austin, N. (1985). *A passion for excellence: The leadership difference.* New York: Random House Inc.

Poling, S., & Borelli, J. Principal Blogs. Retrieved June 2008 from http://www.drjansblog.typepad.com/dr_jans_blog/files/naesp__principal_blogs.pdf

Richardson, W. (2006). *Blogs, wikis, podcasts, and other powerful Web tools for classrooms.* Thousand Oaks, CA: Corwin.

Roberts, C. (2004). *The dissertation journey: A practical and comprehensive guide to planning, writing, and defending your dissertation.* Thousand Oaks, CA: Sage.

Rosenholtz, S. (1989). *Teachers' workplace: The social organization of school.* New York: Longman.

Sailor, W., Zuna, N., Choi, J., Thomas, J., McCart, A., & Roger, B. (2006). Anchoring schoolwide positive behavior support in structural school reform. *Research and Practice for Persons With Severe Disabilities, 31*(1), 18–30.

Schon, D. A. (1983). *The reflective practitioner.* San Francisco: Jossey-Bass.

Schon, D. A. (1987). *Educating the reflective practitioner.* San Francisco: Jossey-Bass.

Schwandt, T. A. (1997). *Qualitative inquiry: A dictionary of terms.* Thousand Oaks, CA: Sage.

Scott, R. (2006, April). *Teaching other people's children: Examining and improving teacher and administrative practices towards African-American students.* Presentation at the second annual University of Florida Center for School Improvement Teaching, Inquiry, and Innovation Showcase, Gainesville, Florida.

Senge, P. M. (1990). *The fifth discipline: The art and practice of the learning organization.* New York: Doubleday/Currency.

Sergiovanni, T. J. (1987). *The principalship: A reflective practice perspective.* Boston: Allyn and Bacon.

Sherman, R. R., & Webb, R. B. (1997). *Qualitative research in education: Focus and methods.* Philadelphia: Falmer.

Short, P. M., & Rhinehart, J. S. (1993). Reflection as a means of developing expertise. *Educational Administration Quarterly, 29*(4), 501–521.

Shulman, L. (1986). Knowledge and teaching: Foundations of the new reform. *Harvard Educational Review, 57*(1), 1–22.

Silva, D. Y., & Dana, N. F. (1999, February). *Cultivating inquiry within a professional development school.* Presentation at the annual meeting of the American Association of Colleges for Teacher Education, Washington, DC.

Smith, S. C., & Scott, J. J. (1990). *The collaborative school: A work environment for effective instruction.* Eugene, OR: ERIC Clearinghouse on Educational Management and the National Association of Secondary School Principals.

Sparks, D. (2002). *Designing powerful professional development for teachers and principals.* Oxford, OH: National Staff Development Council.

Sparks, D., & Hirsh, S. (2000). *Learning to lead, leading to learn.* Oxford, OH: National Staff Development Council. www.nsdc.org/library/leaders/leader_report.cfm

Stevens, K. W. (2001). Collaborative action research: An effective strategy for principal inservice. *Theory Into Practice, 25*(3), 203–206.

Stoicovy, D. (2006, April). *Has the Park Forest Elementary Schoolyard Project affected students' observations of their natural surroundings?* Paper presented at the annual Pennsylvania State University–State College Area School District Inquiry Conference, State College, Pennsylvania.

Stoicovy, D. (2008, March). *We gather together to build a school community.* Paper presented at the annual meeting of the American Educational Research Association, New York, New York.

Stratten, S. (2008). Giving effective PowerPoint presentations. Retrieved June 2008 from http://sbinfocanada.about.com/cs/management/qt/powerptpres.htm

Tucker, M. S., & Codding, J. B. (2002). Preparing principals in the age of accountability. In M. S. Tucker & J. B. Codding (Eds.), *The principal challenge* (pp. 1–42). San Francisco, CA: Jossey-Bass.

Vandiver, F., Durhan, G., Edison, J., Johns, L., Bracewell, M., & Allan, M. (2005, April). *The principals' learning community: Administrators exploring the effectiveness of their roles as instructional leaders.* Presentation at the first annual University of Florida Center for School Improvement Teaching, Inquiry, and Innovation Showcase, Gainesville, Florida.

Walker, B., Cheney, D., Stage, S., & Blum, C. (2005). Schoolwide screening and positive behavior supports: Identifying and supporting students at risk for school failure. *Journal of Positive Behavior Interventions, 7*(4), 194–204.

Walliman, N., & Buckler, B. (2008). *Your dissertation in education.* Thousand Oaks, CA: Sage.

Whitaker, T. (2003). *What great principals do differently: Fifteen things that matter most.* Larchmont, NY: Eye on Education, Inc.

Whitford, B. L., & Wood, D. (In press). *Teachers learning in community: Realities and possibilities.* Albany: State University of New York Press.

Wnek, P. (2007). Facilitating teacher reflection using a collaborative classroom walkthrough model. Unpublished paper, University of Florida.

Wnek, P. (2008, April). *Exploring school-wide positive behavior support (SWPBS) in a special day school.* Paper presented at the fourth annual University of Florida Center for School Improvement Teaching, Inquiry, and Innovation Showcase, Gainesville, Florida.

Wolcott, H. F. (1990). *Writing up qualitative research.* Newbury Park, CA: Sage.

Zappulla, P. (2002). Issues in the development of leadership teams. *Management in Education, 17*(4), 29–34.

Zeichner, K. (2003). Teacher research as professional development for P–12 educators in the USA. *Educational Action Research, 2*(2), 301–326.

Index

CORWIN

A SAGE Company

The Corwin logo—a raven striding across an open book—represents the union of courage and learning. Corwin is committed to improving education for all learners by publishing books and other professional development resources for those serving the field of PreK–12 education. By providing practical, hands-on materials, Corwin continues to carry out the promise of its motto: **"Helping Educators Do Their Work Better."**

**AMERICAN ASSOCIATION
OF SCHOOL ADMINISTRATORS**

The American Association of School Administrators, founded in 1865, is the professional organization for more than 13,000 educational leaders across the United States. AASA's mission is to support and develop effective school system leaders who are dedicated to the highest quality public education for all children. For more information, visit www.aasa.org.